AQUARIUM
OWNER'S
MANUAL

AQUARIUM
OWNER'S
MANUAL

GINA SANDFORD

LONDON, NEW YORK,
MELBOURNE, MUNICH AND DELHI

Project Editor Jill Fornary

Art Editor Helen Diplock

US Editor Alrica Goldstein

Managing Editor Francis Ritter

Managing Art Editor Derek Coombes

DTP Designer Sonia Charbonnier

Tank Set-ups and Special Photography Frank Greenaway

Picture Researcher Mariana Sonnenberg

Production Assistant Kevin Ward

First published in Great Britain in 1999 by
Dorling Kindersley Limited
80 Strand, London, WC2R 0RL

Penguin Group

First American Edition, 1999

Reprinted 2003
2 4 6 8 10 9 7 5 3 1

Published in the United States by
DK Publishing, Inc.
375 Hudson Street
New York, New York 10014

Library of Congress Cataloging-in-Publication Data

Sandford, Gina
Aquarium Owner's Guide / Gina Sandford.
1st American ed.
p.   cm.
Includes index
ISBN 0-7894-9677-1 (alk. paper)
1. Aquarium fishes Handbooks, manuals, etc. 2. Aquarium
plants Handbooks, manuals, etc. 3. Aquarium
Handbooks, manuals, etc. I. Title
SF457.S2454 1999 99-27002   CIP

ISBN 0 7894 9677 1

Reproduced by Colourscan, Singapore
Printed and bound in Italy by L.E.G.O

discover more at
www.dk.com

CONTENTS

INTRODUCTION

A HISTORY OF FISHKEEPING

FISH WERE FIRST KEPT in captivity not for pleasure but for practical reasons, as a food source. The development of fishkeeping as a hobby began when, out of curiosity, unusually colored specimens were isolated from the main stock and then selectively bred. In China, particularly, early aquarists started to produce tank-bred carp in large numbers, not just with enhanced coloration but also with specific body and fin adaptations. By the 16th century, colored carp had been introduced to Japan. Within the next hundred years they had reached Europe and by 1900 the Goldfish had made it to America.

THE BIRTH OF AQUARIUMS

It was probably in the early 19th century that the aquarium as we know it first came into being. Before then, there are only a few records of fish being kept alive for several years in glass jars. The turning point came in 1850, when a Mr. R. Harrington presented a paper to the Chemical Society in London, England, describing how he had successfully maintained a stable aquarium. This sparked great interest, launching fishkeeping as a popular hobby.

In 1852, the London Zoological Society began building the first public aquarium, which was opened the following year. A second facility followed, in the Surrey Zoological Gardens, also in England, and before long public aquariums were established in all the major cities of Europe, their novel freshwater and marine exhibits drawing a steady stream of intrigued visitors.

The first amateur aquarists usually kept native fish. In coastal towns, people tried marine species, while in inland regions virtually all forms of freshwater life were introduced to captivity. Although freshwater fish were generally more accessible and far more widely kept, contemporary aquarium books focussed mainly on coldwater marine fish. Many of the local aquatic plants described in some of these volumes are now rare – sad evidence of the long-term effects of pollution on our waterways.

The aquarium soon became a fashionable household item in Victorian England. There were no

Colorful carp were probably the first fish kept for their aesthetic value. Although closely related, many of today's manmade varieties of Goldfish bear little resemblance to those early specimens. Nevertheless, the fancy Goldfish remains a staple of the hobby, especially with novice fishkeepers.

◁ FOUR-STRIPED DAMSELFISHES SCHOOLING ON A CORAL REEF

ready-made tanks for sale, however, and various books of the day give detailed instructions for constructing an aquarium. These structures were often more decorative than functional. A common design featured a glass front with the other three sides made of wood (coated in pitch to make it watertight) or often slate. Various glass containers and bell jars could be purchased, but tanks were usually oblong and handmade to fit an alcove in the home for prominent display.

Before long, fishkeeping had not only captured the public imagination, but was also posing new challenges for enthusiasts keen to develop ever more ambitious aquariums. In 1857, H. Noel Humphreys wrote *Ocean and River Gardens – A History of*

Early aquarists constructed elaborate stands for their tanks. Unfortunately, the ornate metal frame on this marine tank would have proved toxic to its inhabitants. At that time, both water and livestock could be collected from the unpolluted seashore.

Marine and Freshwater Aquariums, stating: "We shall yet have tropical aquariums, in which the temperature and qualities of the seas between the tropics will be successfully imitated."

LEARNING BASIC PRINCIPLES
The far-sighted Mr. Humphreys not only predicted the invention of the heater and thermostat, which would greatly expand the range of creatures that could be kept in aquariums, but was also among the first to acknowledge the importance of water chemistry in keeping fish. Further, he recognized a principle that is often overlooked by aquarists even today – the critical factor of stocking levels. Commenting on a friend's aquarium, he observed: "Although his interesting tank did not look too overcrowded, yet he soon discovered that a forbidden limit had been passed, and that creatures cannot accommodate themselves to an allotment system in the proportion of a square inch to each individual."

The first days of fishkeeping saw many fanciful creations, such as this decorative tabletop display. Fashioned from a circular container and housing local fish and plant species, it seems to function partly as a vase, and partly as an aquarium.

As Humphreys foresaw, heating, lighting, and filtration systems for aquariums were gradually introduced, though these were initially quite crude. Many early tanks had slate bottoms, and were heated from below by a small burner. As more sophisticated heaters and thermostats were developed, tanks came to be made of glass in a metal frame.

In the days before television, the aquarium was an important focal point for the family. With no modern distractions, early enthusiasts avidly observed their fish, often keeping meticulous records from which we can still learn a great deal.

NEW FISHKEEPING HORIZONS

While aquarium equipment continued to be developed and improved, aquarists began to look farther afield for fish to keep. The hobby had declined somewhat as people tired of the fairly drab native species commonly available. Among the few non-native fish featured in early aquarium literature was the Goldfish: an 1858 US publication and an English work dated 1890 both note that, although considered a coldwater species, the Goldfish originates from warmer climes and can survive at a temperature of 81°F (27°C).

The revival of aquariums came with the introduction of highly colorful tropical species such as the Paradise Fish, which became known in Germany around 1876 and was recorded in England in 1890. From this point on, fishkeeping was to go from strength to strength. Aquatic societies organized competitive fish shows, thus increasing public access to the hobby which managed to flourish even during the austere years of World War II.

As with the Goldfish, it was not long after the introduction of tropical species that importers, breeders, and aquarists began to "improve" them through selective breeding, producing distinctive strains with desirable characteristics. Modern breeding techniques have led to the development of many new varieties of fish. This Orange and Black Sailfin Molly is the highly sellable result of line-breeding for specific traits.

Yet there were still major advances to come. At this time, saltwater aquariums were nearly impossible to maintain, since the metal tank frame would corrode, producing toxins lethal to marine species. To combat this problem, frames were galvanized, polycoated, or made of stainless steel. The real breakthrough, however, came with the development of silicone sealant in the late 1960s. This allowed all-glass aquariums to be manufactured for the first time, and in a variety of shapes and sizes. Tanks could now be moved more easily, without fear of breaking the seal between the glass and the

No aquarium can ever fully capture the splendor and diversity of a coral reef. Technology, however, has allowed us to come close – in the large display tanks of public aquariums, schools of fish are seen interacting almost as they would in nature.

putty. Frames became obsolete, though plastic ones were often added solely as a decorative feature.

MODERN AQUARIUM STYLES

Today, acrylic is used in place of glass to make aquariums in unusual shapes, such as hexagonal. As these "novelty" tanks become increasingly affordable, and as manufacturers produce harder, more scratch-resistant plastics, acrylic aquariums are likely to be regarded as an aesthetically acceptable, lightweight alternative to glass. Traditional angle-iron tank stands have been largely superseded by decorative and functional cabinets designed to coordinate with a variety of decors.

Other tank components, such as heating, lighting, filtration, and

Tropical freshwater fish remain the most popular in the hobby. They are easier to keep and breed than marine species, and have been highly developed by the aquarium trade, resulting in an ever-increasing variety of colorful stock. Most freshwater fish are hardier than marines, and therefore can better withstand the rigors of transport. They also offer aquarists an appealing opportunity to produce their own home-bred broods.

aeration systems, have also been steadily improved for greater safety and efficiency. Apart from advancements in hardware, many species of fish have been "engineered" to have elongated fins, enhanced coloration, and altered body forms (though the ethics of such selective breeding remain debatable). There is now increasing concern for the welfare not just of individual fish but also of entire aquatic species. Many zoos and public aquariums run captive-breeding programs for endangered species, often with the assistance of well-established home aquarists. Cooperative efforts such as this serve both to preserve aquatic life and to widen our knowledge and appreciation of it.

UNDERSTANDING FISH

OF ALL LIVING bony creatures, fish have had the longest period over which to evolve, some 350 million years. This has resulted in a wide variety of species and subspecies, each with its own unique characteristics and adaptations for aquatic life. But why do fish shapes vary so much between species? Why are some fish more brightly colored than others? Why are their fins so diverse in appearance? All of these differences are significant, and a basic knowledge of fish anatomy and physiology will help aquarists to learn why each fish looks and behaves as it does. Understanding how fish function in their natural environment is also a key factor in successful, rewarding fishkeeping.

ANATOMY OF THE FISH

Although fish vary greatly in shape and size, they share the same basic anatomy. The illustration below shows the principal features of a fish's body.

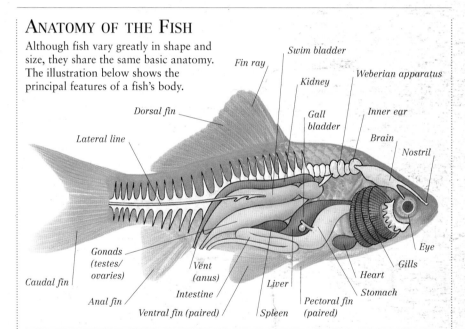

WEIGHTLESS IN WATER

Most fish can maintain their position in the water effortlessly, without floating or sinking, because of a unique organ called the swim bladder. This gas-filled bladder gives the fish neutral buoyancy, equalizing its weight with that of the surrounding water. In some species, the swim bladder is inflated or deflated via an air duct; in others, it is sealed, and filled or emptied by gases in the bloodstream. Bottom-dwelling fish require less buoyancy and have a smaller swim bladder, while active, mid-water species often require oily, meaty foods to boost buoyancy. Certain fish produce a drum-like sound by vibrating the bladder with the supporting muscles. The bladder wall also serves as an eardrum; vibrations are transmitted by a series of bony "levers" or by extensions of the swim bladder to the wall of the inner ear.

◁ SCHOOL OF RUMMY-NOSE TETRAS IN A SOFTWATER AQUARIUM

Body Shape

SINCE WATER IS MUCH denser than air, aquatic organisms must expend far more energy than terrestrial creatures in order to move. A streamlined shape aids locomotion; therefore, the bodies of fish that swim extensively must be more efficient dynamically than those of species that are relatively sedentary. Body form and lifestyle are inextricably linked, reflecting a fish's natural habitat, its diet, and how it locates food.

Fusiform, or Torpedo-shaped

For long periods of constant swimming, the Neon Tetra, like many barbs, rasboras, and other characins, has a body form that presents minimal drag or water resistance. A fusiform shape is the most efficient for active fish from open waters.

Compressed (Tall and Thin)

Fish with tall, thin, compressed bodies, such as angelfish or this Discus, are usually found in slow-moving tracts of water, where they spend a sedentary life drifting among the upper parts of plants. This shape makes them unable to cope with fast currents.

Flattened and Heavily Keeled

The deep, keel-like bodies of hatchetfish are powerfully muscled to enable them to leap from the water, steered by their high-set pectoral fins, either to escape predators or to catch insects hovering just above the surface.

Flattened on Dorsal Surface

Generally found in surface feeders, including freshwater butterflyfish and killifish such as *Aplocheilus lineatus*, shown above, a flat-topped body shape helps the fish to snare food landing on or near the water's surface.

Flat-bottomed

Most bottom-dwelling catfish, such as this Peppered Corydoras, have flat ventral surfaces (undersides) to help keep them stationary in turbid conditions on riverbeds, as hydrodynamic forces press the fish's body to the substrate.

Anguilliform (Eel-like)

Long, eel-like fish such as this marine Gunnell are normally found at or near the bottom, where their sinuous shape allows them to slither through and into narrow crevices. Many small cylindrical species also burrow into the substrate.

MOUTH STRUCTURE

A FISH'S MOUTH dictates what and how it can eat. Species may be piscivorous (fish-eating), insectivorous (requiring a diet of invertebrates), herbivorous (plant-eating), phyto- and zoo-plankton feeders, even scale- and eye-eaters – or may fit into one or several of many other specialized groups. The size and position of the mouth have developed to maximize food-gathering potential, and mirror a fish's eating habits and preferred diet.

TERMINAL MOUTH

Terminal mouths, as seen on this Golden Pencilfish and many mid-water fish, are located at the very tip of the snout, facing directly forward. Upper and lower jaws are of equal length.

INFERIOR MOUTH

Bottom-feeding fish, such as this Weatherloach, have a lower jaw that is shorter than the upper one, to direct the mouth downwards. Taste-sensitive barbels are also commonly featured.

SUPERIOR MOUTH

In surface feeders, such as this Archer, and some specialized plant-eaters (notably *Anostomus* spp.), the lower jaw is longer than the upper, to help gather up food.

PROTRUSILE MOUTH

A protrusile mouth, such as on this Ram, is often seen in predatory species. Its complex structure allows the jaw to thrust forwards as the fish lunges for food, thereby increasing its gape.

SUCKER MOUTH

This *Ancistrus* catfish relies on lip suction to keep it from being swept away by the current. A sucker mouth is filled with small, rasping teeth that can remove algae, on which the fish feeds.

LONG, CONICAL SNOUT

The marine Birdmouth Wrasse's long snout enables it to extract food from the inner niches of corals. Many freshwater fish with such mouths use them to pick nutrients from the substrate.

FISH TEETH

Most fish have teeth, their type and situation determined by diet. In bony fish, teeth consist of an enamel coating over dentine, surrounding a pulp cavity filled with nerves, blood vessels, and connective tissue. Depending on the species, fish may have jaw teeth, mouth teeth, or pharyngeal teeth, or a combination of these types. Teeth can occur in pairs – one operative, the other ready to replace it – or they may be replaced serially. Jaw teeth are either monocuspid (single-tipped), bicuspid (twin-tipped), or tricuspid (triple-tipped). Mouth teeth are found on the roof and floor of the oral cavity; these tooth patches are typical of various catfishes. Pharyngeal teeth are located in the throat. Examples seen on the lower pharyngeal bones of certain cichlids are the fine, tiny teeth of plankton eaters, the long, pointed teeth of predators, and the flat, strong, grinding teeth of molluscivores. Cyprinids lack jaw teeth and have a variety of pharyngeal teeth on one of the gill arches, or supports, to cope with the demands of their particular diet. Carnivorous fish such as the Red Piranha have powerful jaws and sharp, cutting teeth for tearing flesh from their prey. The teeth are often inclined inwards to help keep prey inside the mouth.

Body Coverings

Like all vertebrates, fish are covered with two layers of skin – the inner dermis, containing blood vessels and nerves, and the outer dermis, which is thinner and subject to wear, requiring constant replenishment. Most, but by no means all, fish have some type of squamation, usually in the form of scales. These vary in size, structure, and quantity according to species. Where scaling is absent or only partial, the epidermis is thicker. The dermis is the source of the mucous secretions that make fish feel slippery.

Scales

Most modern bony fish are covered, to varying degrees, by scales. Made of substances resembling enamel or dentine, these form overlapping plates, like tiles on a roof, and offer little resistance to water flow. Benthic, or bottom-dwelling, species often lack scales along the underside, where they would be displaced as the fish is buffeted against the substrate by the current. Some fish, including various armored catfish, have bony dermal plates in place of scales; these are formed from ossified pockets of skin during the early development of the fry. Yet other fish have neither scales nor bony plates, and are instead covered with a thick, tough layer of skin; this is a common feature in many bottom-dwelling species. The number of scales along the length of a fish can be a means of distinguishing species.

Ctenoid Scales

Ctenoid scales have a distinct fine, comb-like structure to the outermost surface, with small teeth on the rear edge of each scale. In aquaria, fish with this type of scaling can easily become entangled when netted.

Cycloid Scales

Cycloid scales are smooth-edged, roughly circular in shape, and overlap heavily, with only about 20 percent exposed. When magnified, growth rings can be seen, showing periods of rapid and slow development.

Ganoid Scales

This is a relatively ancient form of body covering, more basic in structure than either cycloid or ctenoid scales. Most of the scale is visible, with only a small, short attachment hidden in the underlying flesh.

Bony Plates

In armored catfish, the outer layer of skin develops folds soon after the fry hatch. These subsequently harden to form bony plates, or scutes. This covering is not true bone, and is referred to as ossified bone.

Naked

No catfish has true scales; those without bony plates are naked. For protection, the outer skin is thick and sometimes villiform (lumpy, or wart-like). Many other bottom-dwellers are naked on the ventral surface only.

UNUSUAL BODY COVERINGS

Fish without scales can look rather bizarre. The body of the marine Trunkfish is encased in bony slabs, and resembles a box. Some pufferfish and porcupinefish are covered in stout spines that provide a spiky defence as the fish inflates itself to deter predators.

LATERAL LINE

The lateral line system functions as a form of "distant touch." It enables fish to sense vibrations from currents or other fish, and is important in navigation, finding food, and avoiding danger. The lateral line is visible as a row of tiny perforations in the scales or plates along the flank, in either a single or divided line, usually extending from just behind the head to the tail. Water enters these holes, or pores, and fills a series of interconnected ducts under the scales. Inside the ducts are neuromasts, sensory nerve endings that register disturbances in the water surrounding them, and relay this information to the brain. Similar sensory detectors may also be found on the head.

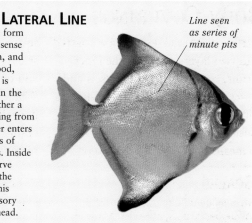

Line seen as series of minute pits

COLORATION

Fish scales are virtually transparent; color derives from cells in the skin, called chromatophores. Pigmented red, orange, yellow, or black, these contract and expand to produce a variety of colors. Light also reflects off a layer in the skin composed of guanin (a by-product of metabolism), making a fish look silvery, chalky white, or iridescent. The Blind Cave Fish, which lives in total darkness, lacks pigment; its pinkish color comes from visible blood vessels.

A fish's color can function as a means of concealment, recognition, or display. Pelagic, or mid-water, species usually have silver or white undersides (to merge with the water surface or sky, thus camouflaging them from fish below), while the upper body is dark, blending with the substrate when seen from above. The Upside-down Catfish, which inverts to feed, is shaded so that its belly is much darker than its back, to conceal it from predators when eating near the surface. On some fish, markings on the flanks disguise the body among

The eye-spot on this butterflyfish fools predators.

rocks or plants, while bottom-dwellers often look dull, to match the substrate. In contrast, species living in dark or muddy waters may be brightly colored so that they are seen by potential mates.

Most fish can change color to suit their daytime or nighttime activities. Some have distinct diurnal patterns: pencilfish exhibit dominant horizontal stripes by day, but adopt shorter, vertical bars at night. Stress and ill health can dull a fish's appearance, while during the breeding season increased hormones intensify the coloration of male fish in particular, to attract a spawning partner.

Color may be used to issue a threat or warning. The Firemouth Cichlid has two spots, one on each gill cover. In posturing to an interloper, the gill covers are opened, revealing the spots as two intimidating, widely spaced eyes. False eye-spots at the base of the tail can also disorientate an attacker, while in schooling species, juvenile markings often serve as a defence, making a huddled group appear to be a single, huge organism. Just as bold color is a common device for signalling to predators that a fish is poisonous, predators may in turn have body patterns designed to deceive prey into mistaking them for harmless companions.

Some deep-sea fish have developed light-producing organs whose function is not clearly understood.

FINS – FORM AND FUNCTION

EACH FIN HAS A ROLE in assisting the fish to swim; their individual actions can be best observed in species such as the slow-moving, highly maneuverable cichlids. Fins are either median or paired. The median fins are the dorsal fin (along the center of the back), the caudal (or tail) fin, and the anal fin (a single fin just behind the vent). The paired fins are the pectorals (equivalent to the arms in humans) and the ventrals (adjacent to the fish's vent). Certain fish lack some of these fins, while others have extras, such as multiple dorsals or an adipose fin – a fleshy appendage behind the dorsal fin whose function is unclear. The true fins are thin membranes of skin, supported by bony rays and controlled by muscles at the fin base.

DORSAL AND ANAL FINS

The dorsal and anal fins help to keep the fish upright, in much the same manner as the keel of a boat. Dorsal fins may have soft rays, both hard and soft rays, spines, or a combination of these, depending on the species. In some fish with very long anal or dorsal fins, locomotion is achieved by a wave of muscular contractions along the fin.

SOFT-RAYED DORSAL FIN

Soft-rayed dorsal fins, as on this Emperor Tetra, are composed mostly of relatively flexible, branched fin rays that support the membrane, with a few simple (unbranched) rays, generally located at the front end of the dorsal fin.

ANAL FIN

As with the dorsal fin, the anal fin (seen clearly on this Humbug) can be either long or short, and constructed of soft rays, hard rays, or a combination of both types. Like the dorsal fin, it acts as a keel to maintain stability.

HARD- AND SOFT-RAYED DORSAL FIN

In certain species, including the coldwater Black-banded Sunfish shown here, the dorsal (and also the anal) fin is constructed of hard, simple rays in the front section, followed by soft, branched rays towards the rear.

ADIPOSE FIN

The adipose fin differs from the other true fins in that it is composed mainly of fatty tissue. In some species, it also contains rudimentary fin spines. Not all fish have an adipose fin, and its shape and size can vary greatly. In species that spend much of their time swimming inverted, such as the Upside-down Catfish, the adipose fin is quite large and serves a purpose much like that of the anal fin on normally orientated fish, to hold a stable position in the water.

CAUDAL FIN

The caudal, or tail, fin acts as the fish's motor mechanism. When flicked from side to side, its thrust propels the fish forwards and initiates a series of S-shaped body sinuations, which sustain movement through the water. In some species, the caudal fin is joined to the dorsal and/or ventral fins to form a single, continuous fin.

FORKED CAUDAL FIN

On fish that swim constantly, including many tetras and rasboras such as this Harlequin, the caudal fin is deeply forked but moderately tall, to provide forward impetus with minimal drag.

BROAD CAUDAL FIN

A caudal fin with a large muscular base, or peduncle, increases drag but imparts a powerful thrust. Broad-tailed fish, including many cichlids, generally move slowly and deliberately.

PECTORAL AND VENTRAL FINS

Fish usually have two sets of paired fins, although some (eels, for example) lack ventral fins. Ventral fins serve as main rudders to steer the fish, while the pectoral fins are used for fine maneuvers, including reversing. To turn right or left, the paired fins are flared, like ailerons on an aircraft. They can also be employed as brakes.

UPRIGHT PECTORAL FINS

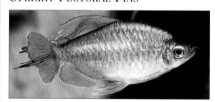

The pectoral fins on most mid-water fish, such as the Congo Tetra pictured above, are vertically disposed to give maximum maneuverability, especially during slow, measured movements.

VENTRAL FINS

A fish can change direction by angling its ventral fins (seen clearly on this damselfish). When moving at speed in a straight line, the ventral fins may be clamped tight to the body to reduce drag.

FLAT PECTORAL FINS

For many bottom-dwellers, such as this Plec, swimming agility is less important than remaining stationary on the substrate. Enlarged, horizontally orientated pectoral fins aid downward force.

SPECIAL FINS

The dorsal fin on most catfish has a stout first ray. This spiny ray, which is often very sharp, can be locked in an erect position to deter predators, to help lodge the fish in crevices, or (in some species) during breeding, either to stimulate the female or to hold her in a mating embrace. This feature, frequently a sexual characteristic, has a wide variety of functions and is sometimes used as a diagnostic tool for identifying species.

BODY PROCESSES

IN ORDER TO MAINTAIN the basic bodily functions necessary for their survival, fish are highly dependent on the medium in which they live. Water conditions – including temperature, chemical composition, and salinity – have a profound effect on the control of physiological processes in aquatic creatures. While most fish have a low tolerance to changes in salinity, some, such as salmon, migrate from fresh water to seawater and back again – a feat that requires alterations to their osmo-regulatory systems.

REGULATION OF BODY FLUIDS AND TEMPERATURE

Both freshwater and marine fish have roughly the same natural levels of salt and water in their bodies, but rely on very different mechanisms to maintain a balance between their body fluids and the saltiness of the external environment. A fish's skin is a semi-permeable membrane, allowing one-way transfer of water. By the natural process of osmosis, when two solutions of different concentration are separated by such a membrane, the weaker solution will flow through the membrane to dilute the stronger solution, until both are of equal strength.

Because the concentration of salts inside a freshwater fish is stronger than that of the water surrounding it, water is absorbed into the fish's body through the skin and gills. The fish does not need to drink any water, and its kidneys retain any essential salts while eliminating copious amounts of weak urine. In contrast, marine fish live in an environment that is saltier than they are, and therefore lose water from their bodies by osmosis. To combat dehydration, they must drink seawater. The unneeded salts are eliminated by the kidneys in small quantities of very concentrated, salty urine. Thus the saying "to drink like a fish" is appropriate only for marine species, which must continually take in water to survive. Because of the fundamental differences in the way they regulate their body fluid levels, freshwater and marine species cannot exist in each other's habitats.

When keeping fish in aquaria, it must be remembered that, in general, they cannot control their body temperature as mammals do. They assume the same temperature as that of the surrounding water, and the biological processes of each species are adapted to function within a particular temperature range. All captive fish should be maintained within limits that they can accommodate comfortably.

FRESHWATER FISH

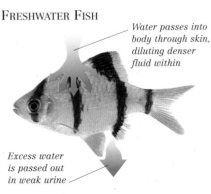

Water passes into body through skin, diluting denser fluid within

Excess water is passed out in weak urine

MARINE FISH

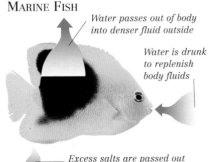

Water passes out of body into denser fluid outside

Water is drunk to replenish body fluids

Excess salts are passed out in very concentrated urine

RESPIRATION

Fish require oxygen every bit as much as humans, and extract it from the water in dissolved form. They lack true lungs as found in terrestrial creatures; instead, water is taken in through the mouth and passed over the gills, located on either side at the back of the head. As water passes over the gills, gases interact with the blood supply: oxygen is diffused across the gill membrane into the circulatory system and carbon dioxide waste is expelled into the water. A certain amount of ammonia may also be released via the gills, along with (in the case of freshwater fish) some water too. The water taken in through the mouth is then pushed out through the gill cover, or operculum. The vascular system distributes the oxygen throughout the fish's body, and picks up carbon dioxide waste to return to the gills for excretion, completing the cycle.

When water is depleted of dissolved oxygen, fish migrate to the surface, where oxygen levels are greatest. Fish seen atypically hanging at the surface are invariably in distress due to oxygen deprivation. In habitats where water levels regularly become low, some species have evolved ancillary means of respiration. *Corydoras* catfish and some loaches are able to gulp in air just above the water surface and then store it in their highly vascular hind guts for gradual dissipation into the bloodstream.

Even more specialized are catfish of the family Clariidae and many anabantids, which have developed a lung-like apparatus behind the gills that allows them to absorb oxygen from atmospheric air. This auxiliary structure, known as the labyrinth organ because of its maze-like construction, must remain damp in order to function; to retain moisture, fish can trap water inside this cavity. The labyrinth organ enables fish to survive periods of oxygen deficiency, usually in waters that are muddy, stagnant, shallow, or very warm.

"BREATHING" WITH GILLS

The gills are composed of highly vascular tissue in which the blood vessels are extremely close to the surface, giving healthy gills a reddish-pink hue. Running along a framework of gill arches, made of cartilage, are comb-like branches called filaments, containing plate-shaped lamellae, which carry large amounts of blood. The lamellae are very delicate, and can be easily damaged by suspended matter in the water; therefore, some fish have fine gill rakers to filter out such material, and to prevent food items from escaping.

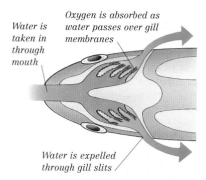

Water is taken in through mouth

Oxygen is absorbed as water passes over gill membranes

Water is expelled through gill slits

SLEEP

Most fish spend at least part of the day or night in a sort of suspended animation; indeed, it is possible to catch a sleeping fish by hand. Since they lack eyelids, fish may appear awake even when asleep. The variety of positions adopted for sleep can also be misleading. Some fish sleep lying on the bottom or hanging vertically – tail up, head down – near the substrate. Others may seek out a bolthole or crevice; yet others will sleep horizontally in mid-water.

In their natural reef environment, certain species of parrotfish hide in a nook and cocoon themselves in a thick, secreted mucus; upon waking, they struggle out of their "sleeping bag" to swim away.

When keeping fish in an aquarium, remember that tankmates may not share the same sleeping patterns. Do not keep small species that rest during the hours of darkness with nocturnal fish that may prey upon them.

SENSES AND INSTINCTS

SINCE THEY LIVE in water rather than on land, fish do not use the five main senses exactly as we do. These faculties have been adapted for an aquatic environment and, often, to suit certain conditions; for example, fish that inhabit murky waters rely more on taste and smell than on sight. A few species have also developed more obscure senses such as electrogenic radar. Each fish's physical attributes, capabilities, and instinctive behaviors are the result of evolution, and are essential to its particular lifestyle.

SIGHT

For most fish, the sense of sight is critical to survival: the ability to see food and potential spawning partners is as vital as the need to detect predators and other dangers. Their aquatic environment makes fish much more short-sighted than terrestrial creatures. Most have monocular vision (with each eye focusing independently), although a few, notably predatory, species are able to focus both eyes on an object. Anableps spp., the Four-eyed Fish, is a surface-dweller, and takes much of its food from above the water. As a result, the eye has developed a split focal length, giving good vision both underwater and above.

The eyes of mid-water fish tend to be large in relation to the size of their head, typically occupying 25–50 percent of the total area. The eyes are placed so that the fish has virtual all-round (monocular) vision. In predators, the eyes are often positioned to allow binocular vision, so that distances can be judged far more accurately, for efficient catching of prey.

Since it is difficult for light to penetrate deep water, bottom-dwelling fish rely less on sight than on the senses of smell and taste. Their eyes are relatively small, and are placed dorsally on the head, for good vision of danger approaching from overhead. Other fish, notably those that live in caves, have reduced eyes, or none at all, and are compensated with an exceptionally well-developed lateral line system for navigation.

Fish have no need for eyelids or tear ducts, since their eyes are constantly moistened by water. However, some species living in shallow, clear waters have a flap that can be lowered across the eye to shade the retina from bright sunlight.

MONOCULAR VISION
(NON-PREDATORY FISH)

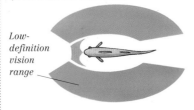

Low-definition vision range

BINOCULAR VISION
(PREDATORY FISH)

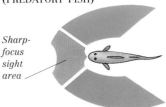

Sharp-focus sight area

In non-predatory fish, the eyes are usually located at the sides of the head. This permits a nearly 360-degree field of view – laterally, above, and below. Such wide-angle vision gives the fish early warning of danger coming from any direction.

In predators, the eyes are often placed side by side, as in humans, so that both eyes can focus on the same object. This stereoscopic sight gives a greatly improved sense of distance and a large area of high-definition vision for catching prey.

HEARING

Although they lack external ears, fish are able to hear through auditory organs found at the back of the skull. Since water is a denser medium than air, sound travels more easily underwater and is more readily sensed than on land. The fish's auditory organ also imparts a sense of balance. In some species, the swim bladder is connected to the inner ear by the Weberian apparatus, a series of small bones (ossicles) that act as levers, transmitting vibrations to the brain.

SMELL AND TASTE

Fish use the sense of smell to locate food at a distance. Unlike humans and other land animals, fish do not have a nose through which to breathe and smell. Instead, they have nostrils containing a number of minute sensory rosettes, liberally covered with smell receptors. These are linked via the neural system to the brain.

Most fish have two connecting pairs of nostrils, front and rear. Water is pumped by muscular action through the front nostril, passes over the sensory rosettes, and exits through the rear nostril. A vast number of catfish, particularly those with reduced vision, have enhanced twin nostrils, with an extended passage between the front and rear nostril, accommodating a greater number of smell rosettes and sensors. This makes the fish's sense of smell more acute. Cichlids, along with other perciformes, have just one pair of nostrils. Water is pumped both in and out of the same aperture.

Humans rely on a single taste organ, the tongue. Fish have a variety of taste receptors – on their lips, in the mouth, on the outside of the head, and, occasionally, on other parts of the body. A barbel is analogous to an external tongue. Simple barbels are often found on bottom-dwelling fish with ventrally placed mouths, and are used to scan the substrate for food. Some catfish, such as Synodontis spp., have relatively short, compound barbels with branches (fimbriations) to increase the surface area for deploying the sensory receptors.

There are other species with membranous barbels, which have a flap of skin to carry the taste receptors, while the large South American catfish Pseudodoras niger has a collection of appendages on the roof and floor of its mouth, all covered in tastebuds. Many gouramis have extensions to their pectoral fins that contain sensory receptors.

SIMPLE BARBELS

COMPOUND BARBELS

FIN EXTENSIONS

TOUCH

Fish do not utilize the sense of touch as we know it. They may flick or brush against objects to alleviate skin irritation caused by parasites, but generally touch is closely allied to taste. Barbels and some filamentous ventral fins are used to touch objects, but since these contain taste receptors, the fish is actually tasting what is available to eat. Nocturnally active, bottom-dwelling species such as many catfish often use their barbels for sensing their way in the dark.

Electric Organs

Inside the bodies of all vertebrates, tiny electrical discharges pass from the nerve endings to the muscles. However, in certain species of fish some muscle cells have been modified into electric organs that amplify these discharges. Fish with large, powerful electric organs, including members of the *Malapterurus* genus (the electric catfish), use them to stun prey and deter predators. The force produced is considerable, and in captivity such species must be handled with due care. Weaker organs (with emissions measurable only by instrumentation) are found in genera such as *Gnathonemus* (the Long-nosed Elephant Fish), and assist navigation by emitting an electrical field around the fish; any detected variations in the returning signals indicate obstacles or other creatures nearby. Such adaptations are of great benefit to electric species, which all have small eyes and live in relatively silty, murky waters, and therefore cannot rely on sight alone for navigation and food-finding.

Sound Making

Some fish can produce sounds, although the function of this behavior is not clear. Noises may be used simply to frighten off potential predators, or perhaps to assist solitary species in contacting a mate. Alternatively, sounds (which travel better underwater than through the air) may aid communication within a group, especially in cloudy waters where sight is of little use.

Since fish have no voice box, they must produce sounds by other means. Some species, particularly many catfish, partially lock the pectoral joint, creating friction between the two bones, resulting in a low, rumbling noise. In other fish, the swim bladder can be caused to vibrate, by using either the muscles attaching it within the body cavity or a complex arrangement of bones at the front of the bladder known as the elastic spring mechanism. In both cases, a growling tone is emitted. Yet other species, notably freshwater Botias and some marine fish, effect a very loud click by rapidly flicking a movable spine below the eye. The function of this noise is unknown.

Body Language

Like most creatures, fish communicate partially through body language. Certain fish will display to each other, sometimes as an aggressive pose or to indicate that they are poisonous, but more frequently as a means of attracting a mate. Many scientists and hobbyists believe that the body language of fish from the same family but inhabiting different continents may be contradictory, whereby a submissive stance by one species could be interpreted as a threat posture by another. Principal contrasts of this nature have been observed between American and African cichlids.

Territorial Behavior

Some species are naturally territorial, and will fend off all other creatures that enter its perceived territory – which in the wild may cover an area many times larger than can be provided in an aquarium. Territorial boundaries are often established at the onset of breeding. Aggression is frequently confined within a species, as with *Ancistrus* catfish, which will fight vehemently among themselves while making their individual homes in hollows or under pieces of wood, yet will virtually ignore all other fish. Fortunately, many fish will acquiesce to co-exist relatively peaceably once a pecking order has been determined.

Certain species are migratory, and in the wild may travel an enormous distance to a remote spawning site. The repression of this instinctive behavior may explain why some fish are unable to breed in captivity.

AN AQUATIC ECOSYSTEM

THE QUALITY OF natural waters is self-regulating. Fresh water is replenished by rainfall, water chemistry (pH and hardness) is controlled by the rocks and minerals over which it flows, and currents ensure that the water surface (the main means of oxygen exchange) is constantly changing. In the enclosed ecosystem of an aquarium, the volume of water is much smaller and far less stable, and water temperature and chemistry must be regulated artificially. Regular partial water changes are also required, to control the build-up of toxins. Finally, filtration is needed to establish and maintain the nitrogen cycle, a natural process that is essential for sustaining aquatic life.

THE NITROGEN CYCLE

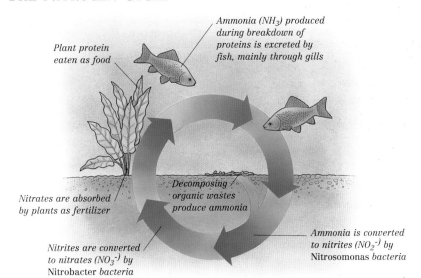

Plant protein eaten as food

Ammonia (NH_3) produced during breakdown of proteins is excreted by fish, mainly through gills

Nitrates are absorbed by plants as fertilizer

Decomposing organic wastes produce ammonia

Nitrites are converted to nitrates (NO_3^-) by Nitrobacter bacteria

Ammonia is converted to nitrites (NO_2^-) by Nitrosomonas bacteria

The nitrogen cycle is a natural chemical process by which dangerous toxins are converted into less harmful and even useful substances, creating a viable aquatic environment. In an aquarium, this cycle takes 36 days to settle and is achieved in three main stages. First, proteins break down to form ammonia (NH_3), which has a high toxicity. Protein sources include fish waste excreted from the vent and gills (the latter being the result of gaseous exchange during respiration) and decaying organic matter (such as bacteria, plants, and, in a stocked tank, any uneaten food or dead fish left in the aquarium). An unhealthy tank will emit a pungent odor of ammonia.

If the cycle is working correctly, the ammonia then converts into nitrites (NO_2^-); though also toxic to fauna, these convert into less harmful nitrates (NO_3^-). The nitrates are ingested as a fertilizer by plants, which flourish, supplying nutrients and dissolved oxygen to the tank, completing the cycle. If there are no plants, nitrates help to sustain beneficial bacteria in the filter. Excess nitrates are removed by water changes.

USING THE SPECIES GUIDES

NO BOOK ABOUT the care of living organisms can ever be more than a guide. Within any given group of creatures, there is always at least one that falls outside any generalizations that are made. While this work aims to provide you with all the basic information you will need to maintain your aquarium fish, invertebrates, and plants, fishkeeping does not strictly follow hard-and-fast rules. Before taking the "plunge" into the hobby, find out as much about it as you can; from there on, your own experience and research will be your guide. To become a successful aquarist, you must first understand and commit yourself to the hobby. Thereafter, the best advice is to never stop learning about your fish.

FRESHWATER AND BRACKISH-WATER AQUARIUM FISH

For the novice aquarist, there is a bewildering array of freshwater and brackish-water species to choose from. Firstly, remember that you cannot mix the two (the latter require conditions midway between freshwater and marine).

DWARF GOURAMI

Some fish have very specific requirements regarding water conditions, diet, and space. By consulting the entries in this book, you should be able to choose fish that you can successfully care for, and to select compatible species that you may mix and match in a community tank to suit your particular needs and taste.

The popularity of freshwater fish is partly owing to their relative hardiness and ease of care. Many species will tolerate minor fluctuations in tank conditions, with no major ill effects, although, as with all fish, it is important to avoid large, and especially sudden, changes. Although it may not be an initial consideration, many freshwater fish can also be aquarium-bred, and the young successfully reared to adulthood.

MONO

MARINE AQUARIUM FISH AND INVERTEBRATES

Often regarded as being the most impressive and desirable of aquariums, marine tanks aren't the easiest to maintain. Water conditions are critical, especially when caring for delicate invertebrates. If you have never kept fish before,

YELLOW TANG

it is advisable to gain some experience first with freshwater species, which are far more forgiving regarding water quality.

Since they are so demanding, marine species must be chosen with particular care. Although the prospect of keeping a reef-type aquarium with both fish and invertebrates is highly appealing, make sure that the inhabitants can co-exist peaceably, or you may witness underwater carnage! In your quest to create the perfect aquatic "picture," resist also the other common error of overstocking your tank. A marine aquarium stocked at the correct level will appear underpopulated, but do not be tempted to exceed the maximum number of creatures that your tank will accommodate, or their health will be at risk.

TOMPOT BLENNY

UNDERSTANDING THE SPECIES PROFILES

For easy reference, each fish or invertebrate featured in the book is individually profiled. Each entry provides all the vital information required for aquarists to maintain that particular species in good health. The tinted panels highlight relevant facts, including preferred tank conditions, while the main text comprises a brief description, with guidance on specific aspects of keeping, or notes on potential problems. To help you interpret each entry correctly, the various elements are defined below.

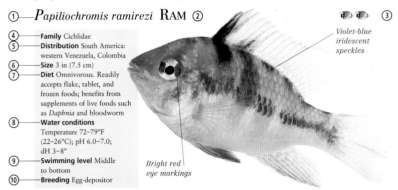

① *Papiliochromis ramirezi* RAM ②

③

Violet-blue iridescent speckles

④ **Family** Cichlidae
⑤ **Distribution** South America: western Venezuela, Colombia
⑥ **Size** 3 in (7.5 cm)
⑦ **Diet** Omnivorous. Readily accepts flake, tablet, and frozen foods; benefits from supplements of live foods such as *Daphnia* and bloodworm
⑧ **Water conditions** Temperature 72–79°F (22–26°C); pH 6.0–7.0; dH 3–8°
⑨ **Swimming level** Middle to bottom
⑩ **Breeding** Egg-depositor

Bright red eye markings

A popular fish, the Ram (also called the Dwarf Butterfly Cichlid) rarely looks its best when kept by novices, who tend to place it in a community tank with too many boisterous companions. ⑪ To feel at home, this somewhat nervous species requires small tetras to act as its lookouts – while they are swimming about happily, it knows it is safe. Provide densely planted shelters, as well as open areas of fine substrate with a few flat stones to rest or spawn on. Breeding pairs will dig pits for rearing and protecting their young.

Remarks: The female Ram is smaller, and has a reddish belly and a shortened second dorsal ray. ⑫ Both parents will tend their eggs and fry.

Softwater tank (pages 186–187) ⑬
Egg-depositors' breeding tank (page 241) ⑭

① **Scientific name** Expressed in Latin, this is the internationally recognized designation for that particular species; no other species will have the same name.

② **Common name** This may vary with locality. The name most commonly used in the aquarium trade is cited.

③ **Care rating** Indicates ease of care: a 1-fish symbol denotes a relatively easy-to-keep species; a 2-fish icon indicates a slightly more difficult species; and a 3-fish symbol designates a fairly challenging species for the more experienced fishkeeper. Factors that may contribute to a higher rating include potential size, specific eating habits, or difficulty in adapting to captivity.

④ **Family** Scientific grouping of closely related species.

⑤ **Distribution** Region, river system, lake, or ocean in which the species is naturally found.

⑥ **Size** Body length of the fish (excluding the caudal fin); unless otherwise stated, size is that which the fish can be expected to attain in an aquarium. Some fish grow larger in captivity than in the wild; others (notably marines) remain much smaller.

⑦ **Diet** The species' diet in the wild (carnivorous, herbivorous, or omnivorous), followed by suitable aquarium alternatives.

⑧ **Water conditions** These are most critical for marine species. Fish kept together must be able to live comfortably within the same ranges of temperature, acidity/alkalinity (pH), hardness (dH), and salinity (SG). See pages 214–215.

⑨ **Swimming level** Region(s) of the tank the fish is most likely to occupy (though in aquariums fish may alter natural habits).

⑩ **Breeding** Details of species' breeding strategy, if known.

⑪ **Profile** Overview of the species (looks, temperament, requirements, advice on keeping, and other considerations).

⑫ **Remarks** Notes on sexing, breeding, or special needs/habits.

⑬ **Recommended tank setup** Refers to featured tank setup (if any) suitable for the species.

⑭ **Recommended breeding tank setup** Refers to suggested breeding tank setup, if any (not relevant for marine species, which are not generally bred in home aquariums).

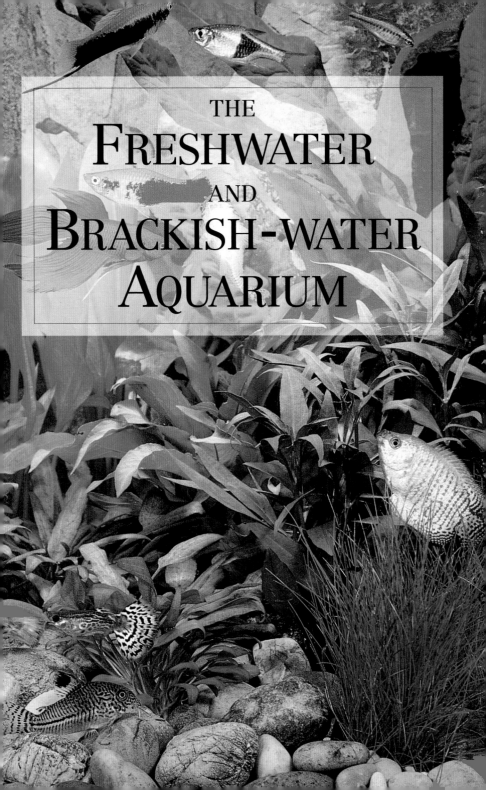

THE
FRESHWATER
AND
BRACKISH-WATER
AQUARIUM

FRESHWATER AND BRACKISH-WATER FISH

With several thousand tropical freshwater species available in the aquarium trade today, and with new varieties continually being developed, it is impossible to discuss the full range here. In the section that follows, many of the most common fish are profiled, with details of their basic requirements to help you make an informed choice when planning your aquarium. When mixing species in a community tank, it is important to ensure that the fish are compatible, not just regarding water conditions but also in size, temperament, lifestyle, required tank setup, and diet. If you are ready for an additional challenge, you may wish to try keeping brackish-water species – interesting fish that occupy specialized niches between a freshwater and marine environment.

◁ LARGE SCHOOL OF NEON TETRAS, AMONG THE MOST POPULAR FISH FOR A FRESHWATER AQUARIUM

ANABANTIDS

THE ANABANTIDS, OR "labyrinth fish," are African and Asian species that belong to the families Anabantidae, Belontiidae, Helostomatidae, and Osphronemidae. Many are highly colored and easy to breed – ideal for the aquarium trade. Others are farmed commercially as food fish, and some of these, notably the Giant Gourami (*Osphronemus* spp.), are also available to the hobbyist – although the Giant Gourami loses much of its charm in adulthood and will quickly outgrow an average-sized tank.

All anabantids have an auxiliary breathing organ, called a "labyrinth," which allows them to survive in inhospitable conditions such as the oxygen-deficient waters of evaporating ponds. Certain species can also migrate across land on humid nights, "walking" on their pectoral fins, in search of more favorable waters.

To help ensure the survival of their offspring, some anabantids construct bubble-nests near the water surface, maximizing the supply of oxygen to eggs and fry. Interestingly, it is the male fish that builds and guards the nest. For successful aquarium breeding, a tight-fitting cover must be used to maintain high humidity levels at the top of the tank; without this, many fry may be lost.

Betta splendens SIAMESE FIGHTER

Family Belontiidae	invertebrates preferred, either live or frozen; will also accept flake foods	75–84°F (24–29°C); pH 6.0–8.0; dH to 25°
Distribution Thailand, Cambodia		
Size 2¾ in (7 cm)		**Swimming level** Middle to top
Diet Omnivorous. Small aquatic	**Water conditions** Temperature	**Breeding** Bubble-nest builder

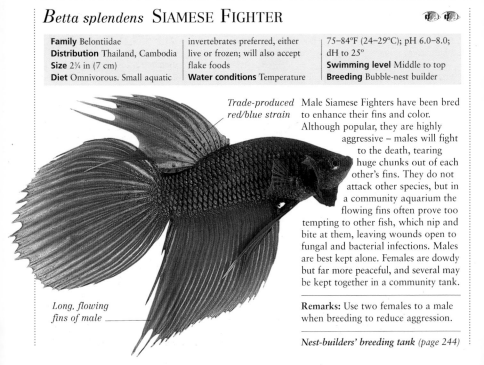

Trade-produced red/blue strain

Long, flowing fins of male

Male Siamese Fighters have been bred to enhance their fins and color. Although popular, they are highly aggressive – males will fight to the death, tearing huge chunks out of each other's fins. They do not attack other species, but in a community aquarium the flowing fins often prove too tempting to other fish, which nip and bite at them, leaving wounds open to fungal and bacterial infections. Males are best kept alone. Females are dowdy but far more peaceful, and several may be kept together in a community tank.

Remarks: Use two females to a male when breeding to reduce aggression.

Nest-builders' breeding tank (page 244)

Colisa lalia DWARF GOURAMI

Family Belontiidae
Distribution India
Size 2 in (5 cm)
Diet Omnivorous. Small aquatic invertebrates such as *Daphnia* and bloodworm, either live or frozen, plus flake foods; supplement with plenty of vegetable matter
Water conditions
Temperature 72–82°F (22–28°C); pH 6.5–7.5; dH to 15°
Swimming level Middle to upper
Breeding Bubble-nest builder

Touch-sensitive cells on ventral fin tips

Usually sold in pairs, the male is more colorful, with red and blue stripes; females are silvery. Orange, thread-like ventral fins carry sensory cells at their tips and are used to help locate food. Keep pairs in an established community tank with other peaceful fish. Commercial breeders have produced several color varieties, including royal blue and red. It is best to avoid crossing these with the original species.

Remarks: Since Dwarf Gouramis are somewhat prone to disease, water quality and careful choice of companions are crucial to their well-being. Any form of stress, such as poor water conditions or bullying, can promote infections. When breeding, ensure that there is plant material available to be incorporated into the bubble-nest.

Nest-builders' breeding tank (page 244)

Sphaerichthys osphromenoides CHOCOLATE GOURAMI

Family Belontiidae
Distribution Sumatra, Borneo, Malay Peninsula
Size 2 in (5 cm)
Diet Omnivorous. Live and frozen foods preferred, but will eventually accept flake foods
Water conditions 77–81°F
(25–27°C); pH 6.0–7.0; dH 2–4°
Swimming level Middle
Breeding Mouthbrooder or bubble-nest builder

Cut your teeth on other species before you try this one! You must maintain optimum water conditions in a mature, planted aquarium to prevent bacterial infections and skin parasites. High temperatures are recommended, but water quality could be more important. Raise the temperature a degree or two above the usual range only for breeding, which can then often be triggered by cooling the tank with a water change.

Remarks: Keep these fish only if you can provide the right conditions; buy a school of 6–10 and let them pair themselves. When spawning, the female broods the eggs in her mouth for 14 days, during which she does not feed; hence she must be in prime condition.

Mouthbrooders' breeding tank (page 243)

Trichogaster trichopterus THREE-SPOT GOURAMI

Family Belontiidae	**Diet** Omnivorous. Live, frozen,	72–82°F (22–28°C); pH 6.0–8.5;
Distribution Southeast Asia to	flake, and pellet foods; supplement	dH to 35°
the Indo-Australian Archipelago	with vegetable matter	**Swimming level** Middle to upper
Size 4 in (10 cm)	**Water conditions** Temperature	**Breeding** Bubble-nest builder

A good fish for the novice aquarist, the Three-spot Gourami is both hardy and easy to breed. Its common name refers to the markings on its flank, which align with the eye, forming a trio of spots. The body is a pale powder-blue color, and males can be distinguished by their longer, more pointed dorsal fin. Somewhat shy, the fish will hide away if bullied, and should be housed with other peaceful species of similar size in a community tank with good filtration. It prefers warm conditions and the cover of plants and caves made from rocks or bogwood.

Remarks: This species is also commonly known as the Blue Gourami because of its body color. It should be bought in pairs; males have a longer, more pointed dorsal fin than females. Males can be aggressive when breeding as they guard the nest; remove females after spawning. The fry are among the easiest anabantids to raise; feed them newly hatched brine shrimp and crumbled flake foods. Infusoria may also be given as a first food.

Tropical freshwater tank (pages 184–185)
Nest-builders' breeding tank (page 244)

GOLD GOURAMI

There are various tank-bred color forms of *Trichogaster trichopterus*, with Gold and Opaline types being more readily available than the true species. The Gold form has distinctive yellow and orange markings on the elongated anal fin, and males are more highly colored.

OPALINE GOURAMI

The Opaline is similar in color to the original species, but has a more marbled or mottled patterning rather than three defined spots. Like other color forms of the Three-spot Gourami, it does not occur in the wild. Females have a slightly more rounded body and anal fin.

Trichogaster leeri LACE GOURAMI

Family Belontiidae
Distribution Sumatra, Borneo, Malay Peninsula
Size 4¾ in (12 cm)
Diet Omnivorous. Small live foods such as mosquito larvae and *Cyclops*; also frozen, flake, tablet, and pellet foods, plus vegetable matter
Water conditions Temperature 72–82°F (22–28°C); pH 6.5–8.0; dH to 30°
Swimming level Middle to upper
Breeding Bubble-nest builder

Also known as Pearl Gouramis or Leeris, these striking fish are ideal for a large community tank with other peaceful species. Like other members of the genus *Trichogaster*, they are easy to keep, being tolerant of most water conditions. Readily sexable, males have longer fins, with a pointed dorsal fin and extended anal fin rays giving a ragged edge, and their throat and body are more red/orange, especially when ready to breed.

Remarks: Keep as pairs. They will often breed in a quiet corner of the community aquarium, either below floating plants or amid vegetation extending to the water surface. To save the fry from larger fish waiting for an easy meal, promptly transfer them to a separate rearing tank.

Tropical freshwater tank (pages 184–185)
Nest-builders' breeding tank (page 244)

Helostoma temminckii KISSING GOURAMI

Family Helostomatidae
Distribution Java, Thailand
Size 4–6 in (10–15 cm)
Diet Omnivorous. Plenty of vegetable foods, plus small aquatic invertebrates, either live or frozen; will also accept flake foods
Water conditions Temperature 72–82°F (22–28°C); pH 6.5–8.5; dH to 30°
Swimming level Middle
Breeding Egg-layer (floating eggs)

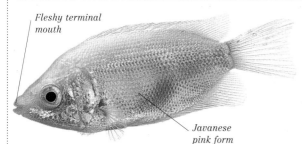

Fleshy terminal mouth

Javanese pink form

CHARACTERISTIC "KISSING"

These fish are often purchased for their novel "kissing" action, which in fact is not a sign of affection but a trial of strength between males and part of the courtship ritual. One of the larger gouramis, this species needs space, but it is not belligerent and can be kept with other similarly sized fish. There are two forms: pink from Java and green from Thailand. Although both are highly adaptable, they are happiest in warm water.

Remarks: Kissing Gouramis are useful for controlling algal growth in new setups, since they delicately pick the algae off plant leaves without damaging them. Keep the species in a large tank, furnished with hardy plants such as Java Fern, Amazon Sword, and Cryptocorynes, or plastic alternatives; soft-leaved plants will be eaten. Specimens of this fish are almost impossible to sex; pairs produce floating eggs.

CATFISH

CATFISH ARE A very diverse group, with over 30 families and in excess of 2,000 species. They are found worldwide (with the exception of the poles) in fresh, brackish, and marine habitats, and come in all shapes and sizes. Catfish are scaleless; some have bony plates, or scutes, on their flanks, formed from ossified skin folds.

A catfish's most notable features are their barbels – thin filaments on the sides of the mouth, resembling feline whiskers (hence "catfish") – and the sharp spines on their fins; beware of these when handling your fish.

Many catfish are nocturnal, though some genera, such as *Corydoras*, are active in the daytime. Most live at or near the bottom of the water and require areas of seclusion where they can hide or rest. One African genus, *Malapterurus*, is able to generate electricity, discharging up to 350 volts!

Feeding habits for catfish vary from out-and-out predators to gentle, grazing herbivores. Generally, fish with long barbels are hunters, using these extensions to locate prey. Members of the Asian genus *Chaca*, however, look unassuming, with very short barbels, but have a capacious mouth – they can swallow fish up to half their size! Check with your dealer before buying a particular species.

Brochis splendens SAILFIN CORYDORAS

Family Callichthyidae	Diet Omnivorous. Small aquatic	Temperature 70–81°F (21–27°C);
Distribution South America:	invertebrates, either live or	pH 6.0–7.5; dH 6–25°
Ecuador, Peru, Brazil	frozen; also flake and tablet foods	Swimming level Bottom
Size 2¾ in (7 cm)	Water conditions	Breeding Egg-depositor

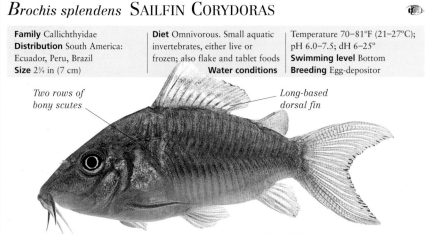

Two rows of bony scutes

Long-based dorsal fin

A splendid fish for the community aquarium, the Sailfin Corydoras should be kept in a group, or with *Corydoras* catfish. It likes to rummage about in the substrate for small invertebrates and bits of food, but will not uproot plants. A soft, sandy substrate is ideal to prevent damage to the barbels. These fish may breed in a tank; the eggs are placed on the underside of broad plant leaves or, sometimes, on the aquarium glass.

Remarks: The fish's common name refers to the large, sail-like dorsal fin of juvenile specimens. Also known as the Emerald or Green Catfish, it is often confused with the similarly colored Bronze Corydoras (*Corydoras aeneus*). However, fish of the genus *Brochis* have 10–18 dorsal fin rays, while *Corydoras* catfish have just 6–8.

Egg-depositors' breeding tank (page 241)

Corydoras barbatus BARBATUS CATFISH

Family Callichthyidae
Distribution South America: Brazil (Rio de Janeiro, São Paulo)
Size 4¾ in (12 cm)
Diet Omnivorous. Small aquatic invertebrates such as *Cyclops, Tubifex,* and *Daphnia,* either live or frozen; supplement with flake and tablet foods
Water conditions Temperature 72–79°F (22–26°C); pH 6.5–7.5; dH to 12°
Swimming level Bottom
Breeding Egg-depositor

Among the larger *Corydoras* species, the Barbatus, or Bearded, Catfish is suitable for the mature community aquarium. There are two color forms, with male specimens from the Rio de Janeiro region having more intense gold reticulations on the head, along with a very distinct golden yellow stripe down the center of the head. In both color forms, males can be distinguished by the bristles on their cheeks when in breeding condition. Fin spines in males are also usually longer than in females.

Remarks: Pairs will often spawn in a community tank, either on the glass or on leaves. The eggs can be removed for hatching in a separate tank.

Tropical freshwater tank (pages 184–185)
Egg-depositors' breeding tank (page 241)

Corydoras paleatus PEPPERED CORYDORAS

Family Callichthyidae
Distribution South America: southeastern Brazil, La Plata river system
Size 2¾ in (7 cm)
Diet Omnivorous. Small aquatic invertebrates, either live or frozen, as well as flake and sinking tablet foods; also include some green foods
Water conditions Temperature 68–75°F (20–24°C); pH 6.5–7.5; dH to 12°
Swimming level Middle to bottom
Breeding Egg-depositor

This species is a mainstay for catfish hobbyists. Specimens often look drab, but in a suitable environment, and if fed plenty of live foods (or frozen equivalents), they develop a beautiful greenish/bronze sheen. These fish will tolerate a wide range of water conditions, as long as extremes of pH and hardness are avoided. Sex them by shape (males are slimmer than females), and by the more pointed anal fins of males.

Remarks: An albino form is available; it requires similar care to its pigmented relative. The species is usually bred in a specially setup tank using a pair, or two males per female. At 73°F (23°C), eggs will hatch in about five days. Once the yolk sac is absorbed, feed newly hatched brine shrimp.

Tropical freshwater tank (pages 184–185)
Egg-depositors' breeding tank (page 241)

Ancistrus spp. BRISTLENOSE CATFISH

Family Loricariidae
Distribution South America:
Guyana and surrounding areas
Size 4¾ in (12 cm)
Diet Herbivorous. Algae, raw
or blanched green vegetables,
as well as frozen and flake
foods; diet should also include
bogwood, which is rasped to
create hollows for shelter
Water conditions
Temperature 72–77°F
(22–25°C); pH 6.5–7.5;
dH to 12°
Swimming level Bottom
Breeding Egg-depositor

Consult your dealer on the many available species of *Ancistrus*, known as the Bushynose Catfish in the US. Some are commonly bred and cheap to buy; others are more specialized, difficult to keep, and expensive. They are suitable for a mature, planted community aquarium. Provide plenty of green foods and some bogwood, which forms part of their diet. An efficient filtration system is essential to maintain water quality.

Remarks: Males are particularly territorial, using their interopercular spines (erectile spines that protrude from the gill area) in disputes. Keep as pairs – mature males develop bushy tubercules on the snout. Breeding is in caves or hollows; eggs are guarded by the male. Feed fry on lettuce and peas.

Tropical freshwater tank (pages 184–185)
Egg-depositors' breeding tank (page 241)

Hypancistrus zebra ZEBRA PLEC

Family Loricariidae
Distribution South America:
Rio Xingu, Brazil
Size 2¾ in (7 cm)
Diet Omnivorous. Small live
aquatic invertebrates such as
Tubifex and *Daphnia*, and
chopped earthworms, plus
frozen and flake foods; meaty
foods preferred to vegetables
Water conditions
Temperature 72–81°F
(22–27°C); pH 6.5–7.0;
dH 5–12°
Swimming level Bottom
Breeding Egg-depositor

Imported as a new species, this fish was marketed as L46 until officially described in 1991. Its bold coloration made it an instant success, and high prices reflected this. Relatively easy to maintain, the Zebra Plec (or Pleco, as it is also known) prefers quiet companions, plenty of hiding places, subdued lighting, and a gentle water flow. Its diet may surprise you; after all, loricariids are supposed to be herbivores – this one likes meat!

Remarks: Mature males have a larger head and longer interopercular spines than females. After spawning, the male guards the eggs. Fry swim after seven days, absorbing the yolk sac in two weeks. Feed newly hatched brine shrimp, followed by vegetable flakes and tiny frozen foods. For breeding, keep at 86°F (30°C); pH 6.5; dH 4°.

Egg-depositors' breeding tank (page 241)

Hypostomus plecostomus PLEC

Family Loricariidae
Distribution Northern
South America
Size 11 in (28 cm)
Diet Omnivorous. Green
foods such as lettuce and
peas, plus vegetable-based
flake foods; will also accept
small live or frozen foods
Water conditions
Temperature 68–82°F (20-
–28°C); pH 6.0–8.0;
dH to 25°
Swimming level Bottom
Breeding Egg-layer (not
bred in aquariums)

This incredibly hardy fish is usually bought as an algae eater for the community aquarium. This is fine, if you have a large tank. Bred commercially in large numbers, small specimens are cheap and endearing, but grow quickly. In six months, 4 in (10 cm) Plecs can almost double in length. Although peaceful, they can be quite destructive when moving about the tank, lashing plants and dislodging rocks with a swipe of their powerful tails. Like all loricariids, they are poor swimmers, frequently anchoring themselves to surfaces with their distinctive underslung sucker mouths. They produce copious amounts of feces; therefore a highly efficient filtration system is needed.

Remarks: Plecs are ideal in a very ample tank, with other large feature fish. Include some wood for them to use as a resting place and retreat.

Otocinclus affinis DWARF OTOCINCLUS

Family Loricariidae
Distribution South America:
southeastern Brazil
Size 1½ in (4 cm)

Diet Herbivorous. Algae and
green foods, but will also take
small live, frozen, and flake foods
Water conditions Temperature

70–79°F (21–26°C); pH 5.5–7.5;
dH to 10°
Swimming level Bottom to/middle
Breeding Egg-depositor

Dark band extends
through eye

Thin, almost
tadpole-like,
body shape

In acclimating this species, water conditions are all-important; also feed plenty of green foods (lettuce and peas are good choices). An external power filter with spray bar return will provide the high oxygen levels these fish need. With too little oxygen, they tend to hang near the surface and may even poke their snouts out of the water. To remedy this, reduce the temperature gradually, increase the water flow, and make sure that the aquarium is not overcrowded. Keep *Otocinclus affinis* as a group in a mature, well-planted tank with other small, peaceful species.

Remarks: Males are slimmer than females; can be tank-bred, but raising the fry is often difficult.

Softwater tank (pages 186–187)
Egg-depositors' breeding tank (page 241)

Synodontis multipunctatus CUCKOO SYNODONTIS

Family Mochokidae
Distribution Africa: Lake Tanganyika
Size 4¾ in (12 cm)
Diet Insectivorous. Small live aquatic invertebrates; will also accept frozen, flake, and tablet foods
Water conditions Temperature 70–77°F (21–25°C); pH 6.8–8.0; dH 15–30°
Swimming level Bottom to middle
Breeding Mouthbrooder (vicariously, as described)

This species is ideal for a Lake Tanganyikan or Lake Malawi aquarium, since extensive rockwork is essential for both the cichlids and the catfish. The latter is relatively easy to maintain and feed, and is active both day and night. Keep in a mature, well-filtered tank; plants are optional.

Remarks: The fish's common name refers to its breeding strategy, similar to that of the cuckoo bird. When the mouthbrooding cichlids are spawning, the Cuckoo Synodontis deposits its eggs among the cichlid eggs, so that both are taken up into the mouth of the cichlid, which then broods and raises the catfish fry along with its own. Since the catfish young hatch first, they prey on the cichlid eggs.

Mouthbrooders' breeding tank (page 243)

Synodontis nigriventris UPSIDE-DOWN CATFISH

Family Mochokidae
Distribution Africa: Zaire Basin
Size Male 3¼ in (8 cm); Female 4 in (10 cm)
Diet Insectivorous. Live, frozen, and flake foods; prefers to take floating material, turning upside down to feed
Water conditions Temperature 72–79°F (22–26°C); pH 6.5–7.5; dH to 12°
Swimming level Middle to top
Breeding Egg-depositor

Peaceful and undemanding, this catfish is happy in a well-maintained community aquarium. It is active only at twilight, when it inverts to feed from the surface. The fish's underside is darker than its back, making it less conspicuous to predators when feeding. In a tank, provide some floating bark and the fish will shelter under this, darting out to feed. If nothing else is available, it will accept tablet foods from the substrate.

Remarks: This species is susceptible to White Spot and, if water conditions deteriorate, bacterial infections. It can be aquarium-bred; males are smaller, slimmer, and more colorful than females. Feed the fry newly hatched brine shrimp. The young do not adopt inverted swimming until they are about two months old.

Egg-depositors' breeding tank (page 241)

Pimelodus pictus ANGELIC PIM

Family Pimelodidae	**Diet** Insectivorous. Live, frozen,	dH to 12°
Distribution South America:	and flake foods	**Swimming level** Middle to upper
Colombia	**Water conditions** Temperature	**Breeding** Egg-layer (details
Size 4¼ in (12 cm)	72–77°F (22–25°C); pH 6.0–6.8;	unknown)

A perennial favorite because of its striking coloration, the Angelic Pim requires diligently maintained water conditions. Although relatively peaceful, it is a hunter by nature, and should be kept only with companions it cannot eat – Neon Tetras and other small fish have been known to disappear overnight into the stomachs of these predatory catfish. They prefer to be kept as a small school and will swim together.

Remarks: The species is prone to disease if water quality deteriorates. Handle with care; these fish have very sharp fin spines which can pierce the skin painfully. If the spines become tangled in a net, put the net and fish back into the tank and leave the fish to free itself. Never attempt to pull the net from the fin; this can damage the musculature that operates the fin spine. Carefully cut away the net instead.

Kryptopterus bicirrhis GLASS CATFISH

Family Siluridae	frozen foods; supplement with	dH to 15°
Distribution India, Southeast Asia	flake foods	**Swimming level** Middle to upper
Size 4 in (10 cm)	**Water conditions** Temperature	**Breeding** Egg-layer (details
Diet Insectivorous. Small live and	72–79°F (22–26°C); pH 6.0–7.0;	unknown)

ANGLED RESTING POSITION

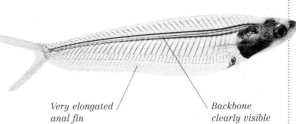

Very elongated / anal fin

Backbone clearly visible

Also known as the Ghost Catfish, this unusual, transparent-bodied fish is commonly bought as a novelty, but deserves greater appreciation. It is best kept as a school – single specimens tend to pine, hide away, and may even die. Allow plenty of swimming space, and maintain water quality to prevent bacterial infections. Provide efficient filtration giving a moderate water flow. The fish prefers small live foods, but will accept frozen substitutes, with flake foods taken as a last resort. Although generally unaggressive, it may eat small fry if the opportunity arises.

Remarks: At rest, these fish hang, tail down, at an angle of about 30° – this is quite normal. When swimming, the body becomes horizontal.

Egg-depositors' breeding tank (page 241)

CHARACINS

CHARACINS ARE A large group of fish native to Africa (about 30 genera and more than 200 species) and South and Central America (250 genera and over 1,000 species). Those kept in aquariums range from tiny tetras to formidable piranhas, and from hatchetfishes to slender pencilfishes. Most characins have teeth and a small, rayless fin (the adipose fin) behind the dorsal fin; its function is unclear. A series of bones linking the swim bladder to the inner ear, called the Weberian apparatus, enhances their hearing. Characins comprise predators, vegetarians, mud-grubbers, filter-feeders, and even some that feed on scales. However, most characins found in the hobby are insectivores, and take live, frozen, and flake foods.

AFRICAN TETRAS

LIKE MANY CHARACINS, African tetras are schooling fish from clear, flowing waters. In aquariums, they need good water quality with high oxygen levels. Active swimmers, these tetras need space and are best kept in a long, well-planted tank. They appreciate a slight current, as provided by a power filter, but can be overwhelmed if the water flow is too strong.

Arnoldichthys spilopterus AFRICAN RED-EYED TETRA

Family Alestidae
Distribution West Africa
Size 3¼ in (8 cm)
Diet Insectivorous. Small live or frozen aquatic invertebrates such as mosquito larvae and bloodworm, supplementing meaty items with flake foods; feed newly hatched fry on brine shrimp nauplii
Water conditions Temperature 73–82°F (23–28°C); pH 6.0–7.5; dH to 20°
Swimming level Middle
Breeding Egg-scatterer

This species requires a relatively large tank offering plenty of swimming space. In the right environment, with a dark substrate, subdued lighting (or the shelter of plants), the water conditions indicated above, and a supply of live or frozen foods, the fish develop very delicate hues of gold, green, and pink along their flanks, and any colours in the finnage deepen. The red-orange upper eye gives the species its common name.

Remarks: The dorsal fin bears a dark blotch. Males have a convex anal fin striped in yellow, red, and black. In females, this fin is mainly clear with a straight rear edge. Soft, acidic conditions are needed for spawning. A pair may produce 1,000 eggs. The fry are timid, and if frightened will not come out to feed. Growth is rapid.

Egg-scatterers' breeding tank (page 240)

Lepidarchus adonis JELLY BEAN TETRA

Family Alestidae
Distribution West Africa
Size ¾ in (2 cm)
Diet Insectivorous. Small live or frozen aquatic invertebrates such as mosquito larvae and bloodworm are beneficial, but will accept flake foods; feed newly hatched fry on brine shrimp nauplii
Water conditions
Temperature 72–79°F (22–26°C); pH 5.5–6.5; dH to 6°
Swimming level Middle
Breeding Egg-depositor

A fish for the specialist, the Jelly Bean Tetra (or Adonis Characin) can be difficult to acclimate but, once settled, it is easy to keep and breed – if suitable water conditions are maintained. Unless you have naturally soft water, be prepared to invest in water-softening equipment. Keep this delicate little fish in a school with other small, peaceful species. The tank should have many fine-leaved plants and very gentle filtration.

Remarks: Males have numerous dark spots on the body; females are virtually transparent. Very soft, acidic conditions (less than 4° dH is fine) are required for breeding, with 20–30 eggs laid on plants. Although tiny, the fry will accept newly hatched brine shrimp. Keep the spawning tank darkened, since the young shy away from light.

Egg-depositors' breeding tank (page 241)

Phenacogrammus interruptus CONGO TETRA

Family Alestidae
Size Male 3¼ in (8.5 cm)
Female 2¼ in (6 cm)
Distribution Zaire
Diet Insectivorous. Live or frozen foods such as mosquito larvae and bloodworm, as well as flake foods; feed fry on infusoria and brine shrimp
Water conditions
Temperature 72–81°F (22–27°C); pH 6.0–7.5; dH 4–18°
Swimming level Middle to top
Breeding Egg-scatterer

This is a prized fish for a large display tank, where adult males can display their flamboyant finnage to their chosen female. Keep in a school with both sexes; young specimens are cheaper to buy. Feed a varied diet, monitor water conditions, and you will raise a group of magnificent fish.

Remarks: Congo Tetras are susceptible to disease if water quality deteriorates. Males may have

their flowing fins nipped – choose companions with care! The drabber females have short fins. Spawning can be initiated by sunlight or a water change. Use the recommended breeding setup to prevent eggs falling to the bottom and being eaten. Feed the fry plenty of brine shrimp.

Tropical freshwater tank (pages 184–185)
Egg-scatterers' breeding tank (page 240)

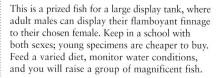

SOUTH AMERICAN TETRAS

ALL TETRAS are popular aquarium fish, but the Neon and Cardinal rank as favorites. Tetras are true schooling fish and should be kept as such, for your benefit as well as theirs – watching a group interact is far more satisfying than searching for the lone specimen cowering behind a plant leaf. Since they prefer the company of their own kind, buy eight to 10 specimens of one species, and perhaps six to eight of another, rather than many types.

Even the hardiest species require soft, slightly acidic conditions and should be introduced to aquariums that have matured for several months. Tetras are happiest in a well-planted tank with subdued or natural lighting.

If using a pale substrate such as sand, carpet part of it with plants to reduce reflected light. Choose companions with care: small tetras frequently become food for larger fish! Tetras themselves will readily accept flake foods, but thrive on supplements of live or frozen aquatic invertebrates.

Males are generally slimmer-bodied than females, and often have long, flowing fins. Although tetras may breed in a community aquarium, the other inhabitants are likely to eat the eggs. It is safer to move the pairs to a special spawning tank; afterwards, return them and raise the fry in the breeding tank. First foods must be very small and finely textured.

Family Characidae	foods such as insect larvae; also	72–79°F (22–26°C); pH 5.0–7.0;
Distribution South America	frozen, flake, and pellet foods,	dH to 10°
Size Varies; see species	supplemented with green foods	**Swimming level** Middle to top
Diet Omnivorous. Small live	**Water conditions** Temperature	**Breeding** Egg-scatterer

Hemigrammus erythrozonus
GLOWLIGHT TETRA

Almost as popular as the Neon and Cardinal Tetras, this 1½ in (4 cm) fish is relatively easy to keep, but can be a challenge to breed. Try pairs set up in a breeding tank with clumps of Java Moss and soft, acidic, warm water. The fish's coloring, distinguished by a red-gold line from snout to tail, gives the impression of a warm filament in a bulb – hence the name "Glowlight."

Hemigrammus pulcher
PRETTY TETRA

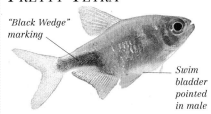

"Black Wedge" marking

Swim bladder pointed in male

Also known as the Black Wedge Tetra, this gentle, 1¾ in (4.5 cm) species is suitable for softwater community aquariums with moderate filtration. If breeding, allow the fish to pair themselves; otherwise, you may find yourself swapping one of the sexes before establishing a compatible pair. As with other *Hemigrammus* species, eggs are laid over and through plants.

Hyphessobrycon erythrostigma
BLEEDING HEART TETRA

The males' extended dorsal and anal fins, along with their attractive coloration, make these fish very popular, but remember to keep the less flamboyant females as well, so that the males have mates to display to. The breeding habits of this 2¼ in (6 cm) species are not well known.

Moenkhausia pittieri
DIAMOND TETRA

Iridescent scales

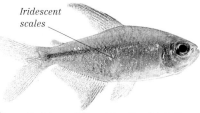

Keep this fish carefully, with a diet rich in live foods, especially black mosquito larvae, and it will develop strong finnage and a beautiful metallic sheen. The species can grow to 2¼ in (6 cm).

Softwater tank (pages 186–187)

Paracheirodon axelrodi
CARDINAL TETRA

Just 2 in (5 cm) long, this vividly colored species is a real gem, shimmering in electric blue and red. Most trade specimens are wild-caught. For best colors (and breeding conditions), provide soft, acidic water; excess calcium salts can lead to internal blockages and "inexplicable" death.

Hyphessobrycon pulchripinnis
LEMON TETRA

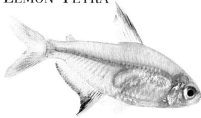

This lovely species is often overlooked because it does not show its best colors in the glare of a dealer's tank. Growing to only 1¾ in (4.5 cm), these fish prefer a tank that is heavily planted at the sides, and relatively soft, acidic conditions. Without such care, they tend to lose their color.

Nematobrycon palmeri
EMPEROR TETRA

Preferring aged water and softer, slightly more acidic, conditions than many other tetras, this fish is fully grown at 2 in (5 cm). Not a very prolific species, it lays its eggs one at a time among fine-leaved plants such as clumps of Java Moss – and then typically eats some!

Paracheirodon innesi
NEON TETRA

The most popular aquarium fish in the hobby today, Neon Tetras are bred by the thousands for shipment worldwide. Their slim bodies sport the same bright blue-green stripe as the Cardinal, but the lower front is silver. Hardy and peaceful, this 1½ in (4 cm) fish can live for over 10 years.

Softwater tank (pages 186–187) **ALL S. A. TETRAS** *Egg-scatterers' breeding tank (page 240)*

HATCHETFISHES

HATCHETFISHES HAVE an unusual shape: compressed laterally, with a straight dorsal profile, a deeply keeled body, and pectoral fins set high like wings. True surface-dwellers, their upturned mouth is designed for feeding from the top of the water. Species vary in size from 1 in (2.5 cm) to 3½ in (9 cm).

Hatchetfishes are notoriously difficult to keep – so much so that some dealers refuse to stock them. However, if you find some that appear healthy and are feeding well, and you can provide the soft, acidic conditions that they prefer, consider trying them once you have fishkeeping experience.

Keep hatchetfishes in schools of six or more; they are not happy in small numbers. Be prepared to feed small live foods or frozen equivalents; flake foods are insufficient, and some species will refuse them.

Prime water conditions must be maintained to keep hatchetfishes in good health. A well-fitting cover is also essential, since these fish can jump; some can even "fly" for several feet by flapping their pectoral fins.

Members of the genus *Carnegiella* are relatively small and suited to quiet community tanks; they lack an adipose fin. Larger hatchetfishes are slightly more robust, but swim quickly and need lots of space, in a tank no shorter than 4 ft (1.25 m). They like a fairly strong flow of well-oxygenated water.

Family Gasteropelecidae **Distribution** Northern South America **Size** Varies; see species	**Diet** Carnivorous. Varied diet of small live or frozen foods; may also accept some flake foods **Water conditions** Temperature	72–82°F (22–28°C); pH 6.0–7.0; dH 5–15° **Swimming level** Top **Breeding** Egg-depositor

Carnegiella strigata
MARBLED HATCHETFISH

Just 1½ in (4 cm) long, this small hatchetfish is prone to White Spot, so avoid all forms of stress. Condition for breeding with black mosquito larvae and small flies. The fry are difficult to raise.

Softwater tank (pages 186–187)

Gasteropelecus sternicula
COMMON HATCHETFISH

This species is slightly more tolerant of water conditions than *G. maculata* (which requires high oxygen levels and regular water changes with aged water), and are 1 in (2.5 cm) smaller, at 2½ in (6.5 cm). Viewed from above, males are more slim than females. Keep in a quiet tank.

PENCILFISHES

PEACEFUL PENCILFISHES of the genera *Nannobrycon* and *Nannostomus* make a welcome addition to a quiet community aquarium. House them in a species tank if you have more boisterous species that may prevent these small, timid fish from feeding.

By day, pencilfishes tend to hide near the surface beneath plant leaves or among trailing roots, resting motionless at an angle in the water. At night they are more active, coming out to search for food, and their daytime color pattern of horizontal stripes fades into vertical blotches. Curiously, some individuals have an adipose fin, while others do not. Keep pencilfishes as a group of six or more in soft, slightly acidic water, free of nitrates. Provide thickets of vegetation and some floating plants to help maintain correct conditions and to give the fish shade and cover. The pH may fluctuate between 5.5 and 7.0, provided any changes are not sudden. Peat filtration is beneficial, and will soften the water. Any rocks, gravel, or sand used must be non-calcareous; a dark substrate is best.

Although pencilfishes will accept most small foods, live foods are essential to condition them for breeding. Set up a tank at pH 6.0 and dH 2° or less, with dim lighting and Java Moss, and remove the parents after spawning. Give the fry tiny foods.

Family Lebiasinidae	depending on species	72–75°F (22–24°C); pH 5.0–6.5;
Distribution Central and	**Diet** Omnivorous. Live, frozen,	dH to 8°
northern South America	and flake foods	**Swimming level** Middle to upper
Size 1½–2¾ in (3.5–7 cm),	**Water conditions** Temperature	**Breeding** Egg-depositor

Nannobrycon eques 🐟 🐟
THREE-STRIPED PENCILFISH

Not often available, this fish, measuring 2 in (5 cm), can be difficult to acclimate and may initially take only small live foods. Males are slimmer and much more colorful than females.

Egg-depositors' breeding tank (page 241)

Nannostomus beckfordi 🐟 🐟
GOLDEN PENCILFISH

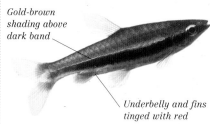

Gold-brown shading above dark band

Underbelly and fins tinged with red

Probably the hardiest of the pencilfishes, this 2¼ in (6 cm) species can be kept in most community tanks, if free of predators. Breed at 86°F (30°C).

Softwater tank (pages 186–187)
Egg-depositors' breeding tank (page 241)

Serrasalmus nattereri RED-BELLIED PIRANHA

Family Characidae	**Diet** Carnivorous. Meaty foods,	73–81°F (23–27°C); pH 5.5–7.5;
Distribution South America:	such as pieces of fish, whole fish,	dH to 20°
Guyana to La Plata river system	worms, flesh of any kind	**Swimming level** All areas
Size 11 in (28 cm)	**Water conditions** Temperature	**Breeding** Egg-depositor

Mature steely gray coloring with iridescent markings

Long anal fin on deep, sturdily-built oval body

Although popular in the hobby because of its fearsome reputation, this fish is banned or restricted for import in several countries, notably the USA, to prevent their escape or release into free waters, where they may survive, multiply, and devastate the native aquatic fauna, as well as posing a risk to human swimmers. Anyone buying a piranha should be aware of the potential dangers in keeping them.

Young piranhas are attractive, silvery fish with numerous black spots and blotches, and red coloring around the anal fin, pectoral fin, and gills. As they mature, the spots fade to a grayish silver, and the throat and belly redden.

Adult piranhas achieve a prodigious size, and should be treated with due respect. In an aquarium they will rarely incite an attack, but may react aggressively if cornered or frightened – and their sharp teeth can inflict a painful wound. Keep your hands, and others', out of the tank. If you need to move a fish, do not support it in the net with your hand – fright may provoke a bite.

Piranhas should be kept in a species aquarium with very efficient filtration, to cope with their high-protein waste. Three or four youngsters can be kept in a 3 ft (90 cm) tank, but will need larger quarters as they grow. Provide a suitable diet, but neither overfeed nor starve your fish.

Remarks: Piranhas can be tank-bred. Males have a gold sheen with a red throat and belly; females are more yellow. The male guards the nest. Fry must be sorted by size and separated, and given plenty of live foods, to prevent cannibalism.

Tropical freshwater tank (pages 184–185)
Egg-depositors' breeding tank (page 241)

SCHOOL OF COLORFUL YOUNG PIRANHAS

Astyanax fasciatus mexicanus BLIND CAVE FISH

Family Characidae
Distribution Texas; Mexico;
Central America
to Panama
Size 3½ in (9 cm)
Diet Omnivorous. Will accept
almost all foods, from flake
to frozen to live, including any
creatures that may fall into the
tank, such as spiders or flies
Water conditions
Temperature 68–77°F
(20–25°C); pH 6.0–7.8;
dH to 30°
Swimming level All areas
Breeding Egg-scatterer

Totally undemanding, this unusual fish is easily accommodated in the average community tank. The species' most notable feature is its lack of eyes – these have become superfluous in its natural habitat, where it navigates pitch-dark underground cave waters using its lateral line system. In captivity, it has no special requirements concerning lighting levels. Keep in mixed-sex schools; males are slimmer than females.

Remarks: At the lower end of its temperature range, the Blind Cave Fish breeds readily. Fry are easy to raise on fine live foods. Interestingly, the young have eyes, which regress as the fish matures. There is also a pigmented, surface-dwelling variety of the species, *Astyanax fasciatus fasciatus*; this is not often available.

Egg-scatterers' breeding tank (page 240)

Chilodus punctatus SPOTTED HEADSTANDER

Family Anostomidae	**Diet** Omnivorous. Vegetable items,	75–82°F (24–28°C); pH 6.0–7.0
Distribution South America:	algae, small live foods such as	dH to 10°
Guyanas and upper Amazon	*Daphnia*, tablet and flake foods	**Swimming level** Middle to bottom
Size 3½ in (9 cm)	**Water conditions** Temperature	**Breeding** Egg-depositor

*Sail-shaped dorsal fin
with dark blotches*

*Spotted pattern
follows central
line along flank*

*Elongate body tapers
into pointed head*

The Spotted Headstander, named for its distinctive head-down swimming position, is a delightful fish for the more experienced hobbyist with a well-established, peaceful aquarium. Keep as a group of 3–4 rather than as single specimens. Water conditions are critical; maintain these with efficient filtration. Keep lighting subdued, or provide thickets of plants, roots, or other shelter; these shy fish usually remain in the shade, emerging to feed.

Remarks: After spawning among the roots of floating plants, parents should be removed. Fry swim head-down from birth; give newly hatched brine shrimp as a first food.

*Egg-depositors' breeding tank
(page 241)*

CICHLIDS

CICHLIDS ARE MAINLY freshwater fish, a few being salt-tolerant. Most come from Africa and South and Central America, although some species are found in Syria, Jordan, Iran, southern India, and Madagascar. Certain cichlids are important food fish, and are farmed in many parts of the world.

There are well over 1,000 species; all have two lateral lines but only one pair of nostrils. Although the largest can reach 20 in (50 cm), most are fairly small, and many are brightly colored, especially when breeding.

Aquarists are often attracted to cichlids by their intriguing behavior, which includes elaborate strategies of parental care. Large specimens that swim in a slow, stately manner make particularly appealing feature fish. Cichlids are territorial, and require a spacious tank providing numerous shelters and designed to accommodate their instinctive habit of digging.

Some species, especially the more diminutive ones, can safely be kept in a general community tank; others are suitable only for a species aquarium or must be housed with companion fish from the same natural habitat. Research carefully before mixing species; cichlids from different environments often have incompatible water requirements and temperaments.

Crenicara filamentosa CHECKERBOARD CICHLID

Family Cichlidae	Female 2¼ in (6 cm)	72–77°F (22–25°C); pH 5.5–6.4;
Distribution South America:	**Diet** Carnivorous. Small live foods	dH to 10°
Orinoco Basin, Rio Negro	preferred; will accept frozen foods	**Swimming level** Middle to bottom
Size Male 3½ in (9 cm)	**Water conditions** Temperature	**Breeding** Egg-depositor

This delightful little fish is suitable for the more experienced aquarist. Pairs or trios (one male to two females) may be kept in a mature, planted aquarium with soft, well-filtered water. Keep them with small tetras; alone, they can be very timid and will retire to secluded areas of the tank. A delicate species, they need close attention to water quality; any deterioration can damage their health. Usually peaceful, they may be territorial when breeding.

Remarks: When spawning, between 50 and 100 eggs are placed on a pre-cleaned leaf or flat rock; the female guards the larvae and fry. Make sure the water is not too hard, or the eggs may develop fungus. The young are fairly easy to raise if given a constant supply of newly hatched brine shrimp.

Softwater tank (pages 186–187)
Egg-depositors' breeding tank (page 241)

Papiliochromis ramirezi RAM

Violet-blue iridescent speckles

Family Cichlidae
Distribution South America: western Venezuela, Colombia
Size 3 in (7.5 cm)
Diet Omnivorous. Readily accepts flake, tablet, and frozen foods; benefits from supplements of live foods such as *Daphnia* and bloodworm
Water conditions Temperature 72–79°F (22–26°C); pH 6.0–7.0; dH 3–8°
Swimming level Middle to bottom
Breeding Egg-depositor

Bright red eye markings

A popular fish, the Ram (also called the Dwarf Butterfly Cichlid) rarely looks its best when kept by novices, who tend to place it in a community tank with too many boisterous companions. To feel at home, this somewhat nervous species requires small tetras to act as its lookouts – while they are swimming about happily, it knows it is safe. Provide some densely planted shelters, as well as open areas of fine substrate with a few flat stones to rest or spawn on. Breeding pairs will dig pits for rearing and protecting their young.

Remarks: The female Ram is smaller, and has a reddish belly and a shortened second dorsal ray. Both parents will tend their eggs and fry.

Softwater tank (pages 186–187)
Egg-depositors' breeding tank (page 241)

Pelvicachromis pulcher KRIBENSIS

Family Cichlidae
Distribution Africa: Nigeria
Size Male 4 in (10 cm)
Female 3¼ in (8 cm)

Diet Omnivorous. Accepts flake, frozen, and live foods, especially bloodworm and *Daphnia*
Water conditions Temperature

75–77°F (24–25°C); pH 6.5–7.5; dH 8–15°
Swimming level Middle to bottom
Breeding Egg-depositor

Kribensis is a fine beginner's fish, but let your tank mature before introducing it. Most specimens for sale are captive-bred, and need a well-planted aquarium with plenty of hiding places and some caves. Use a fine substrate to allow the fish to dig spawning pits. They can be territorial when breeding, but cause no trouble if given adequate shelter.

Remarks: Pairs behave as a close-knit family. Males are larger, with pointed anal and dorsal fins and long central caudal fin rays. Females have more rounded bodies and fins, and a pink belly. Spawning is on cave roofs. The female guards the eggs and fry; the male defends the territory. Both tend the fry; these are easy to raise on brine shrimp.

Egg-depositors' breeding tank (page 241)

Archocentrus spilurus JADE-EYED CICHLID

Family Cichlidae
Distribution Guatemala
Size Male 4¾ in (12 cm)
Female 3¼ in (8 cm)

Diet Omnivorous. Live and frozen foods relished; will also take flake foods and some vegetable matter
Water conditions Temperature

72–77°F (22–25°C); pH 6.8–8.0; dH to 15°
Swimming level Middle to bottom
Breeding Egg-depositor

Though territorial, these beautiful little cichlids are relatively peaceful and may be kept with other similarly sized species. They cause little damage in a planted aquarium, except while breeding, when they may dig. Adult specimens are easy to sex; males have pointed dorsal and ventral fins, and are more colorful, while females are generally smaller yet fuller-bodied, with rounded dorsal and anal fins.

Remarks: Breeding pairs spawn in caves; both parents guard the eggs and fry. The young require algae and plant matter in their diet. Also feed newly hatched brine shrimp, followed by a variety of progressively larger live foods, or frozen equivalents.

Egg-depositors' breeding tank (page 241)

Astronotus ocellatus OSCAR

Rust-colored markings

Family Cichlidae
Distribution South America: Rio Negro, Rio Paraguay, Rio Parana, Amazon
Size 9¾ in (25 cm)
Diet Carnivorous. Will eat anything meaty, alive or dead, plus frozen and pellet foods; earthworms are relished
Water conditions Temperature 72–77°F (22–25°C); pH 6.0–8.0; dH to 25°
Swimming level Middle
Breeding Egg-depositor

Paddle-like caudal fin

Small Oscars are very endearing, but quickly grow into large specimens that can devastate an aquarium with their persistent digging. They are not community fish in the general sense, but may be kept with other large fish in a spacious tank. A species aquarium is the best option. Oscars accept a wide range of water conditions, but stir up much debris; good filtration is essential. Confine decor to immovable objects such as wood and smooth rocks – any plants set in the substrate are likely to be uprooted, while those attached to wood are usually left undisturbed.

Remarks: Generally peaceful when not breeding, Oscars spawn on cleaned rocks, both parents caring diligently for their thousand-odd fry.

Tropical freshwater tank (pages 184–185)

Pterophyllum scalare ANGEL

Family Cichlidae	and most commercial foods; will	75–82°F (24–28°C); pH 6.0–7.5;
Distribution Central Amazon	also pick on lettuce and peas;	dH to 15°
Size 6 in (15 cm); usually smaller	take care not to overfeed	**Swimming level** Middle
Diet Omnivorous. Live, frozen,	**Water conditions** Temperature	**Breeding** Egg-depositor

Hugely popular in the hobby, Angels are selectively bred to enhance color and fins; wild specimens are rare. Select young fish with care; excessive inbreeding can cause deformed fins, poor color, and stunted growth. Keep them in a planted tank, but not with tiny companions; a medium-sized Angel will make a meal of your Neons!

Remarks: Angels are very difficult to sex. Buy a group of young fish and allow them to pair naturally; the pair bond is strong. Eggs are laid on pre-cleaned leaves or other flat surfaces. Since Angels are notorious for eating their eggs, remove the eggs for hatching and growing elsewhere.

Softwater tank (pages 186–187)
Egg-depositors' breeding tank (page 241)

Symphysodon spp. DISCUS

Family Cichlidae	frozen foods preferred, but will	dH 2–6°
Distribution Amazon, Rio Negro	accept flake foods	**Swimming level** Middle
Size 6 in (15 cm)	**Water conditions** Temperature	to bottom
Diet Carnivorous. Small live or	79–86°F (26–30°C); pH 6.0–6.5;	**Breeding** Egg-depositor

To keep Discus well, water conditions are crucial. Nervous fish, they also need peaceful companions; contrary to popular belief, however, it is perfectly safe to keep Angels with Discus. A tall, planted tank with soft, acidic, warm, well-filtered water is ideal. Buy either proven pairs or a group of young fish and allow them to pair themselves.

Remarks: Discus are not easy to sex unless they are breeding. The eggs are laid on a pre-cleaned leaf or other flat surface (sometimes the aquarium glass). The fry must be kept with the parents since, after hatching, they feed by "glancing" on the adults' body slime. Both parents care for the young.

Softwater tank (pages 186–187)
Egg-depositors' breeding tank (page 241)

Julidochromis dickfeldi BROWN JULIE

Family Cichlidae	**Diet** Carnivorous. Small live and	dH 15–20°
Distribution Africa: southwestern	frozen foods; will take flake foods	**Swimming level** Middle
shore of Lake Tanganyika	**Water conditions** Temperature	to bottom
Size 3 in (7.5 cm)	75–79°F (24–26°C); pH 8.0–8.5;	**Breeding** Egg-depositor

Feathered edge on dorsal fin

Pattern of dark stripes

Keep this species as a small group in a tank with plenty of hiding places and space for males to stake territories. Females can be larger than males, but sexing is difficult; allow the fish to pair themselves. The aquarium should be filled with rockwork reaching nearly to the water surface; in the wild, the Brown Julie spends much of its time in and around rock piles. To prevent interbreeding, do not keep this fish with other *Julidochromis* species. Provide plants for cover and a sand substrate to allow digging.

Remarks: Although the pair defend a territory, they do not attend greatly to their fry beyond guarding them for some time in a rearing pit.

Rift Lake tank (pages 188–189)
Egg-depositors' breeding tank (page 241)

Lamprologus sp. DAFFODIL

Family Cichlidae
Distribution Africa: Lake Tanganyika
Size Male 3 in (7.5 cm) Female 2 in (5 cm)
Diet Omnivorous. Live or frozen foods such as bloodworm preferred, but will take flake foods
Water conditions Temperature 75–79°F (24–26°C); pH 8.0–8.5; dH 15–20°
Swimming level Middle to bottom
Breeding Egg-depositor

The delicate coloration and elongated fins of this species make it a firm favorite. Although very peaceful, the Daffodil can hold its own in a community of similarly sized Lake Tanganyikan species. Provide caves and thickets of plants as shelter; small snail shells make suitable refuges. (In the wild, the Daffodil, like members of the *Neolamprologus* genus, shelters and spawns in the empty shells of *Neothauma* snails.)

Remarks: Males are more intensely colored and have more pointed fins than females. Spawning occurs in caves; fry from previous broods often remain in the breeding territory until they reach about 1 in (2.5 cm) and can guard their younger siblings, with or without parental help. The fry will accept newly hatched brine shrimp.

Egg-depositors' breeding tank (page 241)

Neolamprologus brevis

Family Cichlidae
Distribution Africa: Lake Tanganyika
Size 1½ in (4 cm)
Diet Carnivorous. Small live or frozen foods such as *Daphnia* and bloodworm distinctly preferred, but will also accept flake foods
Water conditions Temperature 75–79°F (24–26°C); pH 8.0–8.5; dH 15–20°
Swimming level Middle to bottom
Breeding Egg-depositor

This fish requires open areas of sandy substrate about 2 in (5 cm) deep and some snail shells (those of the Lake Tanganyikan *Neothauma* snail, or edible snails available from restaurants). The cichlid partially buries the shells at an angle in the sand and uses them as a spawning site. A pair will defend a territory up to 7¾ in (20 cm) in diameter; if keeping more than one pair, ensure there is sufficient substrate area for each territory.

Remarks: Males are larger than females and have a yellow-orange edge to the dorsal fin. The female spawns in the shell, while the male, too big to enter the shell, releases his milt above it; this drifts down, fertilizing the eggs. Broods are small; on average, 20 fry may be produced.

Rift Lake tank (pages 188–189)
Egg-depositors' breeding tank (page 241)

Neolamprologus leleupi LEMON CICHLID

Family Cichlidae
Distribution Africa: Lake Tanganyika
Size 2¾ in (7 cm)
Diet Carnivorous. Small live or frozen foods such as *Daphnia* and bloodworm much preferred, but will also take flake foods
Water conditions Temperature 75–79°F (24–26°C); pH 8.0–8.5; dH 15–20°
Swimming level Middle to bottom
Breeding Egg-depositor

A typical Lake Tanganyikan tank with a soft substrate and abundant rock piles is required for this cichlid. The fish's common name refers to its bright yellow coloration, although there are several varieties that are nearer orange in shade. Males can be aggressive toward other males and undesired females. This belligerence can be greatly reduced by providing plenty of hiding places. Caves are needed for spawning.

Remarks: This fish has a long, cylindrical body, and is difficult to sex. Males are usually larger, with a thicker head. After breeding, the female guards the eggs while the male defends the area. Maintain good water quality as the fry (50–100) are very susceptible to bacterial infections.

Rift Lake tank (pages 188–189)
Egg-depositors' breeding tank (page 241)

LAKE MALAWI MBUNA

THE MBUNA ARE a group of highly popular cichlids from Lake Malawi in Africa. They are colorful, breed readily, and may be stocked at higher levels than many other species. Instinctive fighters, they are best kept in a densely populated rock-shore environment, for this curbs their intense competitive urges. Bank rockwork up the back of the tank, almost to the water surface, to provide nooks, crannies, and caves for the fish to swim through and defend. Seat the rocks securely, and choose them with care – tufa, which buffers water conditions, is fine for mouthbrooding species, but is too soft and crumbly for substrate spawners to clean and spawn on.

The water should be hard, alkaline, and highly oxygenated, with a filter that can cope with large amounts of waste. Prepare for weekly water changes of 25–30 percent for mouthbrooders and 10–15 percent for substrate spawners. Do not overcrowd substrate spawners; they require territorial space in which to breed and raise their young. Mouthbrooders need a much smaller area, and only during spawning.

Keep Mbuna as pairs or, better still, allow several females for each male; otherwise, males can be over-attentive.

Family Cichlidae	of frozen, flake, and green foods,	75–79°F (24–26°C); pH 7.5–8.0;
Distribution Africa: Lake Malawi	including algae, but some are	dH 8–10°
Size Varies; see species	specialist feeders; ask your dealer	**Swimming level** All, among rocks
Diet Varies; will usually take a mix	**Water conditions** Temperature	**Breeding** Mouthbrooder

Labeotropheus trewavasae

Labeotropheus trewavasae grows to between 4–5½ in (10–14 cm) and is best kept as a group with at least two females per male. The sexes can be distinguished by the prominent egg-spots on the male's anal fin; these egg-shaped markings are characteristic of male mouthbrooders, and are faint or absent in females. There are several regional color forms, known as morphs, including a white variety. Broods may comprise as many as 40 young; the female should be removed, if practical, after spawning.

Labidochromis caeruleus

One of the most peaceful of the Mbuna, this fish will live either alone or in pairs. It is a fairly small species, measuring 3¼ in (8 cm) at most. Males are slightly larger than females and, when breeding, have more intense coloration. There are two distinct groups: those living in rocky areas feed on small invertebrates among the stony bottom; others inhabit the sandy shoreline, and eat snails found in *Vallisneria* beds. In captivity both types will accept a variety of live, frozen, and flake foods.

Melanochromis johanni

This fish is easy to sex: males are larger at 2¾ in (7 cm), dark blue, and have egg-spots; females are 2¼ in (6 cm) and are orange colored. Keep several females to each male. An average brood may consist of about 30 young and the female is not a very diligent parent, keeping the fry in her mouth for only about a week. (With some Mbuna, the mouthbrooding period can last for 10 days or more.) Fortunately, the young are quite happy to forage for themselves.

Pseudotropheus estherae

Pseudotropheus estherae is an attractive addition to a Lake Malawi tank. Males are bright blue, while females are available in a variety of color forms, from yellow and orange to mottled brown. Purchase in pairs; when buying, check that males and females come from the same shipment, since it is easy to confuse the female of one species with that of another. Adults reach a size of 5 in (12.5 cm) and are typical mouthbrooders, producing about 30 youngsters.

Pseudotropheus livingstonii

Growing to about 5 in (12.5 cm), this fish is less quarrelsome than many other Mbuna. In Lake Malawi, it inhabits the edges of the rocky zone, where there is a sandy substrate. In an aquarium, also include some snail shells; when frightened, small specimens will take refuge in them. Like virtually all Lake Malawi cichlids, *Pseudotropheus livingstonii* is a maternal mouthbrooder, with males displaying egg-spots.

Pseudotropheus zebra

Pseudotropheus zebra comes in several color forms, or morphs, and can be a useful fish in the aquarium, since it likes eating duckweed! Measuring some 4 in (10 cm) long, this rather belligerent species is polygamous, requiring several females for each male. The females will often swim about together in the tank. A brood will be tended by the female for about a week after she has released the fry from her mouth.

FOR ALL MBUNA *Rift Lake tank (pages 188–189), Mouthbrooders' breeding tank (page 243)*

CYPRINIDS

WITH MORE THAN 1,400 species, the family Cyprinidae is found worldwide (apart from South America, Australia, and Antarctica), in lakes, mountain streams, subterranean courses, and virtually all points in between.

Cyprinids lack an adipose fin, and have smooth scales, a single lateral line, and, frequently, up to two pairs of barbels. The mouth is toothless; food is ground up by pharyngeal teeth found in the throat. Most species look archetypally "fish-like," but their size varies greatly: *Barbus tor* from India can attain a length of 8 ft (2.5 m), while the tiny rasboras offered in the trade measure just 1 in (2.5 cm).

Cyprinids include some of the most popular aquarium fish, such as barbs, danios, rasboras, goldfish, and freshwater sharks (which, though shark-shaped, are not true sharks).

Cyprinids are complete omnivores – non-stop eating machines consuming anything that will fit into their mouths, which may include smaller fish and the fry of other species. Feed a varied diet including live or frozen foods to keep them in prime condition.

Largely active, schooling fish, cyprinids should be kept in groups of six to ten in a spacious, planted tank. Many species breed readily, and suit a large community aquarium.

Barbus filamentosus FILAMENT BARB

Family Cyprinidae
Distribution India, Sri Lanka
Size 6 in (15 cm)
Diet Omnivorous. Small aquatic invertebrates, either live or frozen, as well as flake foods; supplement with vegetable matter (green foods preferred)
Water conditions Temperature 68–75°F (20–24°C); pH 6.0–6.5; dH to 15°
Swimming level Middle to upper
Breeding Egg-scatterer

Sometimes referred to as the Black-spot Barb, this active, schooling fish requires plenty of open water to swim in, and suits the larger community aquarium. It will eat soft-leaved plants, but Java Fern, Cryptocornes, and Amazon Swords are usually left undisturbed. To deter plant destruction, include lettuce and peas in the diet. Juvenile specimens are fairly unimpressive, but adults can be spectacular – especially males, with their more intense colors and filamentous dorsal fin extensions (hence the common name).

Remarks: Breeding poses few problems beyond the need for a larger than normal setup with clumps of plants to spawn among. Fry are easy to raise on small live foods such as brine shrimp.

Egg-scatterers' breeding tank (page 240)

Barbus gelius DWARF BARB

Family Cyprinidae
Distribution India
Size 1½ in (4 cm)
Diet Omnivorous. Small live foods such as bloodworm, brine shrimp, and mosquito larvae; also frozen, flake, and green foods; be sure to include algae in the diet, particularly if conditioning fish for breeding
Water conditions Temperature 64–72°F (18–22°C); pH 6.0–7.0; dH to 10°
Swimming level Middle
Breeding Egg-scatterer

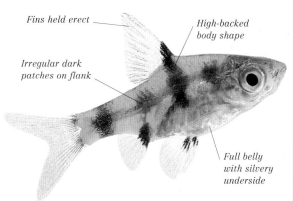

Fins held erect

High-backed body shape

Irregular dark patches on flank

Full belly with silvery underside

Also known as the Golden Dwarf Barb, this small, delicate, yet highly active schooling fish is suitable for a species or community aquarium providing space to swim. It requires good water quality, achieved by very efficient filtration and regular water changes. In soft, acidic conditions the dull yellow stripe on the males develop a beautiful gold or copper shade. Females are deeper-bodied, with less intense coloration.

Remarks: This species is best kept in small groups with peaceful companions of similar size. For breeding, set up a spawning tank with a shallow depth of soft, acidic water, adding plants such as Cryptocornes; the fish will place their eggs on the undersides of the leaves. Eggs hatch in 24 hours, and the fry require very tiny foods.

Egg-scatterers' breeding tank (page 240)

Barbus oligolepis CHECKER BARB

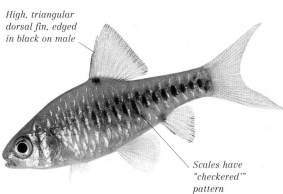

Family Cyprinidae
Distribution Indonesia
Size 2 in (5 cm), although wild specimens can grow as large as 6 in (15 cm)
Diet Omnivorous. Small live foods such as bloodworm, brine shrimp, and mosquito larvae; also frozen, flake, and green foods
Water conditions Temperature 68–75°F (20–24°C); pH 6.0–6.5; dH to 10°
Swimming level Middle
Breeding Egg-scatterer

High, triangular dorsal fin, edged in black on male

Scales have "checkered'" pattern

If you have a mature furnished tank, with plenty of plants and wood, soft, slightly acidic, water, and gentle filtration, give this fish a try. Often overlooked in favor of more colorful species, in the right conditions it is exquisite. Keep a mixed-sex group; the males will spar harmlessly with each other to attract a female. Poor water quality of excess unaged water are not well tolerated; make water changes small and frequent.

Remarks: Checker Barbs will often spawn in a community tank, but the other inhabitants are likely to devour the eggs. Use a spawning setup with soft, acidic, warm water and fine-leaved plants reaching from the substrate to the surface. The eggs are usually laid near the top, and hatch in 36 hours. Feed fry newly hatched brine shrimp.

Egg-scatterers' breeding tank (page 240)

Barbus schwanefeldi TINFOIL BARB

Family Cyprinidae
Distribution Southeast Asia
Size 13¾ in (35 cm)
Diet Omnivorous. Small
aquatic invertebrates, either
live or frozen, as well as
flake foods; supplement
with vegetable matter
(green foods preferred)
Water conditions
Temperature 72–77°F
(22–25°C); pH 6.5–7.0;
dH to 10°
Swimming level Middle
Breeding Egg-layer
(details unknown)

Young specimens of this magnificent species are often bought by novice aquarists and placed in the prized community tank, where, after a few weeks, they proceed to devour all in sight (food as well as most plants), rapidly outgrowing most of their companions until it becomes necessary to rehouse them. To keep these fish, you must provide a very large tank with highly efficient filtration to clear the debris they stir up when foraging for food; use a soft substrate, since they instinctively dig. It is best to keep this active, schooling species as a group. Although they eat plants, it is possible to maintain clumps of Java Fern. Nothing is known of their breeding habits.

Remarks: They jump! Make sure the aquarium is well covered, and try to avoid any sudden movements or noises that might startle them.

Barbus titteya CHERRY BARB

Family Cyprinidae
Distribution India, Sri Lanka
Size 2 in (5 cm)
Diet Omnivorous. Small live
foods such as bloodworm,
brine shrimp, and mosquito
larvae; also frozen and flake
foods and vegetable matter
(green foods preferred)
Water conditions
Temperature 72–79°F
(22–26°C); pH 6.5–7.5;
dH to 12°
Swimming level Middle
to upper
Breeding Egg-scatterer

These fish can be territorial towards their own kind, so it is wise to keep them in pairs rather than as a group predominated by one sex. Provide good filtration and thickets of plants, allowing each pair a separate retreat. Males are far more intensely colored than females; in breeding condition, the males turn a dark cherry red, while females are a duller red-brown. Today, virtually all trade specimens are farm-produced.

Remarks: Cherry Barbs are easy to breed. Use a well-conditioned pair in a specially setup tank planted with Java Moss. The courtship is quite spectacular, with much fin spreading. A pair may produce 300 or so eggs, which hatch in 24 hours. Give newly hatched brine shrimp as a first food.

Tropical freshwater tank (pages 184–185)
Egg-scatterers' breeding tank (page 240)

Barbus tetrazona TIGER BARB

Family Cyprinidae	invertebrates, live or frozen; also	dH to 12°
Distribution Borneo, Indonesia	flake foods and vegetable matter	**Swimming level** Middle
Size 2¾ in (7 cm)	**Water conditions** Temperature	to upper
Diet Omnivorous. Small aquatic	68–79°F (20–26°C); pH 6.5–7.5;	**Breeding** Egg-scatterer

Dorsal fin has distinctive wide, red edging

Dark vertical bands resemble tiger's stripes

You either love or hate these fish! Kept in ones or twos in a community aquarium, they are an absolute menace – picking on their companions, nipping fins, and generally terrorizing smaller fish. Yet, unlikely as it may seem, members of a mixed-sex school of eight or more will spend most of their time displaying to each other and establishing a pecking order within the group, leaving the other tank inhabitants in relative peace. The species' common name is derived from its distinctive striped markings. Male Tiger Barbs are smaller, slimmer, and more colorful than females. Several colour varieties have been produced for the aquarium trade, including green, red, black, and albino strains.

Remarks: If unsure, keep these fish in a species aquarium. To breed, use a spawning setup with soft, acidic, warm water and fine-leaved plants reaching from the substrate to the surface. The eggs are usually laid near the top, and hatch in 36 hours. Feed fry newly hatched brine shrimp.

Egg-scatterers' breeding tank (page 240)

GREEN TIGER BARB

In this strain, also known as the Moss-banded Barb, broad areas of dark color replace the four defined vertical stripes of the Tiger Barb. Body shades and patterns vary somewhat within the variety, although fin color remains constant. Females are plumper when in breeding condition.

RED TIGER BARB

The body of this attractive fish is primarily a deep orange-red, the dark bands of the original species having been suppressed in commercial breeding programs aimed at producing an albino type. Like the other color varieties, the Red Tiger Barb does not occur in the wild.

Brachydanio albolineatus PEARL DANIO

Family Cyprinidae	invertebrates, either live or	70–77°F (21–25°C); pH 6.5–7.0;
Distribution Southeast Asia	frozen, as well as flake foods;	dH to 12°
Size 2¼ in (6 cm)	supplement with vegetable matter	**Swimming level** Middle to upper
Diet Omnivorous. Small aquatic	**Water conditions** Temperature	**Breeding** Egg-scatterer

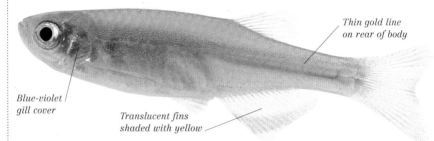

Thin gold line on rear of body

Blue-violet gill cover

Translucent fins shaded with yellow

This small, shoaling fish likes the company of its own kind; keep as a group. Very active, it is well suited to a planted community tank with similarly sized, peaceful species. Water quality is critical; any deterioration will leave specimens highly susceptible to bacterial and viral infections. The species' common name alludes to its iridescent coloration; during spawning the fish assumes an attractive pearly, blue-violet luster.

Remarks: Males are smaller and more colorful than females. For breeding, the water should be warm (79–86°F/26–30°C) and shallow. Pearl Danios spawn as a school, with pairs leaving the group to scatter their eggs over plants. Fry emerge in about 36 hours and should be fed on infusoria and newly hatched brine shrimp.

Egg-scatterers' breeding tank (page 240)

Brachydanio rerio ZEBRA DANIO

Family Cyprinidae	invertebrates, either live or	dH to 12°
Distribution India	frozen; also flake and green foods	**Swimming level** Middle
Size 2¼ in (6 cm)	**Water conditions** Temperature	to upper
Diet Omnivorous. Small aquatic	64–77°F (18–25°C); pH 6.5–7.5;	**Breeding** Egg-scatterer

The Zebra Danio is a popular schooling fish for the community aquarium, strikingly colored with a base shade of silver or gold overlaid from head to fin with bright blue-purple lines. Albino, long-finned, and veil-tailed strains have also been developed. The true species is quite hardy, but the varieties are far more sensitive – in temperatures outside 72–77°F (22–25°C), they may succumb to viral and bacterial infections. Do not keep long-

finned or veil-tailed types with fin-nipping species. Males are generally slimmer than females.

Remarks: Place breeding pairs in a spawning tank with fine-leaved plants; 300–400 eggs are produced. Feed fry as for the Pearl Danio.

Tropical freshwater tank (pages 184–185)
Egg-scatterers' breeding tank (page 240)

Danio aequipinnatus GIANT DANIO

Family Cyprinidae
Distribution India, Sri Lanka
Size 4 in (10 cm)
Diet Omnivorous. Small aquatic invertebrates, live or frozen, plus flake and green foods; for best coloring, give meaty foods such as mosquito larvae and bloodworm
Water conditions Temperature 72–75°F (22–24°C); pH 6.0–7.0; dH to 12°
Swimming level Middle to upper
Breeding Egg-scatterer

Giant Danios are extremely active, and require a large community tank with plenty of swimming space. Keep them in schools, and provide a gentle water current. Since they can jump, install a tight-fitting cover. Males are slimmer and more intensely colored than females, with the blue body stripe extending into the caudal fin. When well fed on live foods, the blue/green background coloration becomes overlaid with golden spots and bars. For good health, ensure regular water changes and good filtration.

Remarks: To stimulate spawning, set up the breeding tank where it will catch sunlight. A pair produces up to 300 eggs, which will hatch in 36 hours. Raise fry on fine live foods.

Egg-scatterers' breeding tank (page 240)

Tanichthys albonubes WHITE CLOUD MOUNTAIN MINNOW

Family Cyprinidae
Distribution White Cloud Mountain, southern China
Size 1½ in (4 cm)
Diet Omnivorous. Small live, frozen, or flake foods
Water conditions Temperature 64–72°F (18–22°C); pH 6.5–7.5;
dH to 15°
Swimming level Middle to upper
Breeding Egg-scatterer

Red surrounds dark patch on caudal fin

Thin gold stripe overlaid with blue lines

This lovely little fish shows its best colors in relatively cool conditions; indeed, if kept too warm (much above 72°F/22°C) for any length of time, it becomes stressed and may even die. Keep in groups of 8–10; single specimens tend to sulk away in the darker regions of the tank. Males are slimmer and more colorful than females. An aquarium-bred long-finned variety is also available, but this is less hardy.

Remarks: The White Cloud is best kept in a well-filtered community tank with other peaceful species, and is easy to breed in cool water. Eggs are scattered over plants, and hatch in 36 hours. Fry should be raised on fine foods: infusoria followed by newly hatched brine shrimp.

Coldwater tank (pages 190–191)
Egg-scatterers' breeding tank (page 240)

Rasbora caudimaculata GREATER SCISSORTAIL

Family Cyprinidae	and flake foods; also include	dH to 12°
Distribution Southeast Asia	some green foods	**Swimming level** Middle to upper
Size 4¾ in (12 cm)	**Water conditions** Temperature	**Breeding** Egg-layer (details
Diet Omnivorous. Live, frozen,	68–77°F (20–25°C); pH 6.5–7.5;	unknown)

Deeply forked
"scissor" tail

Upturned mouth
for surface feeding

If you have a large display aquarium with plenty of open swimming space, then these attractive and very active fish are for you. Keep them as a shoal, and install an efficient external power filter to maintain suitable conditions and water movement – in the wild, the Greater (or Giant) Scissortail inhabits fast-flowing streams and small rivers. A distinctive feature is its deeply forked caudal fin, with a yellow area on each

fork, ending in a white-tipped black patch at each extremity (hence the fish's other common name, the Spot-tail Rasbora). Males are usually slimmer than females, and have a yellowish anal fin and white tips on the caudal fin lobes.

Remarks: These fish are jumpers! Deter this by providing floating plants and fitting a secure cover glass. Few details are known regarding breeding.

Rasbora heteromorpha HARLEQUIN RASBORA

Family Cyprinidae
Distribution Southeast Asia
Size 1¾ in (4.5 cm)
Diet Omnivorous. Live foods preferred (including small aquatic invertebrates and mosquito larvae); also accepts small frozen foods, such as *Daphnia*; offer fry an initial diet of infusoria
Water conditions Temperature 72–77°F (22–25°C); pH 6.0–6.5; dH to 10°
Swimming level Middle
Breeding Egg-depositor

These fish require a mature, well-planted tank with good filtration and regular water changes. Keep in schools of 8–10 with other small, placid species. Although popular, Harlequins (or Red Rasboras) are seldom seen at their best in community aquariums; the water is often too alkaline and the companion fish too boisterous. The species has a blue-black wedge-shaped patch on the flank; females are plumper than males.

Remarks: Breeding is difficult. Set up the tank with a shallow level of warm, very soft, acidic water, and add potted Cryptocorynes (the fish spawn on the undersides of leaves). Pair a two-year-old male with a 9–12-month-old female; condition with live foods. After spawning, remove the pair; keep the tank dark until the eggs hatch.

Egg-depositors' breeding tank (page 241)

Rasbora maculata DWARF RASBORA

Family Cyprinidae
Distribution Southeast Asia,
Malaysia, Singapore, Sumatra
Size 1 in (2.5 cm)
Diet Omnivorous. Will take
small flake and frozen foods,
but live foods (insects, small
invertebrates) much preferred
Water conditions
Temperature 75–79°F
(24–26°C); pH 5.5–6.5;
dH to 10°
Swimming level Middle
Breeding Egg-scatterer (pairs
will not breed until together
for a few days)

This delightful, diminutive fish, also known as
the Pygmy or Spotted Rasbora, is best kept in a
species aquarium or with other peaceful tankmates of similar size. Water quality is particularly
important; provide efficient filtration with a
gentle water flow. Include fine-leaved plants
and give plenty of small live foods, especially
if you wish to breed your Dwarf Rasboras
successfully. Keep in a school of eight or more.

Remarks: These fish are a challenge to keep
properly and on a long-term basis. They can be
bred in a small aquarium with very soft, acidic,
warm water at a shallow depth. Plant large
clumps of Java Moss for them to spawn in.
The young are exceptionally tiny and require
infusoria and other very small live foods.

Egg-scatterers' breeding tank (page 240)

Rasbora pauciperforata RED-LINE RASBORA

Family Cyprinidae
Distribution Southeast Asia
Size 2¾ in (7 cm)
Diet Omnivorous. Will accept
small flake and frozen foods,
but live foods (insects, small
invertebrates) greatly preferred
Water conditions Temperature
72–77°F (22–25°C); pH 6.0–6.5;
dH to 10°
Swimming level Middle to upper
Breeding Egg-scatterer

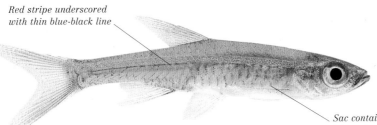

Red stripe underscored
with thin blue-black line

Sac containing
internal organs

The Red-line, or Red-striped, Rasbora is named
for the striking red line extending along its body.
A gregarious fish, single specimens will hide away,
often refuse to feed, and may even die, whereas
a group of 8–10 will swim around as a school.
Keep them in a well-planted community tank
with sufficient open water for activity. Filtration
yielding a slight current is beneficial; water
must be changed regularly to maintain health.

Remarks: Breeding is possible. Provide a tank
with plenty of fine-leaved plants (natural or
synthetic). Male Red-lines can be distinguished
by their slimmer build; allow the fish to pair
themselves. Spawning takes place among the
plants, and the eggs hatch in about 36 hours.
Feed the fry newly hatched brine shrimp.

Egg-scatterers' breeding tank (page 240)

Balanteocheilus melanopterus SILVER SHARK

Family Cyprinidae	and flake foods; supplement with	dH to 10°
Distribution Southeast Asia	vegetable matter	**Swimming level** Middle to upper
Size 13¾ in (35 cm)	**Water conditions** Temperature	**Breeding** Egg-layer (details
Diet Omnivorous. Live, frozen,	72–82°F (22–28°C); pH 6.5–7.0;	unknown)

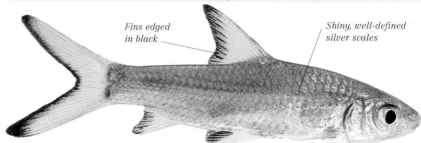

Fins edged in black

Shiny, well-defined silver scales

Constantly on the move, this active, schooling fish requires a large, planted aquarium with plenty of open water to swim in. Despite their size, Silver, or Bala, Sharks are fairly peaceful. Juvenile specimens can be kept in a community tank (in groups of 4–6), but will need more space as they grow. Install a tight-fitting cover, since these fish take fright easily and may leap from the water. Floating plants help to deter jumping.

Provide good filtration giving a steady, gentle current. Silver Sharks have not been bred in aquariums, but can be sexed in the spawning season, when males are slimmer than females.

Remarks: These fish are particularly susceptible to ailments if kept in poor or overcrowded conditions. In water temperatures that are too low, they become prone to White Spot.

Crossocheilus siamensis SIAMESE FLYING FOX

Family Cyprinidae	flake, and green foods	**Swimming level** Bottom
Distribution Southeast Asia	**Water conditions** Temperature	to middle
Size 5½ in (14 cm)	72–79°F (22–26°C); pH 6.5–7.5;	**Breeding** Egg-layer (details
Diet Omnivorous. Live, frozen,	dH to 15°	unknown)

This fish is ideal for the community aquarium, provided you can supply clear, well-oxygenated water. It does best in relatively soft, slightly acidic conditions. Despite a liking for green foods, particularly algae, it does very little damage to aquarium plants, while cleaning algal growth from leaves. If kept as a group of 4–6, they may quarrel among themselves, but rarely harm each other. The Siamese Flying Fox has a torpedo-shaped body marked by a broad, dark band. Nothing is known of its breeding habits.

Remarks: This species can be a useful addition to a tank overrun with thread algae, being one of the few species that will eat it. It will also consume planarian worms (aquatic flatworms).

Tropical freshwater tank (pages 184–185)

Epalzeorhychus bicolor RED-TAILED BLACK SHARK

Family Cyprinidae	flake, and green foods	**Swimming level** Bottom
Distribution Thailand	**Water conditions** Temperature	to middle
Size 4¾ in (12 cm)	72–79°F (22–26°C); pH 6.5–7.5;	**Breeding** Egg-layer (details
Diet Omnivorous. Live, frozen,	dH to 15°	unknown)

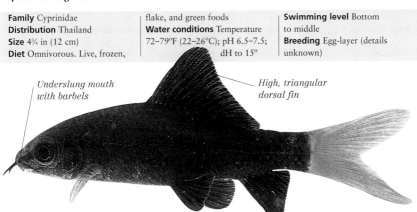

Underslung mouth with barbels

High, triangular dorsal fin

Known by a number of common names, such as the Red-tailed Shark and the Red-tailed Labeo, this popular aquarium fish can be a nightmare – aggressive and quarrelsome with its own kind, and prone to terrorizing companion fish. Keep a group of 5–6 with other species only if they are large enough to fend for themselves. To control belligerence, provide a large tank with plenty of rocks, plants, and wood so that each fish can establish its own territory and refuges in which to hide. With its jet-black body and scarlet caudal fin, the Red-tailed Black Shark is an attractive purchase, but aquarists should beware of its less than appealing nature.

Remarks: Once settled into a tank, this fish poses few problems regarding diet or water quality.

Gyrinocheilus aymonieri SUCKING LOACH

Family Gyrinocheilidae
Distribution Thailand, India
Size 10¾ in (27 cm)
Diet Omnivorous. Predominantly green foods, including algae; will also accept small live or frozen aquatic invertebrates, plus flake, tablet, and pellet foods
Water conditions Temperature 77–82°F (25–28°C); pH 6.0–8.0; dH to 20°
Swimming level Bottom
Breeding Egg-layer (details unknown)

Also sold as the Chinese, or Indian, Algae Eater, this fish is not a true loach, nor does it belong to the family Cyprinidae (it is, however, a close relative). Small, young specimens will feed on algae, "sticking" themselves to the aquarium glass with their sucker mouths, and causing little damage. However, they soon grow into quite destructive adults, excavating pits in the substrate and undermining rocks, wood, and plants. They are happy in a well-planted tank with a few hiding places. Though tolerant of poor water conditions, they stir up much sediment and debris, and will require an efficient external power filter.

Remarks: Mature Sucking Loaches can become territorial and aggressive. They may cling onto the bodies of larger fish such as Angels or Discus, causing irritation or more serious injury.

LOACHES

THE RATHER EEL-LIKE fish commonly called loaches belong to two families: Cobitidae, with about 100 species, and Balitoridae, comprising some 400 species. They are restricted to the fresh waters of Eurasia and the fringe of north Africa (Morocco).

Loaches are bottom-dwellers, and spend much of their time hiding from the light; their bodies are worm-shaped, or triangular in cross-section with a flat belly to hug the substrate. The scales are either absent or reduced to tiny structures buried in the skin, and the mouth is surrounded by up to four pairs of barbels covered in taste receptors, for finding food in the muddy waters they typically inhabit. Although the fins lack spines, cobitid loaches have a sharp spine below each eye that can be erected for defense.

Many species are able to take oxygen from the atmosphere, and so can survive in oxygen-poor waters. All loaches have a swim bladder partly enclosed in bone; this makes them very sensitive to changes in barometric pressure, which alter the volume of the bladder. When pressure changes, as with the passage of a thunderstorm, the fish either rushes to the surface to gulp air or conspicuously bubbles it out from its vent. Weatherloaches are perhaps best known for this behavior.

Botia sidthimunki DWARF CHAIN LOACH

Family Cobitidae	**Diet** Omnivorous. Small live, frozen, flake, and tablet foods	dH to 8°
Distribution Thailand, northern India	**Water conditions** Temperature 72–82°F (22–28°C); pH 6.0–6.5;	**Swimming level** Bottom to middle
Size 2 in (5 cm)		**Breeding** Egg-layer (details unknown)

A delightful fish for the well-planted, mature community aquarium, this small species is also known as the Pygmy Chain Loach. Very active, it is best kept as a school of six or more; the group will be seen scurrying about the substrate in search of food, swimming together, or resting on leaves or wood in the middle of the tank. Unlike larger species of *Botia*, they will not harm other fish but do uproot plants. Be sure to include small live foods such as *Daphnia* and whiteworm (or frozen equivalents) in their diet; flake or tablet foods alone are not sufficient.

Remarks: Regular water changes are essential, as is good filtration. Provide broad-leaved plants as resting surfaces.

Misgurnus anguillicaudatus WEATHERLOACH

Family Cobitidae	**Diet** Omnivorous. Small live,	50–75°F (10–24°C); pH 6.0–8.0;
Distribution Russia, China,	frozen, flake, and tablet foods;	dH to 25°
Korea, Japan	also accepts vegetable matter	**Swimming level** Bottom
Size 19¾ in (50 cm)	**Water conditions** Temperature	**Breeding** Egg-depositor

Short, rounded fins, with dorsal and ventral fins set far back

Long, cylindrical body

Although they can be kept as a coldwater fish, most imported Weatherloaches (or Weatherfish) have been acclimated to tropical conditions and are quite at home in warm, but not very warm, waters. They grow large and can be extremely boisterous, stirring up the substrate in a never-ending search for food; very efficient filtration is required to cope with the displaced debris. Plants should be well-established or potted to avoid being uprooted; use a mud or sand substrate.

Weatherloaches are undemanding and peaceful, and will eat virtually anything. Small specimens may be kept in a community aquarium.

Remarks: Weatherloaches react to barometric changes (hence their common name), becoming more active at low air pressures – they may even jump. Provide hiding places and a well-fit cover. Without sheltered areas, fish can be burned seeking refuge behind or under the tank heater.

Pangio kuhli COOLIE LOACH

Family Cobitidae	invertebrates, live or frozen, plus	75–86°F (24–30°C); pH 6.0–6.5;
Distribution Southeast Asia	flake and tablet foods; given a	dH to 8°
Size 4 in (10 cm)	varied diet, growth is rapid	**Swimming level** Bottom
Diet Omnivorous. Small aquatic	**Water conditions** Temperature	**Breeding** Egg-depositor

Sometimes sold as the Prickly Eye (a reference to the two eye spines), this fish is relatively easy to keep in soft, slightly acidic conditions. It requires a well-planted tank with a fine substrate and lots of pebbles and roots to hide among. The Coolie Loach prefers subdued lighting; this can be achieved even in a brightly lit aquarium by a dense planting of low-growing species, such as certain Cryptocorynes, to carpet part of the

substrate. Since this loach feeds at night, provide food just before the tank lights are switched off. It is especially fond of small worms.

Remarks: It is possible, but difficult, to breed these fish. They produce bright green eggs, which are attached to plants near the water surface. Because the Coolie Loach likes to burrow into the substrate, it can be difficult to catch!

KILLIFISH

KILLIFISH ARE OFTEN referred to as egg-laying toothcarps, since their jaws have teeth. Livebearers form the other major toothcarp group. Killifish are found in North and South America, Africa, and Asia, in rivers, lakes, and seasonal pools; species that live in areas subject to drought survive for just one year, and are called annual killifish.

Killifish are appealingly colorful fish, but can be hard to obtain. They are often regarded as difficult, requiring soft, acidic water conditions, but this does not apply to all species. Although noted as fish for the specialist, there are a few types that are suitable for a peaceful community aquarium.

Most killifish are small and best kept in single-species tanks, to prevent aggression and interbreeding. Species tanks need not be filtered, but should be heated. In the wild, these fish are primarily insectivores, and some tank specimens will accept only live foods.

Killifish are categorized according to spawning method. Egg-depositors place their eggs on plants or artificial spawning mops; peat-divers are annual killifish that must be provided with a peat substrate in which to bury their eggs. The peat is then stored and later rehydrated for hatching. Drought-resistant killifish eggs are often distributed among hobbyists by mail.

Aphyosemion australe CAPE LOPEZ LYRETAIL

Family Aplocheilidae	foods preferred, but will also	dH to 10°
Distribution Western Africa	accept frozen and flake foods	**Swimming level** Middle
Size 2¼ in (6 cm)	**Water conditions** Temperature	**Breeding** Egg-depositor; eggs are
Diet Omnivorous. Small live	70–75°F (21–24°C); pH 5.5–6.5;	laid on spawning mops or plants

Colored bands on fins

Thin body with fairly flat dorsal surface

This beautiful little killifish, also known as the Lyretail Panchax, is frequently available and appears in several naturally occurring color forms. It is a good choice for the novice, and can be kept in a softwater community tank with other small, very peaceful species. Provide soft, slightly acidic water with gentle filtration, and thickets of fine-leaved plants. To bring the fish into breeding condition, give plenty of live foods.

Remarks: Males have extended fins and are more colorful than females. Breed the fish in a specially setup tank with fine-leaved plants or spawning mops; in a community aquarium, few fry will survive. Transfer the eggs to a separate rearing tank; if using spawning mops, replace these daily. Feed fry newly hatched brine shrimp.

Egg-depositors' breeding tank (page 241)

Aplocheilus lineatus SPARKLING PANCHAX

Family Aplocheilidae
Distribution Southern India, Sri Lanka
Size 4 in (10 cm)
Diet Carnivorous. Small live foods such as mosquito larvae, bloodworm, and other insect larvae preferred (will hunt for insects near surface); also takes flake and frozen foods
Water conditions Temperature 72–77°F (22–25°C); pH 6.0–7.0; dH to 12°
Swimming level Upper
Breeding Egg-depositor

The Sparkling Panchax is ideal for a community tank of relatively large fish – it may eat smaller companions and fry. This species can be aggressive, especially with its own kind, so allow plenty of space. Its common name refers to the iridescent yellow spots on the scales, which shimmer in the light. The long, straight body line, dorsal fin set well back, and upturned mouth denote it as a true surface-dweller. Provide a gentle current.

Remarks: To see these fish at their best, keep them in pairs or trios (one male per two females), so that the male is constantly displaying. Beware – they jump! Install a tight-fitting cover; a few floating plants will help to deter leaping. The fish may also shelter in roots near the surface.

Tropical freshwater tank (page 184–185)
Egg-depositors' breeding tank (page 241)

Nothobranchius palmqvisti PALMQVIST'S NOTHOBRANCH

Family Aplocheilidae
Distribution Africa: southern Kenya, Tanzania
Size 2 in (5 cm)
Diet Carnivorous. Small live foods such as mosquito larvae, *Daphnia*, *Cyclops*, and brine shrimp; if fry are not given sufficient live foods, their growth will be stunted
Water conditions Temperature 64–75°F (18–24°C); pH 7.0; dH to 10°
Swimming level Middle to bottom
Breeding Egg-burier

An annual killifish, Palmqvist's Nothobranch should be kept in a species aquarium. Males can be very aggressive and will court females relentlessly. If possible, keep in trios (one male for each two females), and provide ample cover for the females. Males are far more colorful and have larger fins. As with all killifish, feed copious amounts of live foods, or frozen equivalents, to condition adults for spawning.

Remarks: Set up a special tank for spawning, which can usually be induced by raising the water temperature to the upper end of the species' range. Afterwards, remove the females to allow them to recover. Store the eggs for about three months, then rehydrate in soft water to hatch. The fry are easy to raise with a steady supply of live foods.

Egg-buriers' breeding tank (page 242)

LIVEBEARERS

OF THE 22,000 or so species of bony fish, only some 600 bear live young – the rest lay eggs. Most livebearers in the aquarium trade belong to the family Poeciliidae, and many of these, such as the Guppy, Swordtail, and Platy, are popular with novices.

For fry to be born fully formed, the eggs must be fertilized inside the female's body. To insert their sperm, most male livebearers have a modified anal fan called a gonopodium; this has various spines and hooks to help grasp the female during mating. After fertilization, the eggs remain inside the female to develop and hatch. In some livebearers, including the Guppy, the eggs have large yolks that nourish the fry, just like the yolks of eggs laid externally. Other fish have developed the process further: their eggs are small-yolked, and the female feeds the fry directly, as mammals do, through placenta-like structures. A darkened triangular area near the vent, called a gravid patch, can often be seen on pregnant females.

In certain species, such as *Heterandria formosa*, the female can store enough sperm from one mating to produce up to 10 broods. Another fish, the Amazon Molly (*Poecilia formosa*), reproduces without males altogether – it is a female-only species.

Gambusia affinis MOSQUITOFISH

Family Poeciliidae	Diet Carnivorous. Small live foods	64–75°F (18–24°C); pH 6.0–8.0;
Distribution Texas, USA	such as mosquito larvae preferred;	dH to 30°
Size Male 1½ in (4 cm)	also accepts frozen and flake foods	**Swimming level** Middle
Female 2¾ in (7 cm)	**Water conditions** Temperature	**Breeding** Livebearer

Fan-shaped anal fin of female

Rounded abdomen

Also known as the Western Mosquitofish, this species' enormous appetite for mosquito larvae has led to its introduction in many countries to help control malaria. An undemanding fish, it tolerates a wide range of water conditions, and can be kept with other similarly sized species in a well-planted aquarium with good filtration. It is gregarious, and easy to keep and breed. Males display gonopodia, and are smaller than females.

Remarks: If spawning occurs in a community tank, don't expect many fry to survive predation by other fish, including their parents! Some 50–60 young are produced after four weeks' gestation. Transfer the fry to a separate rearing tank for growing, and feed newly hatched brine shrimp.

Coldwater tank (pages 190–191)
Livebearers' breeding tank (page 245)

Heterandria formosa DWARF TOPMINNOW

Family Poeciliidae	Diet Omnivorous. Live, frozen,	63–79°F (17–26°C); pH 6.5–7.5;
Distribution Southeastern USA	flake, and green foods; mosquito	dH to 25°
Size Male ¾ in (2 cm)	larvae is particularly relished	Swimming level Middle
Female 1¾ in (4.5 cm)	Water conditions Temperature	Breeding Livebearer

Also known as the Mosquitofish, this species has the distinction of being not only the eighth smallest vertebrate, but also the smallest vertebrate to give birth to fully formed young. It is a popular aquarium fish that, because of its diminutive size, is usually kept in a species aquarium. Provide a small, densely planted tank with a gentle current. In good water conditions, and if given plenty of small live foods, the Dwarf Topminnow will breed readily; gestation lasts just two weeks.

Remarks: Mosquito larvae in the diet will help maintain the delicate hues of this fish. Like *Gambusia affinis*, it has been exported around the world as a biological mosquito control.

Livebearers' breeding tank (page 245)

Limia melanogaster BLACK-BELLIED LIMIA

Family Poeciliidae
Distribution Haiti, Jamaica
Size Male 1½ in (4 cm)
Female 2½ in (6.5 cm)
Diet Omnivorous. Small aquatic invertebrates such as mosquito larvae, *Daphnia*, and bloodworm, live or frozen; also flake foods and vegetable matter, including algae
Water conditions
Temperature 72–82°F (22–28°C); pH 7.5–8.5; dH 20–30°
Swimming level Middle
Breeding Livebearer

Often available for purchase from specialist outlets or societies, this pretty little fish requires hardwater conditions. It will thrive in a planted tank with a reasonable flow of water. Be sure to use plants that will tolerate hard water, such as Java Fern and *Vallisneria* spp.; you may include a few rocks, but leave enough open space for the fish to swim. The male Black-bellied Limia has a gonopodium and is considerable smaller than the female, which displays a conspicuous gravid patch and is less highly colored overall.

Remarks: If water quality is well maintained, and the fish have a steady supply of small live foods (including bloodworm and mosquito larvae), this species is quite easy to breed.

Livebearers' breeding tank (page 245)

Poecilia reticulata GUPPY

Family Poeciliidae	(3–5 cm); cultivated types larger	fish only) Temperature 72–82°F
Distribution Central America to Brazil	**Diet** Omnivorous. Small live, frozen, flake, and green foods	(22–28°C); pH 7.0–8.5; dH to 30°
Size Wild specimens 1¼–2 in	**Water conditions** (for cultivated	**Swimming level** Middle
		Breeding Livebearer

MALE RED
FANTAIL GUPPY

Round tail (result of line-breeding)

Gonopodium on male fish

MALE BLONDE
GUPPY

FANTAIL GUPPIES

GOLDEN LEOPARD DELTATAIL GUPPIES

The Guppy is a fishkeeping mainstay, and highly popular among novices. Wild Guppies are rarely sold, and are very demanding to keep. Cultivated fish are widely available from specialist breeders. Since Guppies are mature at 3–4 months and yield up to 40 young every 3–4 weeks, within a year several line-bred generations can be produced to establish a new strain, with enhanced color, body size, or fins. Many color forms have been developed, along with numerous fin varieties such as the Fantail, Flagtail, Spadetail, Deltatail, and Roundtail; myriad combinations of these have resulted in types such as the Red Fantail. Males have more color and more flamboyant fins than females. Keep Guppies in a well-planted tank;

ensure the water is not too soft. They eat virtually anything (including their own young), but can digest only small amounts; feed little and often. Give lettuce and peas to deter plant nibbling.

Remarks: Cultivated types make good community fish, provided you have no other species that will nip their trailing fins. If, however, you wish to maintain a certain color strain, keep them in a species tank, or the varieties will interbreed. Provide plants to shelter the young, or move the female to a breeding trap or tank to give birth.

Tropical freshwater tank (pages 184–185)
Livebearers' breeding tank (page 245)

Poecilia sphenops MEXICAN MOLLY

Family Poeciliidae
Distribution Mexico to Colombia
Size 2¼ in (6 cm)
Diet Omnivorous. Small aquatic invertebrates such as insect larvae, either live or frozen; also flake and green foods, including algae, plant material, and peas
Water conditions Temperature 64–82°F (18–28°C); pH 7.0–8.5; dH 12–30°
Swimming level Middle
Breeding Livebearer

Like the Guppy, Mollies have been line-bred, producing Black, Marbled, and Lyretailed varieties. The cultivated forms are prone to disease and require higher temperatures than wild specimens. Adding a little salt to the water helps to keep them healthy. Mollies prefer a planted, hardwater community aquarium; keep hybrids with other fish and plants that can tolerate warm conditions and some salinity.

Remarks: The Mexican Molly is prolific and very easy to breed. Males can be distinguished by their gonopodia; they also have larger fins than females. To aid survival of the young, provide sufficient plant cover in the main aquarium; alternatively, move the female to a large breeding tank to give birth.

Livebearers' breeding tank (page 245)

Poecilia velifera SAILFIN MOLLY

Family Poeciliidae
Distribution Mexico
Size Male 4¾ in (12 cm) Female 7 in (18 cm); usually smaller
Diet Omnivorous. Green foods, especially algae, are an essential part of the diet; will also take small live, frozen, and flake foods
Water conditions Temperature 77–82°F (25–28°C); pH 7.5–8.5; dH 20–35°
Swimming level Middle
Breeding Livebearer

Often confused with another Sailfin Molly (*Poecilia latipinna*), this fish has 18–19 dorsal fin rays, the other 14. *Poecilia velifera* is also known as the Yucatan Molly. Hybrids of these two species come in a variety of color forms. These large fish require hard, clean, flowing water to which a little salt may be added. They also like warmth. Provide a big tank with plenty of swimming space because, in cramped quarters, males do not develop the distinctive sail-like dorsal fin used in displaying to females.

Remarks: Water conditions are vital for breeding success. Females produce up to 100 young after a four-week gestation. The young feed on algae and small live foods such as brine shrimp.

Livebearers' breeding tank (page 245)

Xiphophorus helleri SWORDTAIL

Family Poeciliidae	**Diet** Omnivorous. Small aquatic	68–79°F (20–26°C); pH 7.0–8.0;
Distribution Central America	invertebrates, live or frozen; will	dH 10–30°
Size Male 4 in (10 cm)	also take flake and green foods	**Swimming level** Middle
Female 4¾ in (12 cm)	**Water conditions** Temperature	**Breeding** Livebearer

MALE AND FEMALE PINEAPPLE SWORDTAILS

PAIR OF MARBLED SWORDTAILS

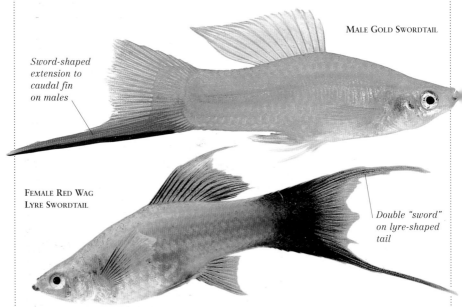

MALE GOLD SWORDTAIL

*Sword-shaped
extension to
caudal fin
on males*

FEMALE RED WAG
LYRE SWORDTAIL

*Double "sword"
on lyre-shaped
tail*

Ever popular, the Swordtail has been bred to produce a number of color and fins forms, including Black, Red, Marbled, High-fin, and Lyre Swordtails, as well as combined varieties such as the Red Lyre. Unfortunately, highly "developed" strains can be prone to disease. The standard-shaped fish, regardless of color, is by far the easiest to keep and is fine for a community aquarium, though males may harass each other or smaller species. Swordtails are very active, and require a fairly large tank, with hard (but not saline) water, lots of swimming space, and thickets of plants to provide refuge for other fish and females pursued by males.

Remarks: Do not buy a small male simply because his sword-like tail extension is well developed. The best stock are those that have grown to a good size before the "sword" is formed. Males can already be recognized by their gonopodia. Females produce large broods of up to 80 young.

Tropical freshwater tank (pages 184–185)
Livebearers' breeding tank (page 245)

Xiphophorus maculatus PLATY

Family Poeciliidae	Female 2¼ in (6 cm)	68–79°F (20–26°C); pH 7.0–8.0;
Distribution Mexico, Guatemala,	**Diet** Omnivorous. Small live,	dH 10–30°
northern Honduras	frozen, flake, and green foods	**Swimming level** Middle
Size Male 1½ in (3.5 cm)	**Water conditions** Temperature	**Breeding** Livebearer

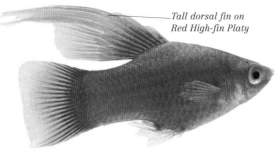

*Tall dorsal fin on
Red High-fin Platy*

FEMALE GOLD PLATY

A good fish for the novice, the Platy comes in many commercially bred color forms, such as the Red Platy, Moon Platy, and Wagtail Platy (with a red or yellow body and a black mouth and fins). It is ideal for a community aquarium, its mild manners allowing it to be kept safely with smaller fish. Wild specimens are more difficult to maintain in captivity, requiring precise water conditions and warmth – at least

82°F (28°C). In nature, Platy populations have distinctive color patterns according to locality.

Remarks: Males, identifiable by their gonopodia, are smaller than females. After a gestation period of 3–4 weeks, up to 80 fry may be produced.

Tropical freshwater tank (pages 184–185)
Livebearers' breeding tank (page 245)

Xiphophorus variatus VARIATUS PLATY

Family Poeciliidae
Distribution Southern Mexico
Size Male 2¼ in (5.5 cm)
Female 2¾ in (7 cm)
Diet Omnivorous. Small live, frozen, flake, and green foods; for all Platies, feed a varied diet for optimum health; all species will graze on plants and algae in aquarium
Water conditions
Temperature 59–77°F
(15–25°C); pH 7.0–8.0;
dH 10–30°
Swimming level Middle
Breeding Livebearer

Like *Xiphophorus maculatus*, the Variatus Platy has been line-bred by the aquarium trade to produce varieties with enhanced color and fins. Popular forms include the Sunset, Marigold, Tiger, and Tuxedo. All varieties make fine community fish, and can be housed with other peaceful species. Provide plant cover and maintain water quality. All Platies prefer hard water, and can tolerate the conditions of a newly

setup aquarium, making them ideal fish to help mature a tank system once nitrites have peaked.

Remarks: Males have gonopodia, while females display a gravid patch. Although they will breed readily in a community tank, use a breeding trap to protect the fry from being eaten by other fish.

Livebearers' breeding tank (page 245)

RAINBOWFISH

THE GROUP OF FISH known by aquarists as rainbowfish comes from three different families: Melanotaeniidae, Pseudomugilidae, and Telmatheriniidae. These fish are native to fresh and brackish waters of eastern and northern Australia, New Guinea, Sulawesi (Celebes), and adjacent islands. Some have a very restricted natural distribution, being found in just one lake or small river. However, since they breed relatively easily in captivity, many species are available to hobbyists.

Rainbowfish were first imported into Europe from Australia in the 1930s, and rapidly endeared

themselves to aquarists. Generally small, peaceful, highly attractive fish, they are named for their brilliant, complex coloration, especially evident in breeding males – red and black pigments augmented by blues and greens produced by light reflections. The majority also have two separate dorsal fins.

Rainbowfish are extremely active fish and require a large, planted tank. Most can be kept in a community aquarium. Although many species are hardy, they are sensitive to water quality, and in poor conditions will remain near the bottom with their fins clamped against their bodies.

Glossolepis incisus RED RAINBOWFISH

Family Melanotaeniidae	Female 4 in (10 cm)	75–79°F (24–26°C); pH 6.8–7.2;
Distribution Indonesia: Irian Jaya (Lake Sentani)	**Diet** Omnivorous. Flake foods and small invertebrates, live or frozen	dH to 15°
Size Male 4¾ in (12 cm)	**Water conditions** Temperature	**Swimming level** Middle to top
		Breeding Egg-depositor

This is a hardy rainbowfish, and one of the best-known species. Avoid the mistake of buying only males because of their bright red coloring; without the drab, silvery females to display to, the males become much paler. Allow plenty of swimming space for these lively fish. Good filtration and gentle water movement are beneficial.

Remarks: Live (or frozen) foods help to maintain the intense coloration of the fish. They breed easily, spawning over a number of days on Java Moss or spawning mops. The fry are tiny and require very fine foods. Culture *Paramecium* as a first offering and follow this with newly hatched brine shrimp. Growth is slow but steady.

Egg-depositors' breeding tank (page 241)

Iriatherina werneri THREADFIN RAINBOWFISH

Family Melanotaeniidae	Diet Omnivorous. Small aquatic	75–81°F (24–27°C); pH 5.5–6.5;
Distribution Indonesia: Irian Jaya	invertebrates, either live or	dH to 10°
Size Male 1½ in (3.5 cm)	frozen; may also take flake foods	**Swimming level** Middle to top
Female 1¼ in (3 cm)	**Water conditions** Temperature	**Breeding** Egg-depositor

A challenge for the more advanced hobbyist, the Threadfin Rainbow is best kept in a species aquarium; in a community, the very long, thread-like extensions on the dorsal and anal fins of males (females lack these fin extensions) may be nipped by other fish. Water conditions are critical; if they deteriorate, this species will be prone to bacterial infections. Provide a very light current. The fish looks its best in sunlight; this also triggers spawning, prompting males to display to females.

Remarks: For breeding, supply Java Moss or spawning mops. Replace these regularly, transferring the eggs; if well fed, the fish will continue to spawn. Give fry infusoria as a first food.

Egg-depositors' breeding tank (page 241)

Melanotaenia boesemani BOESEMAN'S RAINBOWFISH

Family Melanotaeniidae
Distribution Indonesia: Irian Jaya (Ajamaru Lakes)
Size Male 3½ in (9 cm)
Female 2¾ in (7 cm)
Diet Omnivorous. Small aquatic invertebrates, either live or frozen; will also accept flake foods
Water conditions Temperature 81–86°F (27–30°C); pH 6.5–7.0; dH to 10°
Swimming level Middle to top
Breeding Egg-depositor

Boeseman's Rainbow makes a striking centerpiece for the larger furnished aquarium. Males have a distinctive dual color pattern: blue-gray on the front half of the body, gold on the rear, though in captive-bred specimens the intensity of color degenerates with each generation. This species is easy to keep, provided good water quality is maintained; filtration must be efficient but with a gentle flow. Keep as a mixed-sexed school.

Remarks: Males are brighter than females and have longer fins. The fish breed readily; eggs are attached to plants or spawning mops, which can be removed for hatching. The tiny fry can be difficult to rear, requiring the finest of foods. Feed infusoria and brine shrimp nauplii.

Tropical freshwater tank (pages 184–185)
Egg-depositors' breeding tank (page 241)

COLDWATER FISH

THE TERM COLDWATER fish was invented only when heated, or tropical, aquariums became common. Before then, the species now placed in this category were simply the indigenous fish of rivers and lakes in cool climates. In reality, many carps, loaches, trouts, and perches from northern regions can become acclimated to much warmer waters if given time to adapt. Indeed, some extensively line-bred commercial varieties of the Goldfish (originally from coldwater regions of China) can survive only in warm conditions.

Nevertheless, all coldwater fish have a preferred temperature range related to their natural habitats, and must be kept cool in the extreme heat of tropical countries. Trout, introduced to the tropics from cold European waters, live there only at high altitudes in cool, oxygen-rich waters.

Because coldwater fish are widely familiar, some aquarists find them less appealing than exotic tropical imports. Since they have not been so highly developed by the aquarium trade, most species are rather dully colored, as in the wild. However, if kept in optimum conditions, these fish can be very attractive and lively aquarium specimens. Some, such as the Goldfish, are also suitable for novices.

Enneacanthus chaetodon BLACK-BANDED SUNFISH

Family Centrachidae
Distribution US: Maryland, New Jersey, New York
Size 4 in (10 cm)
Diet Carnivorous. Small live aquatic invertebrates such as brine shrimp, bloodworm, and mosquito larvae; only rarely accepts frozen and flake foods
Water conditions Temperature 59–68°F (15–20°C); pH 6.8–7.4; dH 8–20°
Swimming level Middle to bottom
Breeding Egg-depositor

Clean, clear, well-oxygenated water is a must to maintain this fish. It is intolerant of chemicals, rapid temperature fluctuations, and major water changes. Feeding can also be problematic, since it will only rarely accept frozen or flake foods; ensure that you can provide a regular supply of small live foods. Keep either with other small, peaceful fish or in a species aquarium. A planted tank with rocks, wood, and a soft substrate will enable the fish to set up and defend territories, and also provide retreats and spawning sites.

Remarks: When breeding, the male digs a spawning pit for the female to lay her eggs in. He then guards the eggs and subsequent fry.

Coldwater tank (pages 190–191)
Egg-depositors' breeding tank (page 241)

Cobitis taenia SPINED LOACH

Family Cobitidae
Distribution Europe
Size 4¾ in (12 cm)
Diet Carnivorous. Small live aquatic invertebrates such as brine shrimp, bloodworm, and mosquito larvae greatly preferred; may be persuaded to accept frozen foods, but usually refuse flake foods
Water conditions Temperature 57–64°F (14–18°C); pH 5.5–6.5; dH to 10°
Swimming level Bottom
Breeding Egg-scatterer

This species requires a planted tank with oxygen-rich water and cool, clean conditions; if the temperature rises above 68°F (20°C), it will perish. Provide a fine substrate to protect its sensitive barbels, and a gentle current; if the water flow is too strong, this bottom-dwelling fish may struggle to remain on the substrate. Spined Loaches can be difficult to feed, preferring live foods. They are nocturnal, and should be fed after switching off the aquarium lights; keep the room light on to check that they are coming out to feed. Females are larger than males, which have a thickened second pelvic ray.

Remarks: Spawning is in spring or early summer, with the eggs scattered over the substrate.

Egg-scatterers' breeding tank (page 240)

Cottus gobio MILLER'S THUMB

Family Cottidae
Distribution Europe
Size 6 in (15 cm)
Diet Omnivorous. Small aquatic invertebrates, live or frozen; mature specimens in particular will also accept flake and tablet foods
Water conditions Temperature 50–68°F (10–20°C); pH 6.8–7.5; dH to 10°
Swimming level Bottom; fish swims in a scuttling manner along substrate and rocks
Breeding Egg-depositor

Sometimes called the Bullhead (though unrelated to the American catfish of the same name), this fish is found in fast-flowing, oxygen-rich, stony stream beds. In an aquarium, provide a similar environment with gravel and pebbles, a few flat rocks, and some plants. Good-quality, well-oxygenated water with a strong flow is essential. The Miller's Thumb's broad, rounded, rather flattened head gives rise to its common name.

Remarks: This species adapts well to captivity and will breed in shallow water during the spring and summer, especially if given a cooler period during the winter. The fish hollow out a nest underneath a flat stone. Fry prefer small live foods, but will in time take flake and other foods.

Coldwater tank (pages 190–191)
Egg-depositors' breeding tank (page 241)

Carassius auratus GOLDFISH

Family Cyprinidae	pellet foods; also include some	50–68°F (10–20°C); pH 6.5–7.5;
Distribution China	vegetable matter and live or frozen	dH to 15°
Size 9¾ in (25 cm); usually smaller	foods; fish may nibble at plants	**Swimming level** All levels
Diet Omnivorous. Flake and	**Water conditions** Temperature	**Breeding** Egg-scatterer

Long-based dorsal fin

Metallic red-orange coloring

Forked caudal fin is stiffly held

Lateral line clearly visible

COMMON GOLDFISH

Goldfish have been kept in captivity for hundreds of years, and poetic reference has been made to them as early as 800 AD. Originally from China, they were taken to Japan and eventually distributed throughout the Far East. The species was introduced to Europe sometime during the 17th or 18th centuries, and by 1900 the Goldfish had made its way to America.

Although the wild *Carassius auratus* is a dull brown fish, it has been extensively line-bred to enhance color, fins, and body form (including the eyes and scales). Single-tailed varieties are more hardy than twintails and may be kept in a garden pond as well as in the home aquarium; twintails will withstand the summer outside, but prefer indoor warmth in winter.

Twintails have been developed to have a more egg-shaped body than the natural form, and paired or divided caudal and anal fins. Many are bred in the Far East and Florida, with new colors and strains continually being exported to the aquarium trade. Some varieties depart dramatically from the original type, such as the Bubble-eye, developed to have large sacs below its upturned eyes. There are numerous Goldfish societies, which set standards for show specimens regarding shape, number, and length of fins; body form; size; scaling; and many other features.

One of the most popular coldwater fish, the Goldfish is often mistreated, in the mistaken belief that it will live in any conditions. As with any other species, careful maintenance is needed for good health. Goldfish are notoriously filthy, producing much waste, and continually stir up the substrate in their never-ending search for food. A very efficient filtration system and regular water changes of 25 percent per week are essential in the confines of a tank. Do not crowd these fish in water that is depleted of oxygen or too warm, they may gasp at the surface for air.

Remarks: Goldfish breed readily. In the spawning season, males develop tubercules (small white spots on the gill cover and head). At other times, and in common Goldfish with largely unaltered fins, the anal fin of the male is concave, while on the female it is convex. They spawn as waters warm. After courtship, a mature pair may produce over 1,000 eggs which hatch in about five days. The fry are easy to feed on small live foods. Young Goldfish are uniformly dull brown, and need to be grown on for at least eight months before any gold, white, or red colors develop.

Coldwater tank (pages 190–191)
Egg-scatterers' breeding tank (page 240)

COMET

Very slim, elegant fish, Comets have shallow bodies with an elongated caudal fin that can be up to three-quarters the body length, with more pointed lobes than on the common Goldfish. Comets have metallic (highly reflective) scales and are usually red-orange or red-orange and white.

FANTAIL

Highly developed caudal fin

These fish come in both metallic and nacreous forms; nacreous types have clearly distinguished scales with a pearly sheen. Varieties can have normal or telescopic eyes. The main feature of the Fantail is its elaborate caudal fin, which should follow the line of the body without drooping.

MOOR

Metallic-scaled Moors are like early Ford cars; they come in one color – black! Good specimens are velvety black to the very edges of the fins. Like other forms with well-developed or draping, veil-like caudal fins, they are sensitive to prolonged temperatures below 55°F (13°C).

ORANDA

These fish have been bred to accentuate a raspberry-like growth on the head (the hood). The fins are extremely long and delicate-looking, the scales metallic, and the color a deep red-orange or orange and white. A Red-cap variety has a silver body and a scarlet "cap" on its head.

PEARLSCALE

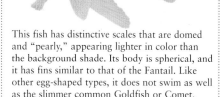

This fish has distinctive scales that are domed and "pearly," appearing lighter in color than the background shade. Its body is spherical, and it has fins similar to that of the Fantail. Like other egg-shaped types, it does not swim as well as the slimmer common Goldfish or Comet.

SHUBUNKIN

Shaped like the common Goldfish, the Shubunkin has a blue/white body with patches of black, red, brown, and yellow, plus black speckles. The scales are either nacreous or matte (invisible, with a dull look). The Bristol has larger, more rounded caudal fin lobes than the London type.

Notropis lutrensis RED SHINER

Family Cyprinidae
Distribution Midwestern US:
from Illinois and Kansas to the
Rio Grande
Size 3¼ in (8 cm)
Diet Omnivorous. Small
aquatic invertebrates, either
live or frozen, plus flake foods;
also accepts vegetable matter
Water conditions
Temperature 59–77°F
(15–25°C); pH 6.8–7.5;
dH 8–20°
Swimming level Middle to top
Breeding Egg-layer
(details unknown)

The Red Shiner is a beautiful schooling fish that
thrives in captivity if kept as a group in a long
aquarium with plenty of open swimming space.
Well-oxygenated water and regular water changes
of about 25 percent per week are required. If
kept at tropical temperatures, the fish's lifespan
is shortened considerably. It prefers uncrowded
conditions with good water flow and filtration,
plus rocks and thickets of plants for cover.

Remarks: Males are more colorful than females,
especially during the spawning season when
they display breeding tubercules around the
snout. At other times, the females are deeper-
bodied than males of a similar length.
If you wish to breed these fish, they require a
cooler period during the winter months.

Coldwater tank (pages 190–191)

Rhodeus spp. BITTERLING

Family Cyprinidae
Distribution Europe,
Far East
Size 2¼–4¼ in (6–12 cm),
depending on species
Diet Omnivorous. Small
aquatic invertebrates such as
insect larvae and bloodworm,
live or frozen; also flake foods
Water conditions
Temperature 59–75°F
(15–24°C); pH 6.5–7.4;
dH to 10°
Swimming level Middle
to bottom
Breeding Egg-depositor

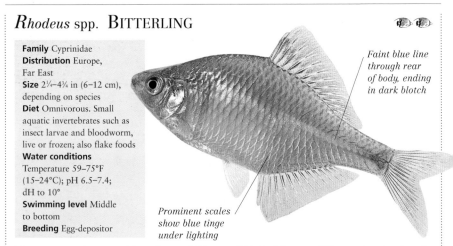

*Faint blue line
through rear
of body, ending
in dark blotch*

*Prominent scales
show blue tinge
under lighting*

There are several species of Bitterling available,
all suitable for a coldwater tank. They require
good water quality and efficient filtration. Provide
plants, a fine gravel or sand substrate, and large
freshwater mussels as a spawning site. Keep as
pairs or buy a school if you cannot sex the fish.

Remarks: Breeding requires a good deal of
fishkeeping skill, to nurture the mussels in

which the fish spawn. When ready to breed, males
exhibit brilliant colors. Pairs are stimulated by
the presence of the mussels, and the female places
her eggs within one, using her ovipositor. The
male's fertilizing milt is drawn in by the mussel,
and subsequent "breathing" aerates the eggs
until they hatch and the fry are expelled.

Coldwater tank (pages 190–191)

Gasterosteus aculeatus THREE-SPINED STICKLEBACK

Family Gasterosteidae
Distribution Europe, northern Asia, Greenland, Iceland, North America, Algeria
Size 4 in (10 cm)
Diet Carnivorous. Small aquatic invertebrates, initally live and, in time, frozen; will take flake foods only rarely; feed fry tiny live foods
Water conditions Temperature 50–68°F (10–20°C); pH 6.0–7.4; dH to 10°
Swimming level All levels
Breeding Nest-builder

Small but endearing, the lively Stickleback is a popular fish with children. Keep a mixed-sex school (ideally with more females than males) in a planted aquarium with fine gravel and well-aerated, clean water. Use native plants, providing hiding places as well as areas of open substrate. This species will initially accept only live foods and needs to be carefully weaned onto frozen foods. Flake is usually ignored.

Remarks: Give them a cold spell in the winter, then warmer water, to encourage breeding. The male (slimmer and more colorful) constructs a nest from and among plants. He entices first one female to spawn therein, then several others. He later guards the eggs (as many as 50) and fry until the young are able to fend for themselves.

Coldwater tank (pages 190–191)

Gymnocephalus cernuus RUFFE

Family Percidae
Distribution Europe, Asia
Size 9¾ in (25 cm)
Diet Carnivorous. Meaty foods such as shrimp, insect larvae, and small fish, either live or frozen (preferably live); will rarely accept flake and tablet foods
Water conditions Temperature 50–68°F (10–20°C); pH 6.5–7.5; dH to 15°
Swimming level Middle to bottom
Breeding Egg-depositor

Also known as the Blacktail, this attractive fish adapts well to aquarium life, provided it has well-filtered water with a high oxygen content. It is an active, schooling species; keep several specimens in a large, planted tank. Feeding can be difficult; Ruffes will readily take almost any live, meaty foods, but only rarely can be persuaded to eat flake and tablet foods. In the wild they are noted for eating fish spawn.

Remarks: The Ruffe's main drawback is its propensity for eating anything alive that it can fit into its mouth, including other fish. Be sure to keep it with species large enough not to be considered as food. If setting up a breeding tank, provide rocks and vegetation as spawning sites.

Coldwater tank (pages 190–191)
Egg-depositors' breeding tank (page 241)

BRACKISH-WATER FISH

NEARLY ALL THE WATERS of the world are either salty (in seas) or fresh (in rivers and lakes). Freshwater fish cannot inhabit the sea, yet there are species that live where rivers run into the sea and the water is brackish, or partially salty. These fish have adapted to tolerate daily fluctuations in salinity and water levels as the tides come and go or as river flows alter. In such changing habitats are found resilient fish such as gobies, the Scat, the Mono, and the Shark Catfish.

Many of these species actually require environmental variations in order to survive, and will die if kept in uniform conditions. Therefore, brackish-water fish need very special care in aquariums. They won't thrive in fresh water even if, in the wild, they spend some of their time there. The temperature ranges given below are critical, but other water values can – indeed should – fluctuate. Use marine salt to maintain pH and hardness at acceptable levels. Not all species can be kept together; check carefully before stocking a community tank.

Frequently overlooked in favor of more colorful marines or easier freshwater fish, brackish-water fish, with their often intriguing looks and lifestyles, make a rewarding challenge for the experienced aquarist.

Anableps spp. FOUR-EYED FISH

Family Anablepidae	**Diet** Carnivorous. Small aquatic invertebrates, live or frozen; will grudgingly take flake foods	75–82°F (24–28°C); pH 7.6–7.8; dH to 15°; SG 1.002–1.007
Distribution Central America, northern South America		**Swimming level** Top
Size 11¾ in (30 cm); usually smaller	**Water conditions** Temperature	**Breeding** Livebearer

Anableps is an interesting fish for the specialist. Its eyes are divided so that it can see above and below water at the same time. Keep in a shallow tank with a tight-fitting cover to maintain humidity above the surface. The water should be warm and well filtered to cope with waste from the species' high-protein diet. Use a gravel substrate and salt-tolerant plants; avoid sharp objects that may damage the fish's eyes. Provide open swimming space and a beach area; *Anableps* will come partially out of the water to rest on this.

Remarks: Keep 6–8, with several of each sex, so the fish can pair naturally: the male's gonopodium bends either right or left; a compatible female will have a genital opening that is oppositely biased.

Livebearers' breeding tank (page 245)

Arius seemani SHARK CATFISH

Family Ariidae	**Diet** Omnivorous. Meaty foods;	dH to 20°; SG 1.002–1.007
Distribution Pacific coast from	also pellet and flake foods	**Swimming level** Middle
California, USA, to Colombia	**Water conditions** Temperature	to bottom
Size 11¾ in (30 cm)	72–82°F (22–28°C); pH 7.0–8.0;	**Breeding** Mouthbrooder

This very active fish likes the company of its own kind, and needs a large tank with lots of swimming space; unlike many catfish, it is not nocturnal. It is easy to keep, as long as water quality does not deteriorate; provide a strong current. Like its namesake, the Shark Catfish cruises unceasingly about the tank and takes most meaty foods, including small fish; do not keep it with tiny species. The fish's silvery color fades with age; to protect its scaleless body, furnish the tank with smooth-edged bogwood. When handling this fish, beware its stout spines.

Remarks: Females are more robust than males and have a small appendage on the ventral fins. There are no reports of captive breeding.

Brackish-water tank (pages 194–195)

Telmatherina ladigesi CELEBES RAINBOWFISH

Family Telmatherinidae **Distribution** Indonesian island of Sulawesi (also called Celebes) **Size** 3 in (7.5 cm) **Diet** Omnivorous. Small aquatic invertebrates such as brine shrimp, bloodworm, and mosquito larvae, live or frozen, to achieve good coloring and size; also accepts flake foods **Water conditions** Temperature 72–82°F (22–28°C); pH 7.0–7.6; dH 12–15°; SG 1.002–1.007 **Swimming level** Middle **Breeding** Egg-depositor	

The Celebes Rainbowfish is a delightful little schooling fish that prefers to be in a group of six or more. It benefits from a careful choice of companions; these should be other small species that will not nip the elongated fins of the males. A planted tank with open swimming areas is best.

Remarks: Take care when making water changes; this fish reacts adversely to sudden alterations in conditions. Breed as pairs or a group in a specially setup tank with fine-leaved and floating plants as spawning sites. After breeding, remove the parents to prevent them from eating their eggs. The fry emerge in a week to 10 days; feed them newly hatched brine shrimp or *Daphnia*.

Brackish-water tank (pages 194–195)
Egg-depositors' breeding tank (page 241)

Chanda ranga GLASSFISH

Family Chandidae	Diet Omnivorous. Small aquatic	68–86°F (20–30°C); pH 7.6–7.8;
Distribution Thailand, India, Burma	invertebrates, live or frozen; also accepts flake and tablet foods	dH to 15°; SG 1.002–1.007
Size 3¼ in (8 cm)	Water conditions Temperature	Swimming level Middle
		Breeding Egg-depositor

Ideal for a planted tank with other peaceful fish, the Glassfish is often kept for its novel transparent body. Males have blue-edged dorsal and anal fins, and their swim bladder (which is easily seen) is more pointed at the rear. They can be territorial; provide space and plenty of hiding places. Live foods are preferred, or frozen if necessary. This fish cannot survive on dry foods alone.

Remarks: The sticky eggs are deposited among plants and hatch in 24 hours. The fry are exceptionally difficult to raise. Use a separate breeding tank and remove the parents after spawning. The eggs are prone to fungal infections; if affected, treat them with a fungicide.

Brackish-water tank (pages 194–195)
Egg-depositors' breeding tank (page 241)

Brachygobius xanthozona BUMBLEBEE GOBY

Family Gobiidae	Diet Carnivorous. Small aquatic	77–86°F (25–30°C); pH 7.6–8.5;
Distribution Southeast Asia, Thailand, southern Vietnam	invertebrates, live or frozen; will accept flake foods only rarely	dH to 15°; SG 1.002–1.007
Size 1¾ in (4.5 cm)	Water conditions Temperature	Swimming level Bottom
		Breeding Egg-depositor

The small Bumblebee Goby, colored with broad yellow and black bands, is best suited to a species tank, or can be kept with mid-water or surface-dwelling fish that will not compete with it for the substrate. Provide many shelters, using pebbles, wood, plants, and flowerpots (as caves). Feeding can be difficult; live foods are preferred, particularly whiteworm and *Tubifex*, but frozen bloodworm or *Daphnia* may also be accepted.

Remarks: A change with fresh water can trigger spawning. Eggs are laid beneath flat stones or in caves. The male guards the fry, which on hatching are free-swimming in lower levels, only later adopting the bottom-dwelling lifestyle of their parents. Feed them brine shrimp nauplii.

Brackish-water tank (pages 194–195)
Egg-depositors' breeding tank (page 241)

Periophthalmus spp. MUDSKIPPER

Family Gobiidae
Distribution Africa through Southeast Asia to Australia
Size 6 in (15 cm)
Diet Carnivorous. Small invertebrates, including worms, crickets, and flies, preferably live; will also accept frozen and flake foods
Water conditions Temperature 77–86°F (25–30°C); pH 8.0–8.5; dH to 15°; SG 1.002–1.007
Swimming level Bottom
Breeding Egg-layer (details unknown)

Mudskippers originate in mangrove swamps, and are sometimes seen resting in shallow water with just their eyes above the water. They require a specially setup tank with a beach area that they can crawl out onto, and rocks and roots for climbing out of the water. The area above the water surface must be kept warm and humid by using a tight-fitting cover; the air temperature should match that of the water.

Also provide very efficient filtration; water quality and cleanliness are of paramount importance. In this type of environment, bacterial infections can quickly take hold. Vary the diet, including plenty of meaty, especially live, foods.

Remarks: These fish become very tame, but if you wish to hand-feed them, use tweezers – Mudskippers have a good set of teeth!

Stigmatogobius sadanundio SPOTTED GOBY

Family Gobiidae
Distribution Philippines, Java, Borneo, Sumatra, Southeast Asia
Size 3¼ in (8.5 cm)
Diet Omnivorous. Small meaty foods such as mosquito larvae and bloodworm, live or frozen; will also eat tank algae
Water conditions Temperature 68–82°F (20–28°C); pH 7.6–8.0; dH to 15°; SG 1.002–1.007
Swimming level Middle to bottom
Breeding Egg-depositor

A placid fish, the Spotted Goby is happiest in a planted aquarium, and may be kept with species that inhabit the upper levels of the tank. Provide many hiding places to accommodate its territorial traits; these can also be used as spawning sites. A diurnal fluctuation in temperature of a couple of degrees, with the daytime warmer than the evening, is beneficial. Under no circumstances try to acclimate this fish to softwater conditions.

Remarks: Males have larger fins; females are generally smaller and more yellow in color. Pairs spawn in warm conditions, laying their eggs (up to 1,000) on the roof of a cave. Both parents guard the fry, which are fairly easy to raise on newly hatched brine shrimp.

Brackish-water tank (pages 194–195)
Egg-depositors' breeding tank (page 241)

Dermogenys pusillus HALFBEAK

Family Hemirhamphidae **Distribution** Southeast Asia, Malaysia, Thailand, Indonesia **Size** 2¾ in (7 cm)	**Diet** Carnivorous. Small live aquatic invertebrates, plus flies; may take frozen and flake foods **Water conditions** Temperature	64–86°F (18–30°C); pH 7.6–7.8; dH to 15°; SG 1.002–1.007 **Swimming level** Top **Breeding** Livebearer

Lower jaw is elongated for surface feeding

Blue patch on males

Thin body with gold line

This unusual-looking fish is best kept in a shallow species tank planted around the edges, leaving plenty of open surface area. Include one or two floating plants on which to place live insects for feeding, and a tight-fitting cover. Although timid if there is insufficient plant cover, males frequently fight using their extended lower jaws, sometimes injuring each other. Keep as a group of just one male and two or three females.

Remarks: Aquarium breeding is difficult. Males are smaller and have a modified anal fin. Some 3–8 weeks after courtship and fertilization, the females produce 10–30 fry. Even after yielding several viable broods, it is not unusual for them to deliver dead fry. The young require very tiny live foods such as newly hatched brine shrimp.

Livebearers' breeding tank (page 245)

Monodactylus argenteus MONO

Family Monodactylidae **Distribution** Eastern coast of Africa to Indonesia **Size** 9¾ in (25 cm)	**Diet** Omnivorous. Live, frozen, flake, and green foods **Water conditions** Temperature 75–82°F (24–28°C); pH 7.6–7.8;	dH to 15°; SG 1.002–1.007 **Swimming level** Middle **Breeding** Egg-layer (details unknown)

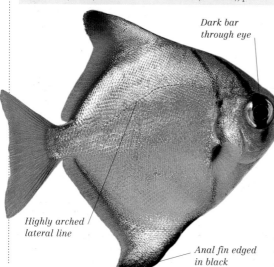

Dark bar through eye

Highly arched lateral line

Anal fin edged in black

The Mono is a most attractive disk-shaped schooling fish that can be shy, particularly if kept with larger, more boisterous species. It is extremely sensitive to poor water conditions, and requires very efficient filtration, plenty of aeration, and regular water changes. If necessary, add a protein skimmer. Keep as a group of 4–6 in a planted tank with room to swim, plus rocks and roots for shelter. The intense black and yellow colors of the juveniles pale with age and remain mainly on the fins in adults.

Remarks: Watch their mouths – Monos are not averse to devouring small fish! They can be greedy eaters; be careful not to overfeed.

Brackish-water tank (pages 194–195)

Poecilia latipinna SAILFIN MOLLY

Family Poeciliidae
Distribution Southern USA
Size Male 4 in (10 cm)
Female 4¾ in (12 cm)
Diet Omnivorous. Vegetable matter, including algae, plus flake, frozen, and live foods; *Daphnia*, bloodworm, and mosquito larvae are relished
Water conditions
Temperature 68–82°F
(20–28°C); pH 7.5–8.5;
dH to 20°; SG 1.002–1.007
Swimming level Middle to top
Breeding Livebearer

Sailfin Mollies are reared on fish farms around the world, and have been selectively bred to produce a number of color forms. They are ideal for a brackish-water aquarium, where they will thrive and multiply readily. (This species can also be kept in fresh water.) Although Sailfin Mollies like to nibble plants, they do not cause too much damage. To protect tank vegetation, include peas or other green foods in the diet. Feed often.

Remarks: Males have gonopodia and flamboyant fins. Use a breeding tank for females to give birth; otherwise, fry will be eaten. Alternatively, catch the young as soon as you see them and grow them elsewhere. Under good conditions, you will have broods of 40 or more each month.

Brackish-water tank (pages 194–195)
Livebearers' breeding tank (page 245)

Scatophagus argus SCAT

Family Scatophagidae
Distribution Indian and Pacific Oceans: Indonesia, Philippines, ranging to Tahiti
Size 11¾ in (30 cm)
Diet Omnivorous. Vary the diet, from live or frozen foods, to algae and vegetable matter, to flake and uncooked oatmeal
Water conditions
Temperature 68–82°F
(20–28°C); pH 7.6–7.8;
dH to 15°; SG 1.002–1.007
Swimming level Middle
Breeding Egg-layer
(details unknown)

Scats eat plants voraciously, making it virtually impossible to maintain a planted tank with these fish. Even the hardy Java Fern will be nibbled at the edges; use rocks or wood as decor. Keep as groups of 3–4, with space to school in and roots to hide among. Provide very efficient filtration and monitor water conditions carefully, since young specimens in particular are badly affected by nitrites. As the fish mature, they prefer greater and greater concentrations of salt until, as adults, they are happiest in seawater.

Remarks: The transformation from juvenile to adult is dramatic: the larvae have large heads and heavy bony plates, like the marine butterflyfish; this armor changes as the fish mature.

Brackish-water tank (pages 194–195)

Brachirus salinarum SOLE

Family Soleidae	invertebrates, live or frozen; may	dH to 15°; SG 1.002–1.007
Distribution Australia	take sinking flake or tablet foods	**Swimming level** Bottom
Size 6 in (15 cm)	**Water conditions** Temperature	**Breeding** Egg-layer
Diet Carnivorous. Small aquatic	72–86°F (22–30°C); pH 7.6–8.0;	(details unknown)

The Sole is also known as the Salt-pan Sole, since in nature it inhabits shallow, brackish waters. A bottom-dweller, it is most active at night; given a sandy substrate, the fish will partially bury itself in this during the day. It is peaceful and can be kept with other small, placid species. Furnish the aquarium with rocks as resting places and plants and wood for decor. Provide good filtration to clear any debris stirred up, and a gentle flow of water that will not sweep the fish away from the bottom.

Remarks: Feed with the tank lights switched off, giving foods that sink to the bottom – this species will not swim in mid-water to catch items. Small worms such as whiteworm are relished, but offer such rich foods sparingly. Nothing is known of the Sole's breeding habits.

Chelonodon nigroviridis GREEN PUFFER

Family Tetraodontidae	**Diet** Omnivorous. Meaty items	74–82°F (24–28°C); pH 7.6–8.0;
Distribution India through	(snails, shrimps, worms), plus	dH to 15°; SG 1.002–1.007
Southeast Asia to Philippines	green, flake, and tablet foods	**Swimming level** Middle
Size 6¾ in (17 cm)	**Water conditions** Temperature	**Breeding** Egg-depositor

A nasty character, the Green Puffer is intolerant and aggressive towards anything and everything. Keep it with other fish at your own risk, and only with similarly sized species that can defend themselves. Provide a planted tank with plenty of open swimming space; use robust plants, since Green Puffers will attack vegetation! Feed a varied diet. Young fish are easier to acclimate than mature specimens.

Remarks: The body partially inflates as a threat or defence mechanism, and each jaw has a pair of teeth. The species has been bred in captivity; eggs are laid on the substrate, and the male guards the fry. The Green Puffer's flesh is toxic to both humans and animals even if cooked; therefore do not feed a dead body to your pet cat!

Toxotes jaculatrix ARCHER

Family Toxotidae
Distribution Asia, India, through Southeast Asia into northern Australia
Size 9½ in (24 cm); usually smaller
Diet Carnivorous. Live foods; in time may take frozen foods
Water conditions
Temperature 77–86°F (25–30°C); pH 7.6–8.0; dH to 15°; SG 1.002–1.007
Swimming level Top
Breeding Egg-layer (details unknown); breeding unlikely in aquariums

Archers are generally peaceful and not too nervous if kept in small groups of like-sized specimens; otherwise, large individuals may pick on smaller ones. They may be housed with fish such as Scats or Monos, although these species can grow incompatibly large and active. Provide a spacious tank with open swimming areas, and maintain conditions carefully; Archers will not survive if kept too cool. They must be given live prey items; buy these from shops selling supplies for reptile-keepers, or hatch maggots for a homegrown crop of flies.

Remarks: Archers like to feed on grasshoppers, crickets, flies, and spiders that fall onto or approach the water surface. If bought as young specimens, they may eventually accept flake foods, but some fish will refuse them altogether.

Brackish-water tank (pages 194–195)

PROJECTILE FEEDING TECHNIQUE

ARCHER JUMPING TO SNARE INSECT

In a specialized tank part-filled with water and having plants above the surface, *Toxotes jaculatrix* can perform its "archery" skills – shooting insects off leaves with an expertly aimed stream of water from its mouth. Shield light fittings, which can make dangerous targets, and install a cover, since the fish may even leap at prey. Both this and the slimmer species of Archer, *Toxotes chatareus*, will also feed more sedentarily from the surface.

FRESHWATER PLANTS

Plants are often regarded as a minor feature in an aquarium, but they play an important role. They not only help to complete an attractive and secure environment for your fish, but also improve tank conditions by absorbing nitrates. Thriving freshwater plants can also curb unsightly algal growth. For success in cultivating tank vegetation, choose true aquatic species, and always purchase healthy specimens without discolored or dead leaves. As you would with fish, choose plants to suit the conditions in your aquarium, and provide appropriate lighting.

The following pages feature plants in a variety of colors, leaf shapes, and heights to suit your particular needs, as well as species able to tolerate cold or brackish water.

◁ LUSH PLANTING IN A FRESHWATER AQUARIUM

Tubers

TUBEROUS PLANTS OF the genus *Aponogeton* are popular in the hobby, though they rarely flourish for more than a season. The tubers, imported damp, may be transferred to a tank, where they will sprout shoots and roots. Alternatively, specimens can be purchased pre-sprouted, ensuring that the plant is viable.

Aponogetons grow well for about eight months, then shed their main leaves, which can be over 20 in (50 cm) long in some species, retaining a basal rosette of leaves. At this time, the plants should be placed in cooler conditions for about eight weeks, then returned to the aquarium. There, they will continue to grow, with some species flowering in the tank. The seeds set are often viable; leave them to germinate and produce plantlets.

Other tuberous plants include *Barclaya* and *Nymphaea* species, members of the Water Lily family. Like Aponogetons, the tubers are imported damp and can be sprouted in the tank. The leaves are tender, and snails are fond of consuming them. *Barclaya* sp. produces long, lanceolate (lancet-shaped) leaves and is one of the most sought-after aquarium plants. It also flowers and sets viable seed underwater. *Nymphaea* species yield a basal rosette of red or green leaves, followed by floating leaves (lily pads). In the aquarium, only the basal rosette should be retained; trim off any growth extending towards the water surface—unless, of course, you want your plant to flower. Propagation is by seed or from shoots separated from the tuber.

Aponogeton rigidiflorius

Aponogetons' long leaves vary in form according to species. They prefer soft water conditions and moderately low lighting levels. Keep the tank clean to prevent the tuber from rotting away and to control algae on the leaves.

Barclaya longifolia

This attractive plant is available in two forms: one has olive-green leaves, the other is deep red. Both varieties require good light to flourish. As a bonus, they may also flower in the aquarium and will set viable seed.

ALSO RECOMMENDED

Aponogeton boivinianus
Aponogeton crispus
Aponogeton madagascariensis (Madagascan Lace Plant)

Aponogeton ulvaceus
Aponogeton undulatus
Nymphaea maculata (African Tiger Lotus)
Nymphaea stellata (Water Lily)

FLOATING PLANTS

MANY FLOATING PLANTS are extremely beneficial in aquaria, providing spawning sites and refuges for vulnerable fry, as well as shaded areas for species of fish requiring shelter and seclusion. They need no anchorage point to grow and thrive, and usually float freely on or in the water column. Some, such as Java Moss and Riccia, attach themselves to wood or rocks, and may even survive out of water, while the adaptable Indian Fern will grow either planted in the substrate, out of water, or floating. A stalwart for coldwater tanks is Hornwort, whose long stems form a thick mat just below the water surface.

These hardy species have minimal requirements: good light, regular water changes, and water movement gentle enough to ensure that they are not swept to the sides of the tank. However, it is important to ensure that water droplets from your condensation tray do not fall onto any floating leaves. This can cause them to rot and, coupled with intense lighting, may also result in the leaves becoming burned.

Most fishkeepers are all too familiar with the highly invasive floating plant Duckweed (*Lemna* spp.), which can proliferate uncontrollably, clogging filtration systems. This plant sticks readily to nets, hands, and arms, and can unwittingly be transferred from one tank to another. Avoid introducing it at all costs – unless you happen to have a fish, such as some of the larger cyprinids, that will eat it!

Pistia stratiotes
WATER LETTUCE

The Water Lettuce is so-named for its broad leaves and radiating structure. Its trailing roots are also useful for shading and sheltering fry.

Salvinia auriculata
BUTTERFLY FERN

Salvinia species have round, hairy leaves that provide good cover for fish. They need fairly bright light and are best suited to medium-hard water.

ALSO RECOMMENDED

Ceratopteris thalictroides (Indian Fern or Water Sprite)
Ceratophyllum spp. (Hornwort)

Riccia fluitans (Riccia)
Vesicularia dubyana (Java Moss)

ROOTED PLANTS

ROOTED PLANTS ESTABLISH themselves with vigor, and quickly become a dominant feature in an aquarium. Plan your plantings carefully; once they have taken root, it is virtually impossible to move them without disrupting the entire tank.

Plants of this type are cultivated for the trade and sold as potted specimens in small, open-mesh baskets. The entire container may be planted in the substrate, but this can be unsightly if the basket is exposed by fish digging. Plants grown in synthetic media, which can irritate fish, should be carefully removed from the media and planted with bare roots. If there is more than one plant in a container, separate and plant them individually to provide more space for growth.

Root disturbance can cause some leaves to die back, but with time the plants will recover to grow new roots and leaves. Once established, feed them every three or four months with a few tablets of aquarium fertilizer or dried rabbit droppings placed within the root run. Conversely, to check the growth of large plants, grasp them at the base and very gently pull upwards, just enough to break a few roots.

Plants such as Java Fern, Dwarf Anubias, and *Bolbitis* sp. have creeping rhizomes with tiny roots by which they will anchor themselves if tied onto rocks or wood. These species are particularly useful for adding height to a planting system and, since they are not bedded in the substrate, will not be uprooted by fish that habitually dig.

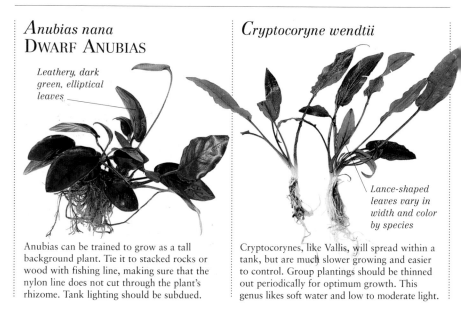

Anubias nana
DWARF ANUBIAS

Leathery, dark
green, elliptical
leaves

Anubias can be trained to grow as a tall background plant. Tie it to stacked rocks or wood with fishing line, making sure that the nylon line does not cut through the plant's rhizome. Tank lighting should be subdued.

Cryptocoryne wendtii

Lance-shaped
leaves vary in
width and color
by species

Cryptocorynes, like Vallis, will spread within a tank, but are much slower growing and easier to control. Group plantings should be thinned out periodically for optimum growth. This genus likes soft water and low to moderate light.

Echinodorus paniculatus
BROAD-LEAF AMAZON SWORD

Long, dagger-shaped leaves on extended stalks give tall profile

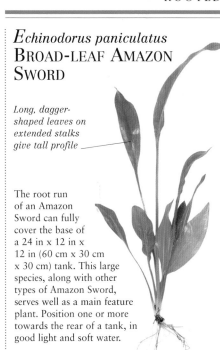

The root run of an Amazon Sword can fully cover the base of a 24 in x 12 in x 12 in (60 cm x 30 cm x 30 cm) tank. This large species, along with other types of Amazon Sword, serves well as a main feature plant. Position one or more towards the rear of a tank, in good light and soft water.

Vallisneria spiralis
STRAIGHT VALLIS

Very elongated, grass-like leaves; related Twisted Vallis grows much shorter

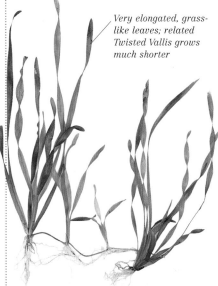

Long-leaved Vallis is invasive; unchecked, it will produce runners that colonize large areas of the tank. It prefers bright light and hard water.

Echinodorus tenellus
PYGMY CHAIN SWORD

This dwarf form of the Amazon Sword is useful for small aquariums or in the foreground of a tank. It suits a well-lit position in soft water, and will withstand low temperatures (59°F/15°C). The plant develops numerous runners.

Microsorium pteropus
JAVA FERN

Tapering foliage will become long in hard water

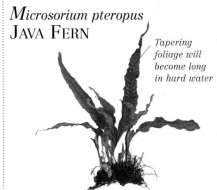

Java Fern's long, "hairy" roots do not extend into the substrate but anchor the plant to rocks or wood. The plant is slow-growing and hardy, requiring only moderate lighting.

ALSO RECOMMENDED

Aglaeonema simplex (Malayan Sword)
Bolbitis heudelotii (African Water Fern)
Cryptocoryne affinis
Cryptocoryne balansae
Cryptocoryne ciliata
Cryptocoryne nevillii (Dwarf Crypt)
Echinodorus cordifolius (Radicans Sword or Spade-leaf Sword)
Echinodorus major (Ruffled Amazon Sword)
Sagittaria platyphylla (Giant Sag)
Sagittaria subulata (Dwarf Sag)
Vallisneria tortifolia (Twisted Vallis)

CUTTINGS

SOME OF THE MOST versatile aquarium plants are purchased as cuttings, which are the unrooted tops of plants. In a tank, these can be used as foreground vegetation (if trimmed regularly) or as backdrop plants. A wide range of colors and leaf shapes are available to lend contrast for massed plantings.

Generally, green-leaved species are easier to cultivate than red varieties, which need far more intense light. Fine-leaved plants such as *Cabomba* spp. require an efficient filtration system to prevent the leaves from becoming clogged with fine matter suspended in the water.

Plant cuttings individually in staggered rows, spaced so that light from above will reach the leaves at the very bottom; if they do not receive light, the lower parts of the plants will turn brown, die, and rot. When viewed from the front of the tank, the cuttings will resemble a solid wall of vegetation. Do not be tempted to save time by planting in bunches; this will bruise the stems and cause them to rot, particularly with tender species such as *Rotala macandra*.

Many plants will grow emersed (out of water) as well as submersed (in water). It is easier to harvest emersed plants, and woody cuttings of these are sometimes available; leaf shapes may differ from submersed growth. When planted in the tank, initially the leaves will fall off. Leave the stems in place, and within a few weeks small growths should appear at some of the leaf joints. When the shoots are long enough, nip them off and plant them as cuttings. Once the cuttings are established, the original woody stems can be removed and discarded. When the plants become too tall, remove them, trim them to the required length, and replant the top sections. Retain the bottom sections for planting in another tank; they will develop side shoots and produce more plants.

Coldwater and brackish-water aquariums require plants that will tolerate, respectively, cool temperatures and a degree of salinity. Some freshwater species can thrive in such conditions; check requirements carefully. Some appropriate choices are listed below right.

RECOMMENDED

Alternanthera rosaefolia (Red Hygrophila)
Ammania senegalensis (Red Ammania)
Ceratophyllum spp. (Hornwort)
Didiplis diandra (Water Hedge)
Egeria densa (Giant Elodea)
Elodea canadensis (Canadian Pondweed)
Heteranthera zosterifolia

Hygrophila polysperma (Dwarf Hygrophila)
Hygrophila salicifolia (Willow-leaf)
Limnophila aquatica (Giant Ambulia)
Ludwigia mullertii
Ludwigia repens
Myriophyllum hippuroides
Synnema triflorum (Water Wisteria)

Bacopa caroliniana

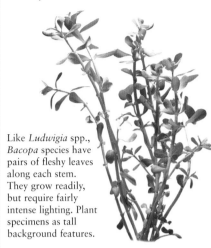

Like *Ludwigia* spp., *Bacopa* species have pairs of fleshy leaves along each stem. They grow readily, but require fairly intense lighting. Plant specimens as tall background features.

Cabomba caroliniana
GREEN CABOMBA

Leaves arranged in pairs

With their fine, feathery leaves, *Cabomba* spp. are useful for filling space but can be difficult to grow. They prefer bright light and soft water. Maintain good tank conditions to prevent debris or algae build-up.

Nomaphila stricta
GIANT HYGROPHILA

Broad leaves serve well as spawning sites

The large leaves of this plant, also known as the Indian Water Star, provide good shelter for fish, which may be tempted to nibble. Hygrophilas do best in strong light and slightly hard water.

Rotala macandra
RED ROTALA

This soft-leaved plant should not be positioned in strong currents, since its delicate foliage is easily damaged. Provide intense lighting; this is critical for Rotala to retain its distinctive red coloration.

BRACKISH-WATER PLANTS

Ceratophyllum spp. (Hornwort)
Cryptocoryne ciliata
Elodea canadensis (Canadian Pondweed)
Hygrophila polysperma (Dwarf Hygrophila)
Microsorium pteropus (Java Fern)

Sagittaria platyphylla (Giant Sag)
Sagittaria subulata (Dwarf Sag)
Vallisneria spirallis (Straight Vallis)
Vallisneria tortifolia (Twisted Vallis)
Vesicularia dubyana (Java Moss)

COLDWATER PLANTS

Ceratophyllum demersum (Hornwort)
Echinodorus tenellus (Pygmy Chain Sword)

Egeria densa (Giant Elodea)
Elodea canadensis (Canadian Pondweed)

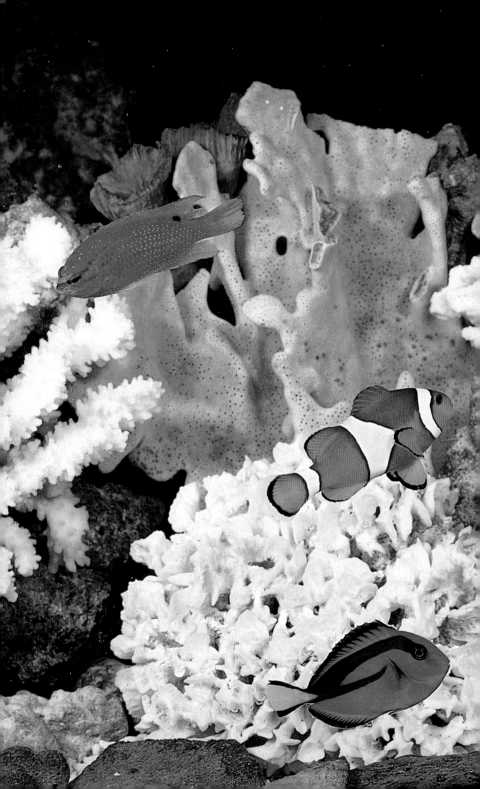

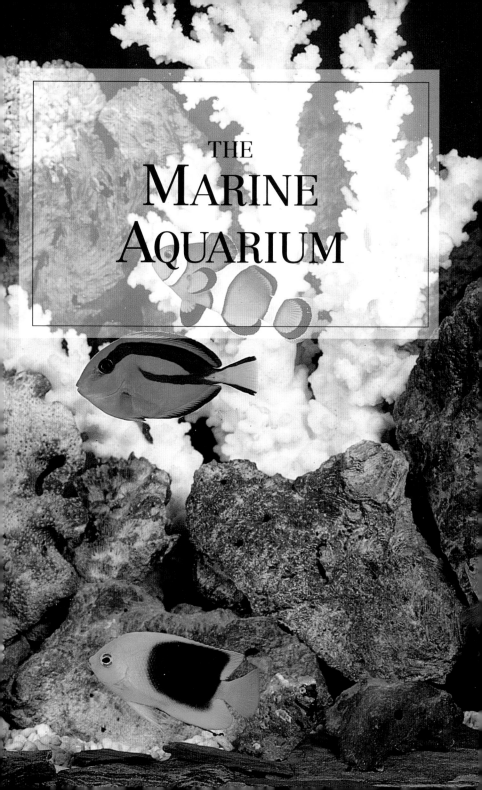

THE
MARINE
AQUARIUM

Marine Fish and Invertebrates

For many fishkeepers, a marine aquarium is the only aquarium to have, since the colors and forms of the fish are so diverse and alluring. There is also the exciting prospect of recreating a coral reef, complete with invertebrates. The species profiled in this section comprise but a small sample of those you may wish to keep. Make your selection with great care; the dietary needs and behavior of some marine species can be problematic. Marine fish also require more space than freshwater fish, and are much more sensitive to poor water quality. Many can be kept only as single specimens, while others are venomous; yet others are predators that can decimate a reef tank, feeding on smaller fish and invertebrates. Invertebrates themselves are highly demanding and should be kept only by experienced aquarists.

◁ Mature tropical marine community tank

ANEMONEFISH

THE FAMILY POMACENTRIDAE divides neatly into two: anemonefish and damselfish. These enjoy equal popularity in the hobby, and provide many an aquarist's first encounter with keeping marine fish.

Anemonefish, also called clownfish because of their comical, waddling swimming style and their bold markings, are best known for their commensal relationship with sea anemones, especially those of the genera *Stoichactis* and *Heteractis*. Although anemones have stinging cells to protect themselves and to stun and capture prey, anemonefish have a mucus coating that renders

them immune to these stings. Thus the anemone does not consider the fish as prey, and the two can live harmoniously. Nevertheless, it is perfectly possible to keep these fish without an anemone, and vice versa. Anemonefish are territorial; keep only one pair per anemone.

Various species will breed in aquariums; buy a pair, or two males; one will develop into a female. If keeping a group, after the dominant pair have spawned the others should be removed to prevent them from being attacked by the very protective male. The fry are not easy to raise, requiring rotifers as a first food.

Amphiprion clarkii BANDED CLOWNFISH

Family Pomacentridae	meaty foods such as fish or	75–79°F (24–26°C); pH 8.3–8.4;
Distribution Indo-Pacific	shellfish, plus algae and vegetable-	SG 1.023–1.027
Size 2 in (5 cm)	based foods; may take flake foods	**Swimming level** Bottom
Diet Omnivorous. Finely chopped	**Water conditions** Temperature	**Breeding** Egg-depositor

The coloration of this widespread species, also called Clark's Clownfish or the Two-banded Clownfish, can vary according to locality. Its body is usually dark brown, with two bright vertical bands on adults; juveniles have a third. The face, belly, and pectoral, anal, and caudal fins are yellow; the dorsal fin is brown. A peaceful, active fish, the Banded Clownfish is suited to a community aquarium. It will eat most small, meaty foods as well as plant matter and, occasionally, flake foods.

Remarks: This fish may be kept with a variety of invertebrates, and has been spawned in tanks. The males tend the eggs and fry. Commercially raised specimens are widely available.

Tropical marine tank (pages 196–197)

Amphiprion ocellaris COMMON CLOWNFISH

Central band "bulges" towards front of body

Relatively blunt head

Rounded fins

Family Pomacentridae
Distribution Indo-Pacific
Size 2 in (5 cm)
Diet Omnivorous. Most small meaty foods, including finely chopped fish, shrimp, mussels, or other shellfish; will generally also take flake foods, especially if fish are tank-bred
Water conditions Temperature 75–79°F (24–26°C); pH 8.3–8.4; SG 1.023–1.027
Swimming level Middle to bottom
Breeding Egg-depositor

This fish is everyone's idea of a clownfish; its striking orange coloration with white bands and black-edged fins makes it almost essential for the marine aquarium. It is a far-ranging species, with the various populations differing widely in coloring. Among the easiest marine fish to maintain, feed, and breed, the Common Clownfish is ideal for keeping with invertebrates. Both wild and tank-bred specimens are sold.

Remarks: For breeding, feed each pair well and provide them with a suitable anemone. When ready to spawn, the pair will clean a rock or shell close to the base of the anemone and deposit their eggs on the cleaned surface. The orange/yellow eggs are fiercely guarded by the male until they hatch in some 7–10 days.

Reef tank (pages 198–199)

Premnas biaculeatus MAROON CLOWNFISH

Family Pomacentridae
Distribution Indo-Pacific, from Madagascar to Solomon Islands (via Philippines and Australia)
Size 4 in (10 cm)
Diet Carnivorous. Finely chopped meaty foods such as fish or shellfish; may also be persuaded to take flake foods
Water conditions Temperature 75–79°F (24–26°C); pH 8.3–8.4; SG 1.023–1.027
Swimming level Middle to bottom
Breeding Egg-depositor

Significantly larger than other anemonefish, this fish is also known as the Spine-cheeked Clownfish, having two prominent spines below the eyes; in *Amphiprion* species these are tiny features on the gill cover. Its deep red color with white stripes makes it popular in the aquarium trade, but it can be aggressive both toward its own kind and other fish, and should be kept only with companions of similar size.

Mated pairs, however, will live together quite peaceably. Maroon Clownfish feed readily, preferring chopped frozen foods to flakes.

Remarks: Although often argumentative with other fish, this species does not usually disturb invertebrates. It may breed in captivity.

Reef tank (pages 198–199)

DAMSELFISH

DAMSELFISH ARE CONSIDERED to be hardy and, therefore, suitable as first fish for a newly setup marine tank or for the novice marine aquarist. This may be so, but their hardiness is no excuse for poor tank management, exposing them to extreme levels of nitrites and ammonia. As with any other fish, poor water quality or excessive stress will leave them susceptible to infections. There are some species that should not be used to mature a marine system; check carefully before you buy.

These are active little fish that in the wild dart among the coral, minding their territories. Aquariums should provide adequate space and shelters for this behavior. Many species sport bright colors, which may fade with stress or to hide from predators. As schooling fish, they are best kept in groups of six or more, if space permits.

Feeding damselfish is simplicity itself. They will take most foods, and benefit from a varied diet, including live, frozen, flake, and green foods. Aquarium breeding is possible. The sexes can be determined by the genital papillae, best seen when the fish are ready to breed. In males, these are narrow and slightly pointed; in females, more broad and blunt. Eggs are laid on a flat rock or shell.

Paraglyphidodon oxyodon BLACK NEON DAMSELFISH

Family Pomacentridae
Distribution Western Pacific
Size 3 in (7.5 cm)
Diet Omnivorous. Small aquatic invertebrates such as *Mysis* and brine shrimp, either live or frozen, plus flake foods; will also accept some vegetable matter, including algae
Water conditions
Temperature 75–79°F (24–26°C); pH 8.3–8.4; SG 1.023–1.027
Swimming level Middle
Breeding Egg-depositor

Bright blue streaks on young fish

Also known as the Blue-velvet Damselfish and the Blue-streak Devil, this is one of the more demanding damselfish. It will not settle well if the water conditions are anything less than perfect. An aggressive fish, it also requires space to stake its territory. The juvenile coloration is a deep bluish black with a paler throat area. A single vertical white and yellow band divides the body just in front of the dorsal fin, and vibrant electric-blue lines can be seen, notably on the head. As the fish matures, these bold markings fade, and adults have a less striking, dull gray appearance. Black Neon Damselfishes are relatively easy to feed in home aquariums, accepting most small foods readily.

Remarks: This species is suitable for keeping with invertebrates in a mixed reef tank.

Chromis cyanea BLUE CHROMIS

Family Pomacentridae	meaty foods such as fish, shrimp,	75–79°F (24–26°C); pH 8.3–8.4;
Distribution Tropical Atlantic	mussels, or other shellfish; will	SG 1.023–1.027
Size 2 in (5 cm)	also take flake and green foods	**Swimming level** Middle
Diet Omnivorous. Finely chopped	**Water conditions** Temperature	**Breeding** Egg-depositor

Colorless edges of fins

A peaceful, schooling fish that prefers to be kept with its own kind, this beautiful species is sometimes sold under the name Blue Reef Fish. The black streaks and speckles on its body, extending into the fins, contrast handsomely with the background coloring, a brilliant blue. The deeply forked caudal fin and horizontal dotted lines along the flank give the fish a streamlined appearance in keeping with its constant activity. It is ideally suited to a reef-type aquarium, with or without invertebrates. Provide well-aerated water and lots of swimming space.

Remarks: Keep as a mixed-sex group if you wish them to breed. At spawning time, the black band at the top of the male's body spreads.

Tropical marine tank (pages 196–197)

Chrysiptera parasema YELLOW-TAILED DAMSELFISH

Family Pomacentridae
Distribution Widespread throughout Indo-Pacific, ranging to Red Sea
Size 2 in (5 cm)
Diet Omnivorous. Finely chopped meaty foods such as fish, shrimp, and mussels; supplement with flake foods and some vegetable matter
Water conditions Temperature 75–79°F (24–26°C); pH 8.3–8.4; SG 1.023–1.027
Swimming level Middle
Breeding Egg-depositor

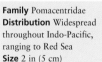

Dark bar on eye

A typical damselfish, this species can be a bit of a troublemaker, picking on any other fish that dare to enter its territory. Extremely hardy, it is an ideal beginner's marine fish, and will eat just about anything, including most commercial marine foods and plant material. As a bonus, the Yellow-tailed Damselfish is very attractive, with most of the body colored a vivid blue, and the rear part bright yellow to orange, fading to clear at the edge of the caudal fin. The scales have a dark center, matched by a dark bar crossing the eye. The dorsal fin is spiny, giving this species a relatively arched profile to echo its often formidable character.

Remarks: Yellow-tailed Damselfishes can share an invertebrate aquarium reasonably harmoniously, usually causing no harm.

Dascyllus aruanus HUMBUG DAMSELFISH

Family Pomacentridae	chopped meaty foods such as	75–79°F (24–26°C); pH 8.3–8.4;
Distribution Indo-Pacific	fish, shrimp, and mussels; also	SG 1.023–1.027
Size 3 in (7.5 cm)	accepts flake and green foods	**Swimming level** Middle
Diet Omnivorous. Finely	**Water conditions** Temperature	**Breeding** Egg-depositor

The distinctive black and white coloration of this species makes it highly desirable; it is also a good choice for marine novices, since it can withstand the rigors of a newly installed system. This is the hardiest of the damselfish, but still deserves well-maintained conditions and a tank with plenty of hiding places for security, simulating its natural coral reef environment. It may also be sold as the White-tailed Damselfish. The very similar-looking Black-tailed Humbug (*Dascyllus melanurus*) can be distinguished by its black caudal fin.

Remarks: This fish is territorial and aggressive towards others of the same species, but will not harm invertebrates.

Tropical marine tank (pages 196–197)

Dascyllus carneus CLOUDY DAMSELFISH

Family Pomacentridae	chopped meaty foods such as	75–79°F (24–26°C); pH 8.3–8.4;
Distribution Indo-Pacific	fish, shrimp, or other shellfish;	SG 1.023–1.027
Size 3 in (7.5 cm)	also takes flake and green foods	**Swimming level** Middle
Diet Omnivorous. Finely	**Water conditions** Temperature	**Breeding** Egg-depositor

Colorless rear section of dorsal fin

Very similar in manner and size to the Humbug, but not quite as robust, the Cloudy Damselfish has more delicate coloration. The front part of the body and much of the fins are dark brown, with the rest a pale, creamy yellow, fading to a transparent caudal fin. Some specimens show a prominent white patch high on the flanks, just below the front part of the dorsal fin, and these fish are grayish-brown. The scales are flecked with blue – hence the other common name, the Blue-spotted Dascyllus.

Remarks. This species is relatively peaceful, but may squabble with its own kind, though less so if group members are of similar size. The fish is compatible with invertebrates.

Dascyllus trimaculatus DOMINO

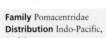

Family Pomacentridae
Distribution Indo-Pacific, Red Sea
Size 3 in (7.5 cm)
Diet Omnivorous. Finely chopped meaty foods such as fish, shrimp, mussels, or other shellfish; will also readily accept flake foods and vegetable matter
Water conditions Temperature 75–79°F (24–26°C); pH 8.3–8.4; SG 1.023 –1.027
Swimming level Middle
Breeding Egg-depositor

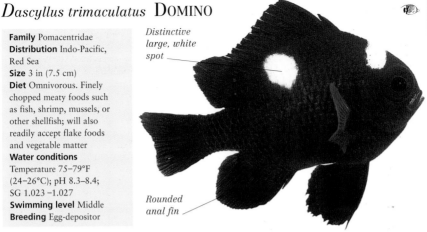

Distinctive large, white spot

Rounded anal fin

As its rather odd name would suggest, this fish is also known as the Three-spot Damselfish. The bright white spots on its flanks sit high on the body midway along the dorsal fin; the third is in the center of the head, above the eyes. These markings fade as the fish ages, and the entire body becomes a beautiful, velvety black. If stressed, it can become dull and grayish in color, with the dark-edged scales increasingly visible; in such cases, check conditions and improve water quality if necessary. The Domino is a commonly available fish, and presents few problems, provided it is given plenty of rocky retreats. It eats well, even greedily.

Remarks: Although often aggressive towards its own kind (and sometimes with others), this species is safe to keep in an invertebrate tank.

Pomacentrus coeruleus BLUE DEVIL

Family Pomacentridae
Distribution Indo-Pacific
Size 2 in (5 cm)
Diet Omnivorous. Finely chopped meaty foods such as fish, shrimp, mussels, or other shellfish, plus *Mysis* and brine shrimp, either live or frozen; supplement with flake foods and vegetable matter
Water conditions Temperature 75–79°F (24–26°C); pH 8.3–8.4; SG 1.023–1.027
Swimming level Middle
Breeding Egg-depositor

Black spot at rear of very long-based dorsal fin

Transparent caudal fin

When young, the Blue Devil is a social fish and enjoys being with members of its own species, but with age comes a degree of intolerance; mature specimens may react aggressively both with each other and with other fish. Avoid choosing tiny companions, which are more likely to be harassed or harmed. Provide a spacious tank with numerous hiding places. Despite its belligerent nature, for which it is aptly named, this fish is popular for its electric-blue coloring, highlighted with yellow-white markings at the center of each scale. Specimens typically have a black line passing from the snout through the eye, though color patterns can vary. The body is rather elongated.

Remarks: Happily, the Blue Devil shows no serious antagonism towards invertebrates.

ANGELFISH

ANGELFISH, BOTH LARGE and dwarf species, are highly popular because of their attractive coloration, but as a rule the larger fish are too demanding for beginners. They are finicky eaters and become listless or ill if water quality deteriorates. Also quite territorial, they are best kept as single specimens. A degree of experience in caring for marine fish is essential.

Dwarf angelfish (*Centropyge* spp.) are far more suited to aquarium life than their larger relatives. They rarely grow in excess of 4 in (10 cm) in a tank, are peaceful, generally easy to feed, and, for the most part, may be kept with invertebrates. They are sociable either in pairs or groups.

Provide angelfish with a reef-type setup with plenty of nooks and crannies to retreat to. In the wild, they pick over reefs, consuming small invertebrates, corals, sponges, and algae. In an aquarium, offer them a wide range of live and frozen foods, such as *Mysis*, brine shrimp, prawns, and mussels, as well as sponge-based foods and algae. Wild-caught adults can be much more difficult to coax into eating than juveniles; when purchasing fish, ask to see them feed.

Some species of angelfish have been bred in aquariums; free-floating eggs are scattered during spawning.

Holacanthus tricolor ROCK BEAUTY

Family Pomacanthidae
Distribution Indo-Pacific
Size 11¾ in (30 cm) in aquariums; 15 in (38 cm) wild
Diet Omnivorous. Sponge-based foods essential; may also take algae and meaty foods such as small pieces of shellfish, plus *Mysis* and brine shrimp, either live or frozen
Water conditions Temperature 75–79°F (24–26°C); pH 8.3–8.4; SG 1.023–1.027
Swimming level All levels
Breeding Egg-scatterer

Rounded, rudder-like anal fin

The Rock Beauty is a very difficult fish because of its strict dietary requirements. Even specimens that have been persuaded to eat the usual commercially available foods may not thrive. It is essential to provide specialized sponge-based foods as a staple. Juveniles are yellow with a blue-edged black spot on the upper rear part of the body. The adult fish has a yellow head, belly, and caudal fin, with the rest of the body and fins black. Mature specimens are territorial and aggressive; keep only one in a community tank. Even young fish can be difficult to acclimate and feed. However, once settled, they will eat live and frozen foods and algae.

Remarks. This quarrelsome fish requires plenty of space and optimum conditions. It is not advisable to keep it with invertebrates.

Pomacanthus annularis BLUE-RINGED ANGELFISH

Family Pomacanthidae
Distribution Indo-Pacific
Size 9¾ in (25 cm) in
aquariums; 15¾ in (40 cm)
wild
Diet Omnivorous. Meaty
foods such as pieces of shrimp
or shellfish, plus live *Mysis*
and brine shrimp; large
quantities of algae are essential
Water conditions
Temperature 75–79°F
(24–26°C); pH 8.3–8.4;
SG 1.023–1.027
Swimming level All levels
Breeding Egg-scatterer

Blue-ringed Angelfish are an eye-catching
species. Juveniles have a dark blue body with
fine, vertical blue and white lines; adults are a
coppery color marked with broader bright blue
lines that turn upwards to converge towards the
rear of the dorsal fin. This fish is very territorial
when kept in an aquarium; keep only one
specimen in a community tank and choose
companion species with care, selecting similarly
sized fishes. Juveniles generally acclimate to
aquarium conditions better than mature fish.
The Blue-ringed Angelfish is fairly delicate in
constitution, and requires large amounts of
algae in the diet. It should also be given plenty
of meaty, and especially live, foods.

Remarks: These are best kept only with other
marine fish and not with invertebrates.

Pomacanthus semicirculatus KORAN ANGELFISH

Family Pomacanthidae
Distribution Indo-Pacific
Size 15 in (38 cm) in
aquariums; 40 cm (15¾ in) wild
Diet Omnivorous. Meaty
foods such as small pieces of
shellfish, plus *Mysis* and brine
shrimp; also takes algae
Water conditions
Temperature 75–79°F
(24–26°C); pH 8.3–8.4;
SG 1.023–1.027
Swimming level All levels
Breeding Egg-scatterer
(as with other angelfishes,
eggs are free-floating)

A popular fish, the juveniles bear virtually no
resemblance to the adults. Young specimens, as
shown above, have a dark blue body covered
with semi-circular white and light blue stripes
(hence the scientific species name). As they
grow, these lines are lost, replaced by patterning
on the caudal fin which is thought to resemble
Arabic script, giving the fish its common name,
in reference to the sacred Muslim volume. The
Koran Angelfish will compete strenuously with
all others to establish and maintain its territory.
Keep this species in a tank that is sufficiently
large to offer copious swimming space, and be
sure to furnish the aquarium with plenty of
shelters, created by using piled rocks.

Remarks: This aggressive fish is not suitable to
be kept in an invertebrate aquarium.

Centropyge argi CHERUBFISH

Family Pomacanthidae	Diet Omnivorous. Small meaty	75–79°F (24–26°C); pH 8.3–8.4;
Distribution Western Atlantic,	items and live or frozen foods; also	SG 1.023–1.027
Caribbean, Gulf of Mexico	plenty of green foods and algae	Swimming level All levels
Size 3 in (7.5 cm)	Water conditions Temperature	Breeding Egg-scatterer

Long-based dorsal fin

Bright blue edging on fin

Also known as the Pygmy Angelfish and the Purple Fireball, this species readily acclimates to aquarium life, is easy to feed, and does not harass invertebrates. The Cherubfish's deep blue-purple body is accented by a yellow head – the extent of this yellow coloration varies considerably according to locality. In the wild, it is usually found in fairly deep waters where there is plenty of rubble to hide among; a tank environment should provide similar shelters.

Remarks: The fish's territorial requirements are not great; if tank size permits, several may be kept together. As with other dwarf angelfish, natural pairing is common, and breeding may occur spontaneously.

Centropyge bicolor BICOLOR CHERUB

Family Pomacanthidae
Distribution Indo-Pacific (except Hawaii)
Size 5 in (12.5 cm)
Diet Omnivorous. Meaty foods such as small pieces of shellfish, plus *Mysis* and brine shrimp, live or frozen; also plenty of green foods and algae (will consume algal growth in tank)
Water conditions Temperature 75–79°F (24–26°C); pH 8.3–8.4; SG 1.023–1.027
Swimming level All levels
Breeding Egg-scatterer

As its common name suggests, this species has a bold dual color pattern, in blue and yellow. Also referred to as the Oriole Angelfish, the Bicolor Cherub will generally settle into a well-established reef-type aquarium and tends to leave invertebrates undisturbed. Although peaceful, it appreciates having hiding places to retire to. The fish readily accepts a variety of foods; the diet should include small meaty items as well as vegetable matter. A typical dwarf angelfish, this species likes to graze on algae.

Remarks: If kept as a group, a dominant male will reign over a harem of females. Interestingly, if that male dies or is removed from the group, one of the females will change sex and take his place. Maintain prime aquarium conditions, since this fish is rather susceptible to disease.

Centropyge bispinosus CORAL BEAUTY

Family Pomacanthidae	Diet Omnivorous. Meaty foods,	75–79°F (24–26°C); pH 8.3–8.4;
Distribution Indo-Pacific,	plus *Mysis* and brine shrimp, live or	SG 1.023–1.027
Australasia	frozen; also green foods and algae	Swimming level All levels
Size 4¾ in (12 cm)	Water conditions Temperature	Breeding Egg-scatterer

Flanks patterned with markings

The Coral Beauty's colors – ranging from purple and red to deep blue and golden yellow, with vertical bars and speckles – vary from juvenile to adult and from population to population. Generally, adults have more gold on the flanks than young fish, while specimens from the Philippines are more red and purple than Australasian ones. A placid, somewhat reclusive fish, it causes little harm to invertebrates and may be kept as pairs or small groups.

Remarks: This species can be difficult to acclimate if there are insufficient hiding places in the aquarium. Its breeding habits are little known.

Dark fins edged in paler blue

Reef tank *(pages 198–199)*

Centropyge eibli EIBL'S ANGELFISH

| Family Pomacanthidae |
| Distribution Indo-Pacific, |
| Australasia |
| Size 6 in (15 cm) |
| Diet Omnivorous. Most small |
| meaty foods, including pieces of |
| shrimp or other shellfish, plus |
| *Mysis* and brine shrimp, live |
| or frozen; also grazes on tank |
| algae (a large part of the diet) |
| Water conditions |
| Temperature 75–79°F |
| (24–26°C); pH 8.3–8.4; |
| SG 1.023–1.027 |
| Swimming level All levels |
| Breeding Egg-scatterer |

Perhaps the main attraction of this peaceful species is its delicate coloration, which varies greatly with locality. Distinctive features include wavy, vertical lines crossing the body, a ringed eye, and a dark rear section with bright-edged fins. Among the largest of the dwarf angelfish, in the wild it is found on coral reefs in depths of over 60 ft (up to 20 m). Named after its discoverer, Eibl's Angelfish is frequently imported for the trade, and adapts well to aquarium conditions. It will happily co-exist with invertebrates in a mixed reef tank, and is not a fussy eater, accepting most small foods.

Remarks: Provide plenty of retreats to simulate the nooks and crannies found in a natural reef. The fish's constant grazing will help to control algal growth. Breeding behavior is unclear.

BUTTERFLYFISH

BUTTERFLYFISH INHABIT coral reefs, where their flamboyant coloring acts as a camouflage; in some species, these patterns darken at night. They resemble angelfishes, but lack their distinctive spine on the gill cover. Butterflyfish's laterally compressed bodies enable them to pass freely between the coral branches, where they feed by poking their long, pointed snouts into crevices in the reef, grazing on algae, coral, sponges, or plankton.

In aquariums, butterflyfish require very stable water conditions and can be erratic eaters; this makes them unsuitable for the novice. Before purchasing a fish, ask to see it feed.

Offer a variety of foods, including sponge-based and frozen items, along with live *Mysis* and brine shrimp. Adults are usually more difficult to acclimate than juveniles, which may require feeding several times a day.

Choose species with care; some are intolerant of other fish. Remember also that juveniles have a different color pattern to adults. Butterflyfish cannot be kept with sea anemones or living corals, which they will consume.

Butterflyfish's captive breeding behavior is not well known; in the wild they spawn as pairs, releasing eggs and sperm simultaneously. The eggs float until ready to hatch.

Chaetodon auriga THREADFIN BUTTERFLYFISH

Family Chaetodontidae
Distribution Indo-Pacific, Red Sea
Size 7¾ in (20 cm) in wild; usually smaller in aquariums
Diet Omnivorous. Coral polyps, crustaceans, and algae; may also accept small live or frozen foods such as *Mysis* and brine shrimp
Water conditions Temperature 75–79°F (24–26°C); pH 8.3–8.4; SG 1.023–1.027
Swimming level Middle
Breeding Egg-scatterer

Thread-like fin extension

Pattern of dark, diagonal lines

The Threadfin Butterflyfish gains its common name from the long, thread-like extension that develops on the rear of the dorsal fin as the fish matures. The front section of the body is white, overlaid with diagonal bands, while the rear is yellow; a dark vertical band passes through the eye. Although coloration varies little with locality, specimens from the Red Sea sometimes lose the distinctive eye-spot on their dorsal fin

as they age. A relatively peaceful fish, the Threadfin Butterflyfish can be retiring if there are insufficient hiding places in the aquarium.

Remarks: Avoid keeping this species with invertebrates, which it may eat. Specimens may be reluctant to accept commercial foods; be patient, and make sure that mealtimes are not monopolized by more outgoing tankmates.

Chaetodon chrysurus PEARLSCALE BUTTERFLYFISH

Family Chaetodontidae
Distribution Indo-Pacific
Size 6 in (15 cm) in wild;
usually smaller in aquariums
Diet Omnivorous. Coral
polyps and small aquatic
invertebrates such as *Mysis*
and brine shrimp, live or
frozen; also plenty of green
foods, including algae
Water conditions
Temperature 75–79°F
(24–26°C); pH 8.3–8.4;
SG 1.023–1.027
Swimming level Middle
Breeding Egg-scatterer

Its beautiful coloration makes the Pearlscale
Butterflyfish a popular choice for aquariums. A
dark "net" pattern covers the flanks, offsetting
large scales that shine pearly white as they
catch the light, giving rise to the fish's common
name. It is a placid species and generally causes
little trouble, unless kept with invertebrates.
The natural range of the Pearlscale Butterflyfish
has not been conclusively established, but its
distribution is believed to be mainly close to
Africa, Mauritius, and the Seychelles, rather
than throughout the Indo-Pacific region.

Remarks: Although it may be coaxed into taking
frozen items, this fish benefits from a diet of
small live foods such as *Mysis* and brine shrimp.

Tropical marine tank (pages 196–197)

Chaetodon collare PAKISTANI BUTTERFLYFISH

Family Chaetodontidae
Distribution Indian Ocean
Size 6 in (15 cm) in wild;
usually smaller in aquariums

Diet Omnivorous. Small live or
frozen foods such as *Mysis* and
brine shrimp, plus green foods
Water conditions Temperature

75–79°F (24–26°C); pH 8.3–8.4;
SG 1.023–1.027
Swimming level Middle
Breeding Egg-scatterer

Although a favorite among hobbyists
because of its striking appearance,
this is one of the more difficult
butterflyfish to keep, primarily
because it is often reluctant to feed.
Also called the Collare Butterflyfish,
the Pakistani Butterflyfish can be
belligerent towards both its own kind
and other species. In nature, some
groups inhabit rocky outcrops rather
than living directly on the coral reef;
these specimens are somewhat easier
to maintain in aquariums, being (very
marginally) better eaters. Fish from
different localities have conflicting
feeding patterns; vary the diet to
determine what your fish prefer.

Remarks: Avoid keeping this fish
with invertebrates. The species is not
recommended for novice aquarists.

Chaetodon melanotus BLACK-BACKED BUTTERFLYFISH

Family Chaetodontidae
Distribution Indo-Pacific
Size 6 in (15 cm) in wild;
usually smaller in aquariums
Diet Omnivorous. Small
aquatic invertebrates such as
Mysis and brine shrimp, live
or frozen; supplement these
with vegetable matter,
including algae
Water conditions
Temperature 75–79°F
(24–26°C); pH 8.3–8.4;
SG 1.023–1.027
Swimming level Middle
Breeding Egg-scatterer

The Black-backed Butterflyfish is appealingly colorful and quite peaceful, but it is also notoriously difficult to keep; aquarists should gain experience with other members of the family Chaetodontidae before trying their hand at these. When purchasing a specimen, it is most important to ensure that it is feeding well and to check that you can provide the same diet that the dealer has been supplying. Fish that are well acclimated in this way are a little easier to maintain. The Black-backed Butterflyfish can change its color pattern dramatically at night or when frightened. At such times, the upper part of the body becomes black, with two white patches – hence the species' common name.

Remarks: This fish is not to be trusted with invertebrates, which it may harass or devour.

Chelmon rostratus COPPERBANDED BUTTERFLYFISH

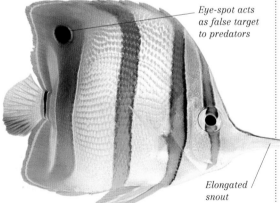

Eye-spot acts as false target to predators

Elongated snout

Family Chaetodontidae
Distribution Indo-Pacific,
Red Sea
Size 6¾ in (17 cm) in wild;
usually smaller in aquariums
Diet Omnivorous. Small
aquatic invertebrates such as
Mysis and brine shrimp, live
or frozen; also plenty of green
foods, including algae
Water conditions
Temperature 75–79°F
(24–26°C); pH 8.3–8.4;
SG 1.023–1.027
Swimming level Middle
Breeding Egg-scatterer

Ever popular for its striking coloration (orange stripes on a silver background) and distinctive long snout, the Copperbanded Butterflyfish is not easy to maintain. Water quality is particularly critical; any deterioration can easily cause illness or even death. In an aquarium, the fish must also be given foods of the correct size or it may starve; in the wild, it uses its narrow snout to delve into coral heads and crevices in search of tiny crustaceans and algae. Individuals can be fussy eaters, often preferring small live foods, though once established in a tank they will usually accept commercial frozen foods.

Remarks: This fish is incompatible with invertebrates, which it will continually pick on. Since it can be aggressive towards its own kind and other species, keep single specimens.

Forcipiger longirostris LONG-NOSED BUTTERFLYFISH

Family Chaetodontidae
Distribution Indo-Pacific:
Great Barrier Reef, New
Guinea, Hawaii
Size 7¾ in (20 cm) in wild;
usually smaller in aquariums
Diet Omnivorous. Small live
or frozen foods such as *Mysis*
and brine shrimp; also plenty
of green foods, including algae
Water conditions
Temperature 75–79°F
(24–26°C); pH 8.3–8.4;
SG 1.023–1.027
Swimming level Middle
Breeding Egg-scatterer

This fish (also referred to as the Forcepsfish, by virtue of its long, thin snout) feeds in the same manner as the Copper-band Butterflyfish but is a little less troublesome to maintain in an aquarium. It is not as aggressive as that species, and generally takes more readily to commercially prepared foods, although it does benefit from having small live foods (such as *Mysis* and brine shrimp) as part of its diet.

Remarks: The Long-nosed Butterflyfish is not suitable for an invertebrate tank. Like the Copper-band Butterflyfish, it has a false eye-spot at the rear of the body (here on the anal, rather than dorsal, fin) to confuse predators, particularly when the fish is feeding head-down among the coral heads. An attacker biting the "eye" will receive only a mouthful of fin tissue and spines, leaving the butterflyfish free to escape.

Heniochus acuminatus WIMPLEFISH

Family Chaetodontidae
Distribution Indo-Pacific,
Red Sea
Size 7 in (18 cm) in wild;
usually smaller in aquariums
Diet Omnivorous. Small
aquatic invertebrates such as
Mysis and brine shrimp, live
or frozen; also plenty of green
foods, including algae
Water conditions
Temperature 75–79°F
(24–26°C); pH 8.3–8.4;
SG 1.023–1.027
Swimming level Middle
Breeding Egg-scatterer

Heniochus acuminatus is also known by a number of other common names: Long-fin Bannerfish, Pennant Coralfish, and Poor Man's Moorish Idol. The fish's unusual extended dorsal fin develops with age. It is a peaceful creature that likes the company of its own kind; indeed, a small school of these in a spacious aquarium makes a very impressive sight. Do not overcrowd the tank, however; this fish requires

plenty of room to swim. Water conditions should also be carefully monitored. The Wimplefish is reasonably easy to feed, accepting many frozen foods as well as grazing on algae.

Remarks: This fish will continually graze along the bodies of invertebrates for food; therefore, avoid housing them together. Young specimens may act as cleaner fish to larger species.

SURGEONS AND TANGS

FISH OF THE FAMILY Acanthuridae are characterized by their laterally compressed ovoid bodies, long-based dorsal and anal fins, and steeply sloping foreheads. The names "surgeon" and "tang" (the latter an Old Norse word for the pointed tip of a tool) allude to the sharp, erectile, scalpel-like spines on the muscular base of the caudal fin. These spiky blades are used in defending territories, and can injure the unwary aquarist.

Surgeons and tangs are constant grazers, and must have a regular supply of algae in the tank to nibble on. Juveniles require several meals a day; the diet should consist largely of green foods such as lettuce or spinach; some species will also take small live or frozen foods and, with persuasion, commercially prepared dry foods.

Unless you can provide a very large aquarium, surgeons and tangs are best kept as single specimens. Although schooling fish by nature, in the confines of a tank they will quarrel with one another. Established individuals are likely to bully and harass any newcomers of similar or smaller size; invertebrates are particularly vulnerable. Give these large, active fish plenty of space and maintain prime water conditions, since they are prone to parasitic infections.

Acanthurus leucosternon POWDER BLUE SURGEON

Family Acanthuridae
Distribution Indo-Pacific
Size 7¾ in (20 cm)
Diet Omnivorous. Small aquatic invertebrates such as *Mysis* or brine shrimp, live or frozen, plus finely chopped shellfish; also give plenty of green foods, including algae
Water conditions Temperature 75–79°F (24–26°C); pH 8.3–8.4; SG 1.023–1.027
Swimming level Middle
Breeding Egg-scatterer (floating eggs)

The brilliant colors of this species, which is also known as the Powder Blue Tang, make it a firm favorite. However, only a single specimen should be kept; two will fight. Even dealers house just one fish per tank to prevent squabbles. The Powder Blue Surgeon can grow up to 9¾ in (25 cm) in the wild, and must be given lots of room to swim. It also requires excellent water quality; provide a very well-established aquarium with stable conditions and a good growth of algae. If there is insufficient algae in the tank, supplement the diet with vegetable matter – lettuce and spinach are suitable substitutes. Young surgeons are voracious eaters, and must be fed little and often.

Remarks: Do not keep with invertebrates. Males are generally larger than females.

Paracanthurus hepatus REGAL TANG

Family Acanthuridae	amounts of algae, supplemented	75–79°F (24–26°C); pH 8.3–8.4;
Distribution Indo-Pacific	with other green foods such as	SG 1.023–1.027
Size 6 in (15 cm)	lettuce, spinach, and peas	**Swimming level** Middle
Diet Herbivorous. Requires large	**Water conditions** Temperature	**Breeding** Egg-scatterer

Easily identified by its royal blue body, distinctive black markings, and bright yellow caudal fin, the Regal Tang makes a stunning addition to a marine aquarium. This beautiful species is also one of the few tangs that can be kept as a small group, provided you have a spacious tank to allow the fish to swim freely. Introduce the school together, as youngsters; after initial wrangling, they should settle down fairly peaceably. It is essential to have copious supplies of algae in the tank, since the Regal Tang grazes almost continuously. Give other green foods to ensure adequate nutrition.

Remarks: It is not advisable to keep this fish with invertebrates.

Tropical marine tank (pages 196–197)

Zebrasoma flavescens YELLOW TANG

Family Acanthuridae	other green foods, including peas,	75–79°F (24–26°C); pH 8.3–8.4;
Distribution Pacific	lettuce, spinach, and vegetable-	SG 1.023–1.027
Size 6 in (15 cm)	based frozen and flake foods	**Swimming level** Middle
Diet Herbivorous. Algae and	**Water conditions** Temperature	**Breeding** Egg-scatterer

Tall fin gives fish exaggerated, disk-shaped profile

If you have adequate space (a 60 in/ 1.5 m aquarium), keep a group of six or more of this striking yellow fish; otherwise, settle for a single specimen, since *Zebrasoma flavescens* is a very territorial species. A large school is generally less aggressive than a small group, since members will be more preoccupied with surveillance than with inflicting serious damage. Yellow Tangs graze ceaselessly; if necessary, culture algae on separate stones and swap these with rocks in the tank to replenish supplies. In addition, offer these herbivores a variety of green foods several times a day.

Remarks: The Yellow Tang is incompatible with invertebrates.

Tropical marine tank (pages 196–197)

TRIGGERFISH

TRIGGERFISH ARE SO named for their ability to raise their first dorsal fin spine and lock it in place as a defence, making their body difficult to remove from a hiding place, or too big for predators for swallow. In nature, triggerfish are intolerant and territorial. Males defend a large area, in which they will allow several females; these in turn have their own smaller territories for breeding. Wild pairs spawn above a pre-dug pit.

With their colorfully patterned, compressed ovoid bodies, triggerfish look stunning in an aquarium, but are unsociable loners, and should be kept only as single specimens, and not with invertebrates. They need rocky crevices in which to rest and retire at night, and are clumsy swimmers: the caudal fin and its muscular base give rapid thrust for territorial defence or escape from a predator, while the undulating dorsal and anal fins and waving pectoral fins provide gentle propulsion for slower, more precise, movements.

Triggerfishes have powerful jaws and teeth for eating molluscs and crustaceans. To feed on spiny creatures such as sea urchins, they will blow jets of water to flip the prey over, exposing its soft underbelly. Some species also eat plankton and algae, while many kept in aquariums will eat frozen foods.

Balistoides conspicillum CLOWN TRIGGERFISH

Family Balistidae
Distribution Indo-Pacific
Size 9¾ in (25 cm), although wild specimens can grow to 19¾ in (50 cm)
Diet Carnivorous. Crustaceans and molluscs; accepts small pieces of shellfish (may become tame enough to hand-feed, but beware the fish's sharp teeth)
Water conditions Temperature 75–79°F (24–26°C); pH 8.3–8.4; SG 1.023–1.027
Swimming level All levels
Breeding Egg-scatterer

Also known as the Big-spotted Triggerfish, this beautiful and very popular fish is highly sought after for its flamboyant coloration, which, in the wild, camouflages it against the coral reefs. Features include a series of white spots along the lower half of the body, a mottled "saddle" marking beneath the dorsal fin, and a yellow lipstick-like band around the mouth. The Clown Triggerfish can grow quite large, and requires a spacious aquarium. Provide plenty of rocky nooks and crannies as resting places and nocturnal refuges. Although this fish generally feeds readily on frozen items, juveniles are often more difficult to acclimate than adults.

Remarks: These fish can be aggressive, both among themselves and with other species. Do not keep them with smaller fish or with invertebrates.

Odonus niger BLACK TRIGGERFISH

Family Balistidae
Distribution Indo-Pacific,
Red Sea
Size 9¾ in (25 cm), although
wild specimens can grow to
19¾ in (50 cm)
Diet Carnivorous. Crustaceans
and molluscs; will take small
pieces of shellfish such as
shrimp or mussels
Water conditions
Temperature 75–79°F
(24–26°C); pH 8.3–8.4;
SG 1.023–1.027
Swimming level All levels
Breeding Egg-scatterer

Despite its common name, the Black Triggerfish is not black; coloration varies with locality, and ranges from dark blue to very deep green (the species is sometimes referred to as the Blue Triggerfish or Green Triggerfish). Interestingly, the color can change with mood. The fish's lyre-shaped caudal fin and conspicuous red teeth are more consistent characteristics. Its scaling is also distinctive, giving a diamond-shaped pattern over the body. For a triggerfish, this is a fairly peaceful and sociable creature. It adapts well to aquarium life, and will happily accept most foods, including frozen items.

Remarks: This fish should not be kept with invertebrates, which are regarded as prey (in the wild, it feeds on sponges). Provide a secure cover, since adult specimens may jump.

Rhinecanthus aculeatus PICASSO TRIGGERFISH

Family Balistidae
Distribution Indo-Pacific
Size 9 in (23 cm), although
wild specimens can grow to
11¾ in (30 cm)
Diet Carnivorous. Crustaceans
and molluscs; will take small
pieces of shellfish such as
shrimp or mussels (fish is a
greedy eater; do not overfeed)
Water conditions
Temperature 75–79°F
(24–26°C); pH 8.3–8.4;
SG 1.023–1.027
Swimming level All levels
Breeding Egg-scatterer

Like the Clown Triggerfish, this species' main attraction is its striking color pattern. The rather bizarre common name, Picasso Triggerfish, refers to the fish's unusual markings. Its distinctive looks make it immensely popular among aquarists. Specimens are easy to feed, taking any of the commercially produced frozen meaty foods available for marines. Do not be surprised if the fish makes a noise when you catch it; this is quite normal. It is thought that bony elements of the pectoral girdle or the skull may play a part in sound production, by causing the swim bladder to resonate.

Remarks: An intolerant species, it will pick on both its own kind and other fish, even if they are of a similar size. Do not keep the Picasso Triggerfish with invertebrates; it will eat them.

WRASSES

THERE ARE OVER 400 species of wrasse, many of which grow too large for a home aquarium. Generally, these are elongate fish – cylindrical or somewhat deeper-bodied. They are often brightly colored, changing dramatically in appearance from juvenile to adult.

Wrasses spend much of their time buried in the substrate; tanks must provide a sand substrate to allow digging. Some wrasses spin cocoons in which to rest in safety, and many, such as the Cleaner Wrasse, have the unusual habit of picking unwanted parasites from the bodies of larger fish.

Wrasses are easily fed in captivity, eating predominantly crustaceans and accepting frozen foods readily. However, enthusiasts should take note: wrasses are extremely active and rather boisterous; as they mature and grow, they can undermine rockwork and wreak havoc in a tank. Youngsters kept in a community aquarium may need to be removed when full-sized.

Interestingly, all wrasses begin life as females but, if kept in a group, one fish will change into a male to make spawning possible. Breeding strategies vary: some spawn in pairs, others in groups. Certain species release eggs and milt as they spiral towards the water surface, while others construct nests of sand, gravel, and algae.

Coris gaimard CLOWN WRASSE

Family Labridae	**Diet** Carnivorous. Meaty foods	75–79°F (24–26°C); pH 8.3–8.4;
Distribution Indo-Pacific	such as chopped fish, shrimp,	SG 1.023–1.027
Size 11¾ in (30 cm) in wild;	mussels, or other shellfish	**Swimming** Bottom
usually smaller in aquariums	**Water conditions** Temperature	**Breeding** Egg-scatterer

Also known as the Red Labrid (although only the dorsal and anal fins of adults are strongly red), this species can be very quarrelsome with its own kind. Keep single specimens to prevent fighting. Young fish are bright orange with white and dark brown/black markings, before developing their mature colors: a dark body dotted with blue speckles, an orange/red head, red dorsal and anal fins, and a vivid yellow caudal fin.

Remarks: Clown Wrasses are easily frightened, and mature specimens can be quite destructive; only juvenile fish are suitable for a community aquarium. Youngsters are often misidentified as *Coris formosa*. This related species has a brown (not deep orange) body, with a central white marking that extends the full length of the fish.

Tropical marine tank (pages 196–197)

Gomphosus varius BIRDMOUTH WRASSE

Family Labridae
Distribution Indo-Pacific
Size 9¾ in (25 cm) in wild;
usually smaller in aquariums
Diet Carnivorous. Meaty
foods such as chopped fish,
shrimp, mussels, or other
shellfish, plus *Mysis* or brine
shrimp, either live or frozen;
will also graze on algae in tank
Water conditions
Temperature 75–79°F
(24–26°C); pH 8.3–8.4;
SG 1.023–1.027
Swimming level Bottom
Breeding Egg-scatterer

The beautiful blue-green coloration of the adult male Birdmouth Wrasse makes this a popular aquarium fish; juveniles and females are duller-looking – more brown in appearance. In its natural reef habitat, the fish's elongated snout enables it to pluck morsels such as shrimp from tiny crevices in the coral branches. Although this wrasse is generally peaceful, its constant activity may be an irritant to other species.

Remarks: Although young specimens can safely be kept with invertebrates, older fish may harm them. Large wrasses have a robust appetite, and will pick at and eat invertebrates in order to satisfy it. They have sharp teeth and are not averse to nibbling fingers either! Juveniles act as "cleaners" for larger fish; adults do not perform this role.

Tropical marine tank (pages 196–197)

Labroides dimidiatus CLEANER WRASSE

Family Labridae
Distribution Indo-Pacific
Size 4 in (10 cm) in wild
Diet Carnivorous. Finely chopped

fish, shrimp, mussels, or other shellfish, to supplement natural diet of skin parasites from other fish
Water conditions Temperature

75–79°F (24–26°C); pH 8.3–8.4; SG 1.023–1.027
Swimming level All levels
Breeding Egg-scatterer

Perhaps the best known of the wrasses, the Cleaner Wrasse is accepted by large fish, which respond to its approach by spreading their fins and remaining still while the wrasse performs its parasite-removal service. (The colors of the "client" fish may even fade to make the parasites more visible.) It is peaceful and may be kept with invertebrates.

Remarks: Make certain that you do not acquire the False Cleaner Wrasse (*Aspidontus taeniatus*), which looks very similar but is a predator. The true Cleaner Wrasse has a horizontal black band extending from the caudal fin to the tip of the snout, and the mouth is located at the end of the snout rather than below it, for picking up parasites.

Tropical marine tank (pages 196–197)

OTHER TROPICAL MARINE FISH

THERE ARE A NUMBER of other tropical marine fish that are suited to aquarium life, but cannot easily be grouped by type. The largest category comprises predatory fish known as bass and grouper. Within this very broad classification, several small to medium-sized species (and juvenile specimens of some larger fish) have become popular with marine aquarists. Certain species are hermaphrodites, making specimens almost impossible to sex unless they are breeding or preparing to spawn. Females can be identified by their rounded, egg-filled bodies, and males by their more intense coloration. In other species, differences in fins help to indicate gender. Bass and grouper cause little trouble in aquariums if provided with plenty of space and companions too large for them to eat.

Others in this miscellany include some of the more flamboyant marine fish, the best known of which are seahorses and the Lionfish. Both are difficult to keep, the former because of its precise food requirements and the latter because of its venomous spines and tendency to devour tankmates. There are, however, several other smaller, innocuous species that make welcome additions to the community aquarium, whether a fish-only tank or a mixed invertebrate and fish setup.

Calloplesiops altivelis MARINE BETTA

Family Plesiopidae
Distribution Indo-Pacific
Size 6 in (15 cm) in wild; usually smaller in aquariums
Diet Carnivorous. Meaty foods such as small pieces of fish, shrimp, or other shellfish; live foods preferred, but in time dead items usually taken
Water conditions Temperature 75–79°F (24–26°C); pH 8.3–8.4; SG 1.023–1.027
Swimming level Middle to bottom
Breeding Egg-depositor

This fish is a hunter, and will drift through the tank with its head down in predatory mode; make sure companions are large enough not to be eaten. The Marine Betta (or Comet Grouper) has a striking body camouflage; the white spots that cover it disguise its real eye while attackers are lured off target, towards the false eye-spot at the rear of the dorsal fin. This pattern also deceives prey into misjudging the fish's orientation.

Remarks: Marine Bettas will eat virtually all meaty foods. Although they may initially accept only live foods, eventually most specimens can be weaned onto dead items. Individuals take some time to settle in an aquarium, and will feel most secure if given the shelter of extensive rockwork. They are compatible with invertebrates.

Tropical marine tank (pages 196–197)

Anthias squamipinnis WRECKFISH

Family Serrandiae
Distribution Indo-Pacific
Size 5 in (12.5 cm) in wild;
usually smaller in aquariums
Diet Carnivorous. Meaty
foods such as small pieces of
fish, shrimp, or other shellfish;
live foods preferred, but
specimens can be trained
to accept dead items
Water conditions
Temperature 75–79°F
(24–26°C); pH 8.3–8.4;
SG 1.023–1.027
Swimming level All levels
Breeding Egg-scatterer

Also referred to as Anthias, the Orange Sea Perch, and the Lyretail Coralfish, the Wreckfish is a popular choice for marine aquariums. This beautiful species is bright orange-yellow with a deeply forked, lyre-shaped caudal fin and long ventral fins, giving it an extremely graceful profile. It is a schooling fish and should be kept as a group of 3–4. Male fish have an elongated third dorsal fin spine and are usually more highly colored than females. In a school, the dominant male will take command and establish a harem.

Remarks: This fish prefers live foods, but will take frozen items if they are dropped into the flow of water from the filter, so that they appear to move. It is peaceful and may be kept with invertebrates.

Tropical marine tank (pages 196–197)

Chromileptis altivelis PANTHERFISH

Family Serranidae
Distribution Indo-Pacific
Size 19¾ in (50 cm) in wild;
usually smaller in aquariums
Diet Carnivorous. Meaty
foods such as small pieces of
fish, shrimp, or other shellfish;
live foods preferred, but may be
persuaded to take dead items
Water conditions
Temperature 75–79°F
(24–26°C); pH 8.3–8.4;
SG 1.023–1.027
Swimming level All levels
Breeding Egg-layer
(details unknown)

Aquarists who have not done their homework before buying a specimen of this very attractive species (also known as the Polka-dot Grouper) may subsequently wonder why their smaller fish are slowly disappearing! The Pantherfish is an active predator, and will consume anything that fits into its capacious mouth. It will accept dead foods, and can become tame enough to feed from your fingers. The spotted pattern acts as a hunting disguise, to break up the outline of the body; these black spots are larger on small fish but more numerous on large specimens.

Remarks: Do not keep this species with small fish or invertebrates. If tankmates are of a suitable size and temperament to avoid predation, a Pantherfish can make an excellent addition that will constantly prowl the tank.

Sphaeramia nematoptera SPOTTED CARDINALFISH

Family Apogonidae
Distribution Indo-Pacific
Size 3 in (7.5 cm)
Diet Carnivorous. Small aquatic invertebrates such as *Mysis* and brine shrimp, initially live; once acclimated, specimens will accept frozen alternatives, but flake foods are flatly rejected
Water conditions
Temperature 75–79°F (24–26°C); pH 8.3–8.4; SG 1.023–1.027
Swimming level Middle
Breeding Mouthbrooder

Both this and the other commonly available cardinalfish, the Flamefish (*Apogon maculatus*), are hardy species characterized by a second dorsal fin and a large head, eyes, and mouth. They are peaceful fish needing quiet companions. Mostly nocturnal, cardinalfishes may take some time to acclimate to a brightly lit aquarium. Feed newly imported specimens in the evening; once settled, they will eat at other times. They may accept only live foods initially, but will eventually take frozen substitutes. Flake foods are refused even if on the verge of starvation.

Remarks: The Spotted Cardinalfish is at home in an invertebrate tank, where it will shelter among rocks or coral heads during the day.

Reef tank (pages 198–199)

Ecsenius midas MIDAS BLENNY

Family Blenniidae
Distribution Indian Ocean, Red Sea
Size 4 in (10 cm)
Diet Omnivorous. Small aquatic invertebrates such as *Mysis* and brine shrimp, either live or frozen; also readily accepts flake foods and will graze on algae in tank
Water conditions
Temperature 75–79°F (24–26°C); pH 8.3–8.4; SG 1.023–1.027
Swimming level Bottom
Breeding Egg-depositor

This is a lovely, peaceful little fish for the beginner. Though a bottom-dweller, it likes to rest on rocks with its head held high so it can survey the area and guard its territory. Above its eyes can be seen two small, hair-like growths. The Midas Blenny (named for its golden yellow color) adapts well to an aquarium if given plenty of boltholes to retreat to. It feeds on algae and small invertebrates and will even take frozen and flake foods.

Remarks: Some prefer to keep this blenny in a species aquarium rather than with a community of larger fish; tankmates must be very placid. Several species of blenny have been tank-bred. Males, which are generally larger than females, may go through a succession of color changes when breeding. Most species lay adhesive eggs in the shelter of caves or under stones. The Midas Blenny can safely be kept with invertebrates.

Synchiropus splendidus MANDARINFISH

Family Callionymidae	frozen foods, preferably	SG 1.023–1.027
Distribution Pacific	crustaceans; also fond of algae	**Swimming level** Bottom
Size 4 in (10 cm)	**Water conditions** Temperature	**Breeding** Egg-scatterer
Diet Omnivorous. Small live and	75–79°F (24–26°C); pH 8.3–8.4;	(floating eggs)

These highly colored, retiring little fish prefer a quiet tank with similarly sized, peaceful species. Provide plenty of rocks as cover, and a sand substrate. Once established in the aquarium, the Mandarinfish spends much of its time perched on rocks. If frightened, it will hide in a crevice or bury itself in the sand. It is rather intolerant of its own kind; keep either single specimens or matched pairs: two males may fight. Males can be easily identified by the extended spine on their dorsal fin.

Remarks: This species is well suited to an invertebrate tank. Handle with care; the body mucus is believed to be poisonous. To date, these fish have not been successfully aquarium-bred.

Reef tank (pages 198–199)

Oxycirrhites typus LONG-NOSED HAWKFISH

Family Cirrhitidae	foods such as brine shrimp; also	SG 1.023–1.027
Distribution Indian Ocean	frozen foods, including plankton	**Swimming level** Bottom (but
Size 4 in (10 cm)	**Water conditions** Temperature	may perch at higher levels)
Diet Carnivorous. Small live	75–79°F (24–26°C); pH 8.3–8.4;	**Breeding** Egg-depositor

A social character, the Long-nosed Hawkfish may be kept with others of its own species in a mature tank with very clear, well-oxygenated water. A bottom-dweller, it will nevertheless perch on rocks and among corals at various levels. Like its bird namesake, it is a keen hunter, lurking until small prey pass close by, then lunging out to take them. Its natural diet is small shrimp and other live invertebrates, but it will accept frozen substitutes. Each of the fish's dorsal fin spines is tipped with a tuft of filaments. Males are smaller than females, and have black-edged ventral and caudal fins; the lower jaw is also a deeper red.

Remarks: This distinctive-looking species may be kept with invertebrates; indeed, its long snout is ideal for probing in the cracks and crevices of a reef tank in search of tiny morsels of food.

Lythrypnus dalli CATALINA GOBY

Family Gobiidae	**Diet** Carnivorous. Very small live	68–72°F (20–22°C); pH 8.3–8.4;
Distribution Pacific coast	and frozen foods; also meaty foods	SG 1.023–1.027
of California, USA	such as shrimp, if finely chopped	**Swimming level** Bottom
Size 2¼ in (6 cm)	**Water conditions** Temperature	**Breeding** Egg-depositor

This little species, with its brilliant pattern of blue stripes, is also known as the Blue-banded Goby. It requires cooler temperatures than most tropical marine fish, but may be kept with other compatible small, placid species. Provide a sand substrate, as it likes to dig burrows, as well as caves into which the fish can retreat, to rest or to spawn; hiding places are essential to avoid territorial disputes. Breeding is best achieved in a species aquarium; keep several, and condition them with copious live foods. These fish are easy to feed, provided they are given very small items.

Remarks: Catalina Gobies can be kept with invertebrates. Though short-lived, they may well breed in the aquarium. Eggs are laid in caves or burrows, and then guarded by the male. The fry can be quite a challenge to raise, as they are tiny.

Gramma loreto ROYAL GRAMMA

Family Grammidae
Distribution Western Atlantic, Caribbean
Size 5 in (12.5 cm)
Diet Omnivorous. Small live and frozen foods, plus flake foods commercially prepared for marine species; ensure that some vegetable matter is included in the diet
Water conditions
Temperature 75–79°F (24–26°C); pH 8.3–8.4; SG 1.023–1.027
Swimming level Middle
Breeding Egg-depositor

These vividly colored fish normally inhabit dark caves and crevices on reefs. Create a similar environment in an aquarium to make them feel secure, and they will venture out even under bright lighting. If your tank is big enough, you can keep two, but they may be very aggressive with each other; if in doubt, confine yourself to one specimen. Once settled, the Royal Gramma is relatively simple to feed and trouble-free.

Remarks: This species is fine in an invertebrate tank. There are conflicting reports of aquarium breeding; despite alleged hatchings, no fry have successfully been reared. By one account, the male fish was seen to line a cave with algae, and was subsequently observed mouthbrooding eggs. In another instance, eggs were reportedly laid inside an algae-lined pit, where they were later guarded by what was presumed to be the male.

Nemateleotris magnifica FIREFISH

Family Microdesmidae	frozen foods, plus flake foods;	SG 1.023–1.027
Distribution Indo-Pacific	give brine shrimp twice a week	**Swimming level** Bottom
Size 2¼ in (6 cm)	**Water conditions** Temperature	**Breeding** Egg-layer (details
Diet Omnivorous. Small live and	75–79°F (24–26°C); pH 8.3–8.4;	unknown)

Also referred to as the Magnificent Hover Goby, this is another small fish that retreats into burrows when danger threatens. Provide a deep sand substrate to allow digging; if it cannot find or make boltholes for itself, the Firefish never really settles into aquarium life. Do not keep it with boisterous species, or it may be reluctant to emerge from its hideaways. It may need live foods when first introduced to the tank, but will soon adapt to frozen foods, which it takes from, or close to, the bottom. The fish flicks its extended dorsal fin ray as a signal to others of its kind; keep just one or two to reduce fighting.

Remarks: This is a suitable species for an invertebrate aquarium. Install a tight-fitting cover, since Firefish will jump if they become frightened.

Opistognathus aurifrons YELLOW-HEADED JAWFISH

Family Opistognathidae
Distribution Western Atlantic
Size 5 in (12.5 cm)
Diet Carnivorous. Meaty foods such as small pieces of fish, shrimp, or other shellfish (crustaceans are particularly liked); will also take live and frozen foods, plus tiny fish or fry if the opportunity arises
Water conditions Temperature 75–79°F (24–26°C); pH 8.3–8.4; SG 1.023–1.027
Swimming level Bottom
Breeding Mouthbrooder

The only part of this fish that you normally see is its head sticking out of its burrow. It only seems to come part-way out, even when lunging at passing food. If caught outside its hole, it has the endearing habit of disappearing back into it, tail-first, at breakneck speed! It may even cover the entrance with a pebble or shell. Several can be kept, provided each has enough room to make its own home and stake its own territory. They tolerate other fish well; allow sufficient sandy substrate for all burrow-dwelling species.

Remarks: The Jawfish will live happily with invertebrates. Take care when catching it, since it may jump; it will also leap if startled, so make sure that the aquarium is securely covered.

Reef tank (pages 198–199)

Lactoria cornuta COWFISH

Family Ostraciidae
Distribution Indo-Pacific
Size 15¾ in (40 cm)
Diet Omnivorous. Small live and frozen foods, plus algae; fish is slow-moving and may not receive enough food; watch for signs of starvation (sides of body appear concave)
Water conditions Temperature 75–79°F (24–26°C); pH 8.3–8.4; SG 1.023–1.027
Swimming level Middle
Breeding Egg-layer (details unknown)

The Cowfish (or Longhorned Cowfish) is easily recognizable, with its two pairs of bony "horns" – one on the head (hence the common name) and one at the tail. Its box-shaped body is made up of bony plates covered with a thin skin; the hard projections and encased structure afford the fish great protection against predators. Only its fins are movable; these are used to propel it slowly and deliberately through the water. Take care if you have any "cleaner" fish in the aquarium, since the Cowfish's delicate skin may be damaged by their attentions. Beware also that this species' own flesh is poisonous, and that if threatened it will release toxins into the water; these can be lethal to both the Cowfish and its tankmates.

Remarks: This fish may be kept with some invertebrates, but it might pick at Tubeworms.

Pterois volitans LIONFISH

Family Scorpaenidae
Distribution Indo-Pacific
Size 13¾ in (35 cm)
Diet Carnivorous. Live and frozen foods; meaty foods such as small pieces of fish and shrimp
Water conditions Temperature 75–79°F (24–26°C); pH 8.3–8.4; SG 1.023–1.027
Swimming level Middle
Breeding Egg-layer (eggs in floating gelatinous ball)

Long, spiny rays of dorsal fin

Extended pectoral fin

Also known as the Scorpionfish, the Lionfish is exciting in appearance and size; its flamboyant fins and striped color pattern (which can vary greatly) make it a firm favorite. Its main drawbacks are its eating habits – it will swallow anything it can get into its mouth – and the venomous stinging cells on the fins. These fish are hunters that in the wild stalk prey in packs. In a tank, they drift, apparently aimlessly, towards their prey until close enough to lunge and engulf the hapless victim in one swift movement. Do not keep the fish with small companions that can be eaten.

Remarks: This fish can inflict painful stings. If stung, bathe the affected area in very hot water to coagulate the poison; seek medical advice if unsure.

Siganus vulpinus FOXFACE

Family Siganidae	frozen foods, plus green foods;	pH 8.3–8.4; SG 1.023–1.027
Distribution Pacific	will graze on algae in tank	Swimming level Middle
Size 9¾ in (25 cm)	Water conditions	Breeding Egg-layer (details
Diet Omnivorous. Small live and	Temperature 75–79°F (24–26°C);	unknown)

Dorsal fin
swept back

Terminal
mouth

Also known as the Foxfish or the Badgerfish (a reference to its striped face), this is a relatively amenable fish for the community aquarium. It is generally peaceful and settles well, but can be a bit intolerant and argumentative with others of its own kind. The Foxface is an active fish, and will be content if given lots of swimming space. Although this species will accept most foods, be sure to provide plenty of vegetable matter in the diet. A tank containing algae is particularly suitable, since the fish likes to graze.

Remarks: It is best not to keep the Foxface with invertebrates, as it tends to pick at some of the more sedentary creatures. There are no reports of this species breeding in an aquarium, but studies of other fish of the same family suggest that spawning may be triggered by water changes.

Hippocampus kuda YELLOW SEAHORSE

Family Syngnathidae	foods such as *Mysis* and brine	SG 1.023–1.027
Distribution Indo-Pacific	shrimp; rarely takes frozen foods	Swimming level Middle
Size 9¾ in (25 cm)	Water conditions Temperature	and lower
Diet Carnivorous. Small live	75–79°F (24–26°C); pH 8.3–8.4;	Breeding Pouchbrooder

This seahorse is known by a number of other common names, including the Golden Seahorse and the Pacific Seahorse. Its unusual shape makes it a very appealing aquarium specimen, but this is not the easiest of fish to maintain properly. Unless you are prepared to invest the time in providing a suitable supply of food, do not even consider keeping it. Yellow Seahorses are best kept in a species tank. Be sure to provide coral branches for them to hold on to, as in the wild.

Remarks: These fish have been bred in captivity. The male broods the eggs in its pouch and releases the fry after about four weeks. Seahorses' mouths are small, and both adults and fry need copious amounts of small (in the case of fry, tiny) live foods to thrive.

COLDWATER MARINE FISH

AQUARISTS WHO LIVE in the temperate zones – the northern US, southern Canada, northwestern Europe, and all regions of similar climate – may choose to keep coldwater marine species. These are not usually offered for sale in retail outlets; instead, enthusiasts collect both fish and invertebrates from coastal rockpools.

Beware, however, when collecting specimens. The young of many large fish are often found in rockpools; if introduced to your aquarium, these may quickly outgrow the tank or prey on the other inhabitants. Choose from the species recommended below; they are relatively small, and should

not cause too much trouble. Always obtain permission from the relevant government authority before taking any fish from the seashore.

Coldwater marine fish require an aquarium setup similar to that used for tropical species, except that a cooling system must usually be installed in place of a tank heater.

Fishkeepers frequently disregard coldwater marines, since they are quite dully colored. Nevertheless, these interesting and subtly attractive fish are well worth keeping, and can be used, along with compatible coldwater invertebrates, to stock a habitat-themed coastal rockpool tank.

Lipophrys pholis SHANNY

Family Blenniidae	Size 6¼ in (16 cm)	54–59°F (12–15°C); pH 8.0–8.4;
Distribution Mediterranean, eastern Atlantic coast from western Africa to Scotland	Diet Carnivorous. Small meaty foods, either live or frozen	SG 1.024–1.025
	Water conditions Temperature	Swimming level Bottom
		Breeding Egg-depositor

Coldwater blennies are active little fish that will delve among rocky crevices at the bottom of a tank. The Shanny is a typical blenny in that it likes having a bolthole or two, and this species is particularly fussy about its boltholes. Include some fairly large mollusc shells in the aquarium, since Shannies will sometimes prefer to take up residence inside these. Provide at least one shell for each fish, along with numerous caves and

hollows as retreats. They like the company of their own kind, and should be kept in a group.

Remarks: Shannies lack the small cirri (hair-like growths) above the eyes that are characteristic of most blennies. They also have the somewhat disconcerting habit of hauling themselves slightly out of the water to bask on rocks; this can look strange, but is perfectly normal for the species.

Parablennius gattorugine TOMPOT BLENNY

Family Blenniidae	**Size** 7¾ in (20 cm)	54–59°F (12–15°C); pH 8.0–8.4;
Distribution Eastern Atlantic	**Diet** Carnivorous. Meaty foods	SG 1.024–1.025
coast from Mediterranean to	such as fish, shrimp, and mussels	**Swimming level** Bottom
northern Scotland	**Water conditions** Temperature	**Breeding** Egg-depositor

Very long dorsal fin with hard and soft rays

The small Tompot Blenny can be very territorial and will sometimes pester smaller fish, though it may in turn be picked on by larger species. To prevent either problem, keep it in a species tank or provide plenty of rocks under which the fish can hide and to which it can stake a claim. You may also construct a few caves and tunnels as retreats. When feeding, ensure that enough food reaches the bottom for the blenny, which will feed from the substrate. Tompots are inquisitive and will come out from their shelters to see what is going on around them, especially once they grow accustomed to your presence.

Remarks: Like all blennies, the Tompot's stocky, cylindrical body is covered with a thick skin in place of scales. The bristly crests, or cirri, above its eyes are also a common blenny feature.

Spinachia spinachia FIFTEEN-SPINED STICKLEBACK

Family Gasterosteidae
Distribution Northeastern Atlantic coast from Bay of Biscay to Norway
Size 7¾ in (20 cm)
Diet Carnivorous. Small live foods such as *Mysis* and brine shrimp; may reluctantly take frozen items, but will rarely accept flake foods
Water conditions Temperature 54–59°F (12–15°C); pH 8.0–8.4; SG 1.024–1.025
Swimming level Middle
Breeding Nest-builder

This fish's common name refers to the 15 short spines that form its dorsal fin. The body is long and thin, tapering to a very spindly section at the rear. The only member of the family Gasterosteidae that lives in marine conditions, it poses a challenge to the aquarist, mainly because of its feeding requirements: small live foods must be offered several times a day. It is a short-lived species, with wild specimens surviving for possibly two years at the most. If kept in a community tank, choose companion fish carefully, as this stickleback is apt to nip fins.

Remarks: If you can manage to feed this fish well, breeding may be possible. Like their freshwater relatives, the spawning pair work together to construct a nest of plant material, which they stick together with a secreted fluid.

Lepadogaster candollei CONNEMARA CLINGFISH

Family Gobiesocidae	**Diet** Carnivorous. Small live and	54–59°F (12–15°C); pH 8.0–8.4;
Distribution Eastern Atlantic,	frozen foods; also meaty foods	SG 1.024–1.025
Mediterranean, Black Sea	such as fish, shrimp, and mussels	**Swimming level** Bottom
Size 3 in (7.5 cm)	**Water conditions** Temperature	**Breeding** Egg-depositor

This is a secretive fish that in the wild inhabits rocky shallows and prefers the shelter of rocks and seaweed. To prevent it from being swept away by the surging sea, the aptly named Connemara Clingfish has pelvic fins that are combined to form a sucker-like disk that "sticks" the fish to rocks, plants, and other surfaces. Like other species of clingfish, it lacks scales, the body being covered by a thick skin. Its eyes protrude notably. Although similar in appearance to blennies, clingfish are more brightly colored, this species ranging from green to reddish brown, with various spots or stripes. Mature males may have large spots on the head.

Remarks: Choose tankmates with care, since this fish is predatory and a natural scavenger, as its capacious mouth clearly attests.

Gobius niger BLACK GOBY

Family Gobiidae	**Diet** Carnivorous. Small live and	54–59°F (12–15°C); pH 8.0–8.4;
Distribution Eastern Atlantic,	frozen foods; also meaty foods	SG 1.024–1.025
Mediterranean, Black Sea	such as fish, shrimp, and mussels	**Swimming level** Bottom
Size 6 in (15 cm)	**Water conditions** Temperature	**Breeding** Egg-depositor

With such a wide-ranging distribution, it is not surprising that this species shows geographical variations in color. Coloration may also differ within the same local population, to match the appearance of the surrounding rocks, so that each group blends into its particular domain. Despite the fish's common name (as well as its scientific name, *niger* meaning black), truly black forms of the Black Goby are rarely found.

Remarks: Gobies have two dorsal fins and can be distinguished easily from blennies, which have only one. Typical of the gobies, this little fish is territorial, so provide nooks and crannies in which individual specimens can retreat. If keeping a group of Black Gobies, house them in a reasonably large aquarium, or mayhem will ensue: they are liable to bicker with each other when establishing and defending territories.

Coris julis RAINBOW WRASSE

Family Labridae	**Diet** Carnivorous. Small live and	SG 1.024–1.025
Distribution Eastern Atlantic,	frozen foods; also meaty foods	**Swimming level** Bottom
Mediterranean	**Water conditions** Temperature	to middle
Size 9¾ in (25 cm)	54–59°F (12–15°C); pH 8.0–8.4;	**Breeding** Egg-scatterer

Despite its potentially large size, the Rainbow Wrasse is generally peaceful, if at times a little boisterous. Much of the day is spent swimming about in the lower regions of the aquarium, but at night it may bury itself in the substrate, easily undermining rocks in the process. As with other wrasses, coloration varies according to locality, gender, age, readiness to breed, and even the mood the fish is in! This species is easy to feed.

Remarks: These fish are hermaphrodites: it is fairly common for females to become fully functional males in order to facilitate spawning within a school. Wrasses breed in either of two ways: a group may swim towards the water surface and release eggs and milt together, or a pair may perform a courtship display prior to spawning at the surface. The eggs drift in the current, hatching into planktonic larvae.

Pholis gunnellus GUNNELL

Family Pholididae
Distribution Western and eastern Atlantic, northern Pacific coast of USA
Size 9¾ in (25 cm)
Diet Carnivorous. Meaty foods such as finely chopped fish, shrimp, mussels, or other shellfish; also *Mysis* or brine shrimp, either live or frozen
Water conditions Temperature 54–59°F (12–15°C); pH 8.0–8.4; SG 1.024–1.025
Swimming level Bottom
Breeding Egg-depositor

A slippery character, this eel-like creature is also known as the Butterfish. Like gobies, the Gunnell's natural habitat is rocky areas with nooks and overhangs, where it can hide away. The body is slim and sinuous, with long-based dorsal and anal fins that are joined to the small, rounded caudal fin. Adult Gunnells are brown and gold, with pale-rimmed dark spots along the dorsal fin and a bar through the eye. Juveniles have dark vertical bands that disappear as the fish mature. Provide tank specimens with plenty of hiding places, and give small, meaty foods.

Remarks: This species should not be kept with small invertebrates, since they form a major part of its diet in the wild. It is thought that the fish breed by laying eggs in clumps under stones, and that either parent tends the eggs until hatching.

TROPICAL INVERTEBRATES

THE IDEA OF KEEPING invertebrates in a tropical marine aquarium conjures up a vision of a coral reef, with a whole community of creatures living together in harmony. To turn this into a reality will require patience and experience. Invertebrates are more delicate than fish, and need closer attention to water quality; they must also be provided with more intense lighting. Do not attempt to keep them until you have successfully maintained a fish-only marine tank.

Many invertebrates need a constant supply of fine live cultured foods; others have diets that are even more specialized. In the sea, some species will feed continuously for hours; in a tank environment, these specimens must be fed two or three times a day.

There is a wide variety of tropical invertebrates available to hobbyists; some of the hardier species are profiled below. Research your choices with care; even related species can vary enormously in character and requirements. For example, some sea slugs are peaceful herbivores, while others are carnivorous and will consume tankmates. Conversely, certain fish eat invertebrates in the wild, and should not be kept with them. If in any doubt about compatibility, seek advice from your dealer.

Sabellastarte spp. TUBEWORM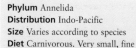

Phylum Annelida	live foods such as brine shrimp	SG 1.020–1.024
Distribution Indo-Pacific	nauplii, rotifers, and plankton	**Breeding** May breed in tank,
Size Varies according to species	**Water conditions** Temperature	spawning at dawn; clouds of eggs
Diet Carnivorous. Very small, fine	75–79°F (24–26°C); pH 8.2–8.4;	and sperm emerge from the body

Popular invertebrates imported from Singapore, Indonesia, and Sri Lanka, Tubeworms are also sold as Fanworms or Featherduster Worms (referring to the feathery tentacles on their heads).

This creature's body is encased in a parchment-like tube that is partially buried in the substrate. To feed, the Tubeworm extends its head from the tube, and the tentacles wave in the water flow, trapping small prey and channeling it into the mouth. At any hint of danger, the tentacles are quickly withdrawn into the tube. Tentacles may be bitten off by predators or shed in poor water conditions, but will regenerate if the tube is left in place. Adults often shed their feathery heads so they cannot eat their own larvae.

Reef tank (pages 198–199)

Heteractis malu MALU ANEMONE

Phylum Cnidaria	**Diet** Carnivorous. Meaty foods	benefits from vitamin supplements
Distribution Indo-Pacific:	such as small pieces of raw fish,	**Water conditions** Temperature
Philippines, Indonesia, Singapore	shrimp, squid, and mussels,	75–79°F (24–26°C); pH 8.2–8.4;
Size 4–15¾ in (10–40 cm) diameter	sprinkled over tentacles; also	SG 1.020–1.024

This widely available sea anemone is often kept as a home for clownfishes. Large, with long, purple-tipped tentacles, its body color can vary from cream to brown. Intense lighting will encourage the growth of zooxanthellae algae, which may cover the anemone, darkening its appearance. The algae gives the anemone some nourishment.

Place an anemone with its tentacles pointing upwards. Anemones "breathe" via their tentacles, and may suffocate if water cannot flow through them; provide a constant current. This species often stays where it is put, but can move, particularly if stressed. Occasionally, it will collapse, releasing foul water and wastes. If this occurs more than once in 24 hours, change the tank water.

Reef tank (pages 198–199)

Dardanus megistos RED HERMIT CRAB

Phylum Crustacea	such as small pieces of raw fish,	**Water conditions** Temperature
Distribution Caribbean	shrimp, squid, and mussels; will	75–79°F (24–26°C); pH 8.2–8.4;
Size 4–6 in (10–15 cm)	also accept a wide range of	SG 1.020–1.024
Diet Carnivorous. Meaty foods	commercial foods	**Breeding** Difficult in aquariums

Although their bright color and lively behavior make them very appealing for the home aquarium, Red Hermit Crabs can develop into quite large and powerful creatures capable of wrecking a reef tank. They are more suited to the role of scavenger in a large aquarium with fish of a reasonable size that can manage to keep out of harm's way.

When purchasing a young crab, remember that it will outgrow its original shell and will need a selection of larger shells for it to move into. If this is not provided, a Hermit Crab may eat another shell-dweller in the aquarium in order to occupy its shell.

Even with the encumbrance of a shell, these creatures can move rather quickly and are not averse to capturing small fish or other invertebrates that they regard as a meal.

Lysmata amboinensis CLEANER SHRIMP

Phylum Crustacea	**Diet** Carnivorous. Meaty foods	**Water conditions** Temperature
Distribution Indo-Pacific	such as small pieces of raw fish,	75–79°F (24–26°C); pH 8.2–8.4;
Size 1¼–3¼ in (3–8 cm),	shrimp, and mussels; also accepts	SG 1.020–1.024
excluding antennae	a wide range of commercial foods	**Breeding** Common in aquariums

The Cleaner Shrimp's common name comes from its habit of picking skin parasites and other matter from the bodies of large fish that, fortunately, do not consider the shrimp as food! In an aquarium, it may still perform this service.

The Cleaner Shrimp is popular with hobbyists because of its striking coloration – two scarlet stripes flanking a bright white stripe along the back. Active and gregarious, it will scavenge in all regions of the tank. Provide numerous shelters; shrimp are most vulnerable at molting times, when the shell is shed to accommodate growth. Females can sometimes be seen carrying clusters of green eggs under their abdomen, but it is unlikely that any young will escape being eaten by the other aquarium inhabitants.

Reef tank (pages 198–199)

Fromia monilis ORANGE STARFISH

Phylum Echinodermata	such as small pieces of raw fish,	**Water conditions** Temperature
Distribution Indonesia, Sri Lanka	shrimp, squid, and mussels,	75–79°F (24–26°C); pH 8.2–8.4;
Size 2¼–4 in (6–10 cm) diameter	placed near arms; may also	SG 1.020–1.024
Diet Carnivorous. Meaty foods	accept some commercial foods	**Breeding** Rare in aquariums

Popular for its beautiful spotted orange and red coloring, the placid, harmless Orange Starfish is an ideal addition to an invertebrate tank, being relatively easy to keep and feed. Other species, such as the commonly named Feather Starfish or Brittle Starfish, have more specific needs and are suitable only for the experienced aquarist.

When purchasing any starfish, check carefully that it has not been damaged, especially on the tips of its arms. Ensure also that the body is rigid and not limp; a starfish's vascular system is easily harmed. Do not buy an injured specimen, as it will have a slim chance of survival. Feed sparingly, once every other day. As with all invertebrates, maintain water quality.

Reef tank (pages 198–199)

Pseudocolochirus axiologus SEA APPLE

Phylum Echinodermata	fine live or frozen foods such as	commercial foods
Distribution Indonesia	brine shrimp nauplii and rotifers;	**Water conditions** Temperature
Size 6–7¾ in (15–20 cm)	diet may be supplemented with	75–79°F (24–26°C); pH 8.2–8.4;
Diet Carnivorous. Very small,	specialized suspension-type	SG 1.020–1.024

Of all the Sea Cucumbers, Sea Apples are the most colorful, with a pinkish gray body up to 4 in (10 cm) in length and rows of yellow, pink, or orange tubular feet. At the front end is an array of delicate, feathery tentacles, ranging in color from yellow to deep red and used for filter feeding. Food is trapped by the tentacles; this is then thrust into the mouth and consumed.

The Sea Apple has great appeal for hobbyists, but its dietary requirements are fairly demanding. It must be given small, fine foods at regular intervals several times a day; many specimens slowly starve to death in aquariums because this regime is not observed. Avoid keeping a Sea Apple with fish that may attack or pick at its tentacles.

Reef tank (pages 198–199)

Aplysia spp. SEA HARE

Phylum Mollusca	exclusively on algae (grazing on	75–79°F (24–26°C); pH 8.2–8.4;
Distribution Worldwide	algal growth in the tank), but may	SG 1.020–1.024
Size 2¼–11¾ in (6–30 cm)	also accept other plant matter	**Breeding** May breed in home
Diet Herbivorous. Feeds almost	**Water conditions** Temperature	aquariums

Although not particularly attractive, these greenish brown-colored sea slugs can be extremely useful to marine aquarists. They graze almost continuously on algae, which if left unchecked can easily overrun an invertebrate tank. Given plenty of algae and good water conditions, Sea Hares can live for over two years.

Those offered for sale are usually of Caribbean origin. The Caribbean Sea Hare (*Aplysia dactylomela*) is widely available as small specimens 2¼–3¼ in (6–8 cm) long. Be prepared, however, for these to grow to 11¾ in (30 cm) or more. Like snails, Sea Hares have a muscular foot with which they glide over rocks and vegetation in search of food. The ear-like projections on their heads, and their habit of grazing on algae, give them their name.

COLDWATER INVERTEBRATES

THERE ARE MANY small coldwater invertebrates that make good subjects for home aquariums. Like coldwater fish, they are, for the most part, less colorful than their often vivid tropical counterparts.

Coldwater invertebrates are not usually sold in aquarium shops but are collected directly from rockpools along the seashore. Take care when searching for specimens; rockpools often contain the fry of large fish, which, if added to your tank, may soon outgrow it or become a danger to the other inhabitants. Remember also that many marine invertebrate species are becoming rare; before

collecting any creature, make sure that it is not an endangered species. Obtain permission from the relevant government authority, and restrict yourself to taking a few specimens.

As with tropical invertebrates, one can make no generalizations regarding feeding or maintenance; research carefully the particular requirements and behavior of each species you would like to keep. A steady supply of the correct foods is essential, and this may mean culturing your own. Until you are sure that you can provide the right diet, resist taking any invertebrates home; otherwise, they may starve to death.

SEA ANEMONES

Phylum Cnidaria	**Size** Varies according to species	**Water conditions** Temperature 54–59°F (12–15°C); pH 8.0–8.4; SG 1.024–1.025
Distribution Mediterranean, Atlantic, and northeastern Pacific coasts	**Diet** Carnivorous. Small pieces of raw fish, shrimp, squid, or mussels, sprinkled over tentacles	**Breeding** Often divide if well fed

The Beadlet Anemone (*Actinia equina*) has two subspecies: *A. e. var. mesembryanthemum*, which is common in rockpools; and *A. e. var. fragracea*, inhabiting deeper waters. Both make excellent subjects for the home aquarium. They can be found in a number of colors, including green, brown, and red. Alternatives to these are the red and white Dahlia Anemones. *Urticina felina* is seen on both the eastern and western coasts of the north Atlantic, and on the northeastern Pacific shoreline, while *Urticina crassicornis* lives on the eastern coast of North America. All anemones have a tubular body, multiple tentacles, and a disk-like sucker foot. They require a steady, reasonably strong flow of water to enable them to respire and feed.

PRAWNS AND SHRIMPS

Phylum Crustacea	**Diet** Carnivorous. Meaty foods	**Water conditions** Temperature
Distribution Mediterranean,	such as small pieces of raw fish,	54–59°F (12–15°C); pH 8.0–8.4;
Atlantic, and Pacific coasts	shrimp, squid, and mussels; will	SG 1.024–1.025
Size Varies according to species	also accept some commercial foods	**Breeding** Common in aquariums

Any of the prawns and shrimps belonging to the genera *Palaemon*, *Crangon*, and *Hippolyte* make wonderful scavengers for the aquarium, and may also become cleaners for fish in the tank. They can be caught quite easily with a net in rockpools but must be transported with care; they will quickly die if the water becomes too warm. Like the more spectacularly colored tropical shrimps, they are an interesting and lively addition to an invertebrate tank, moving constantly about the aquarium in pursuit of titbits. Be sure to provide plenty of hiding places where they may seek refuge, particularly during molting periods, when their shells are shed, exposing the soft body. If breeding occurs, females can be observed carrying eggs beneath their abdomen, but any young will be highly vulnerable to predation by larger tankmates.

STARFISHES

Phylum Echinodermata	**Diet** Carnivorous. Meaty foods	also accept some commercial foods
Distribution Mediterranean,	such as small pieces of raw fish,	**Water conditions** Temperature
Atlantic, and Pacific coasts	shrimp, scallops, and mussels,	54–59°F (12–15°C); pH 8.0–8.4;
Size Varies according to species	placed near arms of starfish; may	SG 1.024–1.025

It is quite common to find small starfish specimens in rockpools, and it is very tempting to take them home for the aquarium. This is fine, provided you do not keep them with anything they are likely to feed on, such as scallops and mussels. A hungry *Asteria rubens* starfish, native to the northeastern Atlantic, will readily pry open a mollusc, invert its stomach into the shell, and devour the contents. Starfishes move slowly over any underwater surface in search of food, using their five sucker-covered limbs; these can be regenerated if damaged.

Starfishes are somewhat easier to keep than other rockpool inhabitants such as limpets, winkles, scallops, and mussels. House these separately, and provide tiny, fine foods. Maintain water conditions as for starfishes.

MARINE ALGAE

ALGAE ARE NOT true plants, but form a kingdom of their own; however, they are just as important as plants to any reef setup. Some colonize rocks, while others live within anemones, providing them with nourishment and utilizing their waste. Small encrusting and filamentous algal species may be inadvertently introduced to the aquarium, along with tiny invertebrates, when adding rock collected from the sea. The larger, more decorative varieties, as pictured below, are sold like freshwater plants.

Green, brown, or red algae are beneficial to the tank, and many invertebrates and fish love grazing on them. However, the development of film-like, brownish-purple algae can indicate a variety of problems in the aquarium, including overstocking, poor water quality, overfeeding, or incorrect lighting. Promptly siphon out this type of algal growth and rectify the causes.

Algae need strong light, the waste products from fish and invertebrates, and various trace elements found in seawater. Of all algae, members of the genus *Caulerpa* are the most numerous; these can be difficult to identify, since a single species may assume different forms. Factors such as lighting, substrate, and nutrients all contribute to this diversity of growth. Some species of algae are sensitive to temperature changes, with a 9°F (5°C) fluctuation proving fatal, while others, such as *Caulerpa prolifera*, can withstand substantial variations.

Acetebularia spp.
MERMAID'S CUP

This attractive, small, blue-green alga, resembling little toadstools, is delicate and may easily be damaged in transit and by tank livestock. It requires good light and gentle water movement.

Caulerpa prolifera

The most commonly seen green alga in marine aquariums is this hardy species ideal for novices, although, once established, it can grow wildly! Maintain control with regular harvests.

Codiacea spp.
CALCAREOUS ALGAE

Calcareous Algae are so-called because they
absorb calcium from seawater to reinforce their
leaves, a process that makes them more rigid
than *Caulerpa* species. Given strong lighting
and high pH levels, they are easy to keep.

Pencillus capitatus
SHAVING BRUSH

Popular for its unusual shape, this alga is usually
imported from the Caribbean, where it is found
on sand or mud substrates. Before buying a
specimen, check that it is undamaged. With luck,
it will propagate via small shoots near the base.

Rhodophyceae spp.
RED ALGAE

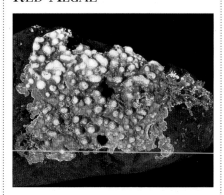

Red Algae are firm favorites, since they contrast
well in a reef aquarium. In healthy plants, the
red color extends to the very edges of the fronds.
Specimens are best purchased attached to a rock,
but even so can be difficult to maintain.

Valonia ventricosa
SAILOR'S EYEBALLS

Each of the ball-shaped growths on this alga is a
single cell reaching up to 2 in (5 cm) in diameter,
the largest single-celled development in nature.
The cells are readily punctured; take extra care
when handling the plant or working in the tank.

ALSO RECOMMENDED

Caulerpa peltata
Caulerpa pinnata
Caulerpa racemosa
Caulerpa scalpelliformis

Caulerpa sertularioides
Caulerpa taxifolia
Halimeda opuntia (Cactus Alga)
Halymenia spp. (Red Seaweed Algae)

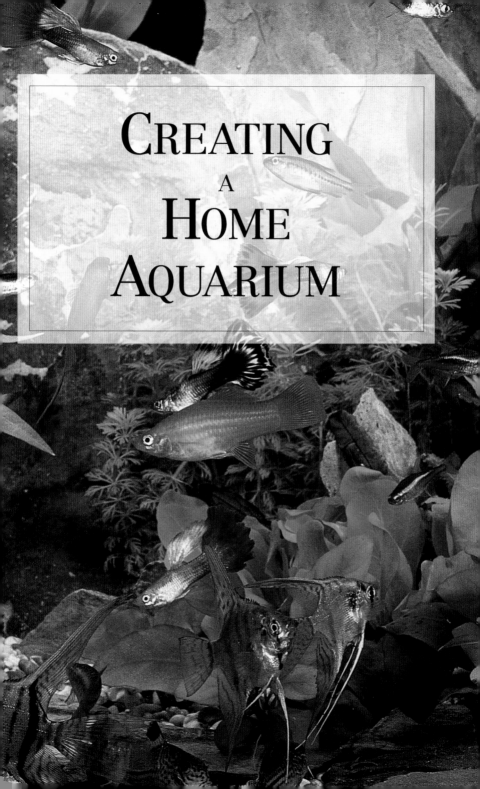

CREATING
A
HOME
AQUARIUM

AQUARIUM EQUIPMENT

Novice aquarists can be daunted
by the vast range of equipment
available. If you are on a budget,
don't despair – the most expensive
item is not necessarily the best, and
no amount of costly gadgets will
ensure fishkeeping success. Basic
equipment allied with effort and a
desire to learn are all you need. Begin
by researching the various operating
systems – how they work and how
they can be most effectively used.
Before purchasing anything, plan
your aquarium carefully, selecting
both hardware and decor that will
create the right environment for your
fish. If in doubt about the suitability,
convenience, or reliability of any
item, seek advice from your dealer
or experienced hobbyists.

◁ TROPICAL FRESHWATER AQUARIUM WITH DECORATIVE
STREAM OF BUBBLES CREATED USING A LONG AIR STONE

TANKS AND STANDS

WHEN PLANNING YOUR aquarium, the tank and stand are the first items you will have to consider. Take account of your budget, and the space available in your home. The tank size will also partially govern the type and number of fish you can keep. A community of small tropical freshwater fish, or a modest number of fancy goldfish, could easily be accommodated in a 24 x 12 x 12 in (60 x 30 x 30 cm) aquarium. This setup, however, would be inadequate for housing most marine species, which require a greater surface area and, generally, more precise water conditions; to maintain these fish, you will need a relatively large aquarium.

Tanks and stands are available in many styles to suit a variety of tastes. If none matches the design or dimensions you require, you may, with care, construct a tank to your own specifications. Ensure that the stand and floor can support the finished aquarium, and put the tank where it will be safe, secure, and accessible for installation and maintenance.

TANK CONSTRUCTION

Arguably the greatest advance in the fishkeeping hobby has been the use of silicone sealant in the construction of tanks. Prior to its development in the late 1960s, tanks were made of angle-iron frames with the glass sealed in place with special linseed-free putty. The steel frames were prone to corrosion, particularly if used for marine aquariums, while the putty was not leakproof, losing its sealing efficacy once hardened. At that time, tanks had a maximum lifespan of 10 years.

All this changed when silicone rubber was developed in a semi-fluid form that would molecularly bond pieces of glass, and, once set, retain a degree of resilience. Nowadays, tank frames are rare, and added solely for decorative purposes.

Modern construction methods have allowed boundless possibilities in aquarium design. Now there are aquariums with angled side walls (for placing in a corner), bow-fronted aquariums, hexagonal tanks, and others with inbuilt biological filtration compartments. There is a tank for virtually every need and purpose, and most suppliers will build tanks to meet individual requirements.

If constructing your own tank, choose carefully the type and thickness of glass to be used, and purchase the silicone from an aquarium shop; similar products sold as a bathroom sealant or for building purposes are not suitable, since they often contain toxic fungicides. Silicone rubber contains acetic acid, and in its liquid form can give off a pungent smell; always read and follow the instructions on the container. Do not use secondhand glass; it may be weakened by exposure to sunlight or heat. If you are not confident handling the glass, have it cut to size and the edges ground smooth for safety.

Although glass is still the most common material used to make aquariums, newer acrylics are becoming popular. Early plastic tanks yellowed and became brittle with age, and were easily scratched by gravel or cleaning tools. Today's acrylic aquariums are strong yet light, with none of the sealing problems of glass tanks.

To protect the fish and minimize water evaporation, many tanks have integrated hoods, which also hold lights and wiring. A sheet of glass, or cover, can be placed on top of the tank instead, or set on runners inside the tank so a hood can also be fitted.

TANK STANDS

Tanks, particularly glass types, are heavy even before they have been filled with water, substrate, and rockwork. Since a gallon of fresh water weighs 8.3 lb (3.8 kg), a complete furnished aquarium can tip the scales at 1,100 lb (500 kg) or more. The stand it is seated on must bear this load, and should be flat and level; otherwise, the tanks distort or leak, or the glass cracks.

Many tanks are offered with a separate cabinet in different styles and finishes to match your room decor. These have been designed to evenly support the weight of the aquarium. The cupboard can be used to store fish food, nets, and other equipment, or to hide an external power filter or air pump. In the latter case, fit a non-return valve in the air line running from the pump, to prevent back-siphoning of water from the tank. To avoid overheating, make sure there is adequate air circulation to both the pump and any powered filter in the cabinet.

Simple metal tank stands are available as a cheaper option, or you may construct your own stand from wood, brick, or concrete blocks – indeed, any material capable of sustaining the weight of the tank and its contents. The stand must be secure; if using bricks or decorative concrete blocks, bond the elements together with mortar. Remember that a collapsed aquarium can cause a great deal of damage and injury.

A good-quality cabinet can enhance the overall appearance of your aquarium, as well as conveniently concealing and storing equipment.

Whether your stand is ready-made or self-built, do not place the tank directly on it. The smallest bit of debris can impart point stresses in the glass bottom, causing it to crack. Always place a piece of expanded polystyrene between the base of the tank and its stand. As a precaution, retailers often supply polystyrene tiles with any tank.

Consider the strength not just of your tank stand, but also of the floor. Although a solid, level concrete floor is fine, timbered flooring must be tested to ensure that it can withstand the weight. If the stand imparts point-loading – for instance, has four legs instead of a continuous plinth – these points should be positioned so that they stand over, and not between, the floor joists.

When buying a tank or stand, note that the standard metric sizes sold do not correspond exactly to imperial sizes. As a rule of thumb when choosing the size of an aquarium, large tanks are easier to maintain than smaller ones; in a greater volume of water, fluctuations in chemistry tend to be gradual and more manageable. Of course, a tank and stand of any size can be difficult to lift and move; arrange to have someone help you if possible.

FILTERS

AQUARIUM FILTERS ARE used to clean the water and work by trapping solid waste and converting it into a harmless form that can be returned to the tank. This conversion is performed by the natural process known as the nitrogen cycle (*see page 27*).

The efficiency of a filter is primarily related to the filtration surface area and the quantity of water passed through it. There are two basic means of pumping water through a filter: by applying an electric pump, or by using an airlift system. Although electric pump-driven filters are usually more effective (and more expensive), airlift versions may be appropriate where more gradual water movement is required, such as in a tank containing fry. Depending on design, filters can be situated inside or outside the tank; external filters are rarely run on airlift systems, and generally require the use of an electric pump. Filters that use electric pumps to draw water through the system are known as power filters.

EXTERNAL FILTERS

External filters are usually more effective than internal filters, and easier to maintain. A further advantage is that the media can be changed to alter water chemistry (for example, added peat will make the water more acidic, while coral sand will harden it). Aquarists may combine the two systems, perhaps using an external power unit as the main filter, with the water returned to the tank via a trickle filter and/or UV sterilizer.

ELECTRIC POWER FILTERS

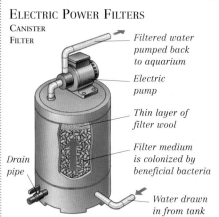

CANISTER FILTER

Filtered water pumped back to aquarium

Electric pump

Thin layer of filter wool

Drain pipe

Filter medium is colonized by beneficial bacteria

Water drawn in from tank

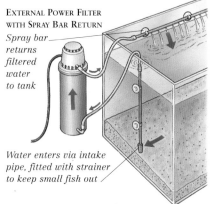

EXTERNAL POWER FILTER WITH SPRAY BAR RETURN

Spray bar returns filtered water to tank

Water enters via intake pipe, fitted with strainer to keep small fish out

External power filters feature a canister into which the filter media (usually carbon and filter wool) and any water conditioning additives are placed. On top of the canister sits an electric pump. Water flows into the filter via the intake pipe from the tank, entering through a port near the bottom of the canister. It then passes through the media, and is pumped back to the aquarium. To prime such a filter, it is necessary to start a siphon by sucking on the outlet pipe. For effective priming, the filter must be positioned so that the pump lies below the water level. Although the pump may be a sealed unit, it must not be placed inside the tank.

GRAVITY-FED RAPID SAND FILTER

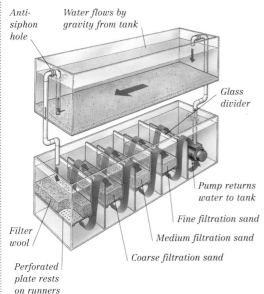

Anti-siphon hole

Water flows by gravity from tank

Glass divider

Pump returns water to tank

Fine filtration sand

Medium filtration sand

Coarse filtration sand

Filter wool

Perforated plate rests on runners

Internal undergravel filters can be disturbed by fish digging in the substrate, and may impede plant growth. External versions use a gravity-fed rapid sand filter. This consists of a special tank or ready-made trough, compartmentalized so that water flows through various beds of gravel and sand, which can be graded in size along the length of the filter. The filter sits under the tank and, unlike a power filter, is fed not by a siphon but by an overflow system, whereby water returns from the filter via a submersible electric pump, and overflows the aquarium through a specially designed labyrinth or an overflow pipe to the filter. The end compartment of the filter can be used for heaters and thermostats, and the entire unit is concealed in the aquarium stand. Such filters are effective for both freshwater and marine setups. Large models are often used by public aquariums for filtering entire systems.

WET/DRY FILTER

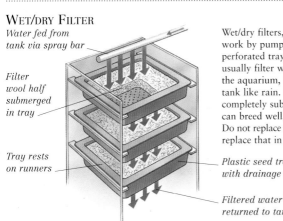

Water fed from tank via spray bar

Filter wool half submerged in tray

Tray rests on runners

Plastic seed trays with drainage holes

Filtered water returned to tank

Wet/dry filters, also referred to as trickle filters, work by pumping water through a series of perforated trays containing the filter medium, usually filter wool. The filter is located above the aquarium, so that the water returns to the tank like rain. Since the filter wool is never completely submerged, oxygen-loving bacteria can breed well, aiding the nitrification process. Do not replace all of the medium at once. Instead, replace that in the top tray only, and transfer this to the bottom position, moving the other two trays up. With this method, the beneficial bacteria colony will be retained.

ULTRA-VIOLET STERILIZERS

Although not true filters, ultra-violet (UV) sterilizers are sometimes used in conjunction with external power filters to remove free-swimming pathogens, including algal spores. They are useful accessories for both marine and freshwater systems. Usually, the UV-emitting fluorescent tube is surrounded by a clear quartz tube and a protective opaque outer casing. Water returning to the aquarium enters a port at one end of the case and travels along a narrow channel between the case and the quartz tube. As it passes through the sterilizer, it is irradiated by UV light emissions, which kill any pathogens. A UV tube has a defined, and fairly short, useful life, after which its effectiveness quickly degrades. At the end of this period, the tube should be replaced.

Internal Filters

Internal filters come in various shapes and sizes to suit most tanks. With the exception of undergravel filters, air-operated internal units are generally suited only to small, lightly stocked aquariums. Internal power filters are submersible water pumps that fit onto a filter capsule, and can be used for small to medium-sized tanks. The primary drawback of any filter positioned inside an aquarium is that when the unit is removed for cleaning, some debris will inevitably drain back into the tank. The only way to clean an internal filter thoroughly is to dismantle the entire aquarium and, in effect, begin again. However, this will not be necessary very often, provided that you neither overfeed your fish nor keep your tank overstocked.

Sponge Filter

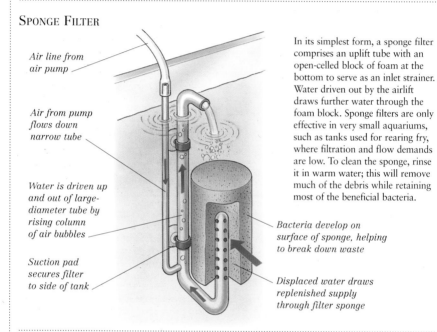

Air line from
air pump

Air from pump
flows down
narrow tube

Water is driven up
and out of large-
diameter tube by
rising column
of air bubbles

Suction pad
secures filter
to side of tank

In its simplest form, a sponge filter comprises an uplift tube with an open-celled block of foam at the bottom to serve as an inlet strainer. Water driven out by the airlift draws further water through the foam block. Sponge filters are only effective in very small aquariums, such as tanks used for rearing fry, where filtration and flow demands are low. To clean the sponge, rinse it in warm water; this will remove much of the debris while retaining most of the beneficial bacteria.

Bacteria develop on
surface of sponge, helping
to break down waste

Displaced water draws
replenished supply
through filter sponge

Box Filter

Small corner box filters, using a simple airlift, are also ideal for smaller tanks. These consist of a box with slots (usually on the top face, but sometimes also on the sides) through which the water enters. Inside, filter wool is packed over a slightly raised bottom plate, which also has slots for water movement. From the raised bottom plate rises an uplift tube containing an air stone connected to an air pump. As the water in this tube is driven out by the rising stream of air bubbles, so water passes through the filter box to replenish it. Waste material carried by the current becomes trapped in the filter wool, where the nitrogen cycle converts it to harmless salts. Box filters usually sit on the substrate; you may need to place some marbles or a stone inside the box as ballast. A few types are provided with rubber suction cups to attach them to the tank glass.

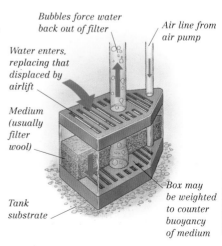

Bubbles force water
back out of filter

Air line from
air pump

Water enters,
replacing that
displaced by
airlift

Medium
(usually
filter
wool)

Tank
substrate

Box may
be weighted
to counter
buoyancy
of medium

UNDERGRAVEL FILTER

Simple airlift pumps water from under filter plate(s)

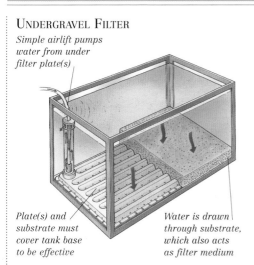

Plate(s) and substrate must cover tank base to be effective

Water is drawn through substrate, which also acts as filter medium

Undergravel filters consist of one or more plates installed under the substrate. These should cover the entire base of the tank, spaced about ¼–½ in (5–10 mm) apart. There are generally two uplift tubes that rise from these plates, reaching almost to the surface of the water. The tubes operate via either an airlift system or a submersible electric pump, and draw water out from under the substrate. As additional water is forced through the substrate to displace it, solids are trapped and then broken down to a harmless form by nitrifying bacteria. A gravel tidy may be used to prevent fine substrates from clogging the filter plate(s). This is simply a piece of perforated plastic sheeting that is typically placed to separate two grades of substrate: say, coarse gravel at the base of a tank and a top layer of sand.

INTERNAL POWER FILTER

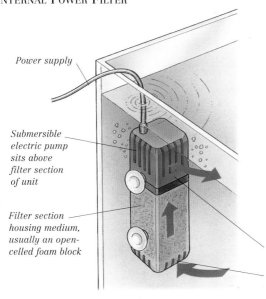

Power supply

Submersible electric pump sits above filter section of unit

Filter section housing medium, usually an open-celled foam block

Pump expels clean water

Tank water is drawn into filter canister

There is a selection of reasonably priced internal filters powered by small, sealed, submersible electric pumps. The water flow is similar in principle to that provided by an airlift corner filter, but with the pump replacing the airlift system. An open-celled foam block is frequently used as the filter medium instead of filter wool. Since the flow is typically greater than with an airlift-type filter, internal power filters are usually placed not on the substrate but nearer the water surface, to prevent rapid clogging of the medium. Suction devices are supplied to secure the filter to the side of the tank.

PROTEIN SKIMMERS

Protein skimmers are generally used in marine setups to remove accumulated proteins. The skimming device lies just below the water surface. Water, usually pumped by an airlift fitted with an air stone, cascades into the upper compartment of the skimmer, where the proteins collect as a froth, which can then be removed. To maintain the efficiency of the unit, the wooden air stone should be replaced every two months. If dosing your tank to treat fish ailments, switch off the skimmer for 12 hours so it does not eradicate the medication.

AIR PUMPS

CONTRARY TO POPULAR belief, the stream of bubbles from an air stone does little to increase the dissolved oxygen level in the aquarium water. The bubbles reach the surface too quickly for oxygen to diffuse. It is the ripples that form on the water surface that increase the area over which oxygen exchange can take place. Thus, it is perfectly possible to run an aquarium without an air pump, provided you have another means of creating water movement (for example, by using a spray bar from a power filter). Air pumps are essential, however, to power certain types of filtration systems. The current produced by an air stone improves water circulation around heaters, preventing hot spots, and ensures that oxygen-rich surface water is circulated to the entire aquarium.

DIAPHRAGM AND PISTON PUMPS

Most air pumps available to the aquarist are diaphragm types. Since they operate via an arm vibrating a diaphragm, they are often quite noisy, although regular maintenance can dramatically reduce sound levels. The constant movement also leads to fatigue, and the diaphragm and flaps should be replaced periodically. Always keep spares in case of emergency. Air pumps can be used as power sources for filtration systems, the rising bubbles drawing water through the filtration bed. Pumps used in this way should be switched off only briefly, for servicing; otherwise, the filtration will fail.

Piston pumps are much quieter than diaphragm pumps, but tend to be less efficient. If the pump is placed below the water level (as is common if it is housed in a cabinet), fit an inline non-return valve between it and the air stone, uplift tube, or other unit being powered. This will enable air to pass freely from the pump, while preventing any return flow of water or air. Without a valve, if the pump should fail, water may siphon back up the tube and into the pump, either flooding the floor or emptying the tank. If it is fitted the wrong way around, no air will reach the tank, while water may enter the pump.

DIAPHRAGM PUMP

USING AN AIR STONE

Air stones have several uses in aquariums. A long air stone can be employed to produce a stream of small bubbles as a decorative feature. An air stone may also be used to power an undergravel or small internal box filter, or in a protein skimmer on a marine tank. Air stones are available in a variety of shapes, and their porosity determines the size of the bubbles created: coarse-grained air stones yield larger bubbles than fine-textured wooden ones. Air stones do deteriorate with time, so remember to replace them regularly.

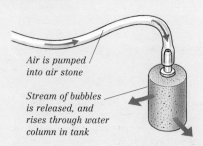

Air is pumped into air stone

Stream of bubbles is released, and rises through water column in tank

HEATERS AND COOLERS

EARLY HEATERS AND thermostats were encased in glass tubes, sealed with a rubber stopper; these units were fragile, and easily broken by large fish. By the mid-1970s, government regulations led to dramatic improvements in the robustness and safety of heaters and thermostats. With continued development, today's equipment is more reliable, more accurate, and safer than ever before.

HEATERS AND THERMOSTATS

A small heater is adequate for small volumes of water; a large tank requires a large heater or, preferably, two smaller-wattage units. This has a safety advantage: should one heater become stuck while switched either off or on, the other will correspondingly hold the temperature within acceptable limits, or shut off so that the other unit does not overheat the aquarium.

Thermostats are often operated by a bi-metallic strip that reacts to temperature and opens or closes to regulate electricity flow to the heater. Submersible units feature a temperature dial; modern external thermostats have tamper-proof safety dials. The latest thermostats use microchip technology and are worth the added expense for their superior accuracy and reliability. A small sensor, either placed in the water or fixed to the outside of the aquarium glass, relays the water temperature to an external thermostat, which then switches the heater on or off as required. Some models also have a built-in temperature display. Combined heater/thermostat units are also available.

Undertank heating mats are controlled by a separate thermostat. They are not submersible, and should be placed underneath the aquarium. A significant inconvenience when using heating mats is that if one should fail, then the whole tank must be dismantled to replace it.

THERMOMETERS

Thermometers are essential in regulating aquarium temperature. Since they are inexpensive, it is worth investing in two so that you can cross-reference them to double-check readings. Glass alcohol thermometers are popular, reasonably accurate, and quick to react, and the red or blue fluid they contain makes them easy to read. Alternatively, there are thin plastic strips that can be attached to the outside of the tank. Each section responds to a different temperature. The strips will quickly alert you to any problems, but position them with care, since direct sunlight can cause a false reading. Accurate, battery-powered LCD thermometers may also be purchased.

THERMOMETERS: EXTERNAL (NEAR RIGHT) AND INTERNAL (FAR RIGHT)

COOLERS

Just as we need to warm up water for tropical fish, so we may have to cool water for coldwater fish, especially marine species. This is particularly relevant in the summer months, when temperatures in the aquarium can exceed those that the fish would encounter in the wild. Some aquarists construct their own refrigeration systems, but there are custom-built units available that are fully controllable.

LIGHTING

LIGHT RAYS DO NOT EASILY penetrate water; the deeper the tank, the more intense the light source required to illuminate the bottom. If you merely wish to view your fish, a single fluorescent tube will suffice. If you also want to grow plants with any degree of success, or to keep marine invertebrates, some further understanding of light is required.

Visible light forms only a small part of electromagnetic radiation which, in simple terms, consists of cosmic rays at the short-wave end of the scale and radio waves at the long-wave end. The colors of the visible spectrum combine to form white light. Plants utilize the blue and orange-red range of the spectrum, while invertebrates require the blue to violet range to thrive; fluorescent tubes covering the appropriate ranges should be installed.

When keeping fish, invertebrates, or plants native to tropical regions, where a day contains 12 hours of light and 12 of darkness, the aquarist must simulate that environment by leaving a single light on for 12 hours a day, or by sequencing several fluorescent tubes using time switches to come on and off to mimic dawn and dusk.

FLUORESCENT LIGHTING

Fluorescent lighting is probably the easiest, most efficient, and most uniform method of illuminating an aquarium. Fluorescent lights are available in a range of colors, which the aquarist can combine to achieve the desired spectral coverage for the organisms in a tank. Several types of full-spectrum white lights are available, but none adequately simulates daylight. They are more expensive than standard tubes and need replacing after about 6–8 months, although they may still appear to work efficiently. Standard tubes should also be routinely changed every 12–18 months.

Most tanks are supplied with an integral hood, allowing the use of one or more fluorescent tubes. Before purchasing your aquarium, check that you will be able to fit the required amount of lighting into the hood and that it can be accessed easily for maintenance.

SPOTLIGHTS

Spotlights can be used to create an alternative look, placing emphasis on a particular section of the aquarium and highlighting water movement. These are not housed in a hood, but suspended above the tank. If the lights are fairly close to the water surface, a cover glass is needed to prevent water from splashing onto them. Spotlights are extremely useful for illuminating deep tanks. Always ensure that tank spotlights are positioned so they do not shine into people's eyes.

Mercury vapor lamps may use bulbs either with or without a built-in reflector; most aquarists prefer the latter. The efficient life of the bulb is short, and it should be replaced every six months. Metal halide lamps provide a much more intense light and are highly valued for use with invertebrate aquariums. They are costly and need replacing every 8–10 months, but the expense is worthwhile.

TUNGSTEN LAMPS

Tungsten lamps are not ideal for aquarium use. Although economical to buy and easy to install, they run hot and have a short life in the confines of a tank hood. Condensation can easily render the fittings hazardous, and the spectrum of light emitted is not well suited to plant growth.

CONDENSATION TRAYS

Condensation trays prevent water from evaporating and condensing onto light fittings. They may be plastic or, more usually, glass. Anything positioned between the light source and the water will reduce the amount of light reaching the water. Be sure to keep condensation trays scrupulously clean, removing any salt and algal build-up regularly.

In order to cover a more complete portion of the visible spectrum, and thus to sustain a wider variety of life forms, different types of tank lighting may be combined. This can result in some very dramatic effects, particularly in heavily planted freshwater aquariums and in tropical marine setups featuring invertebrates.

SUBSTRATES

A SUBSTRATE IS VITAL to make fish feel secure, to serve as a bedding material for plants and other decor items, and to provide a home for essential tank bacteria. All substrates must be thoroughly washed in hot, but not soapy, water before use to remove dirt and debris. Pick out any small pieces of metal from substrates for marine or brackish-water aquariums; these particles can react with salt water to produce toxins.

GRAVEL

Gravel is the most commonly used freshwater aquarium substrate. It comes in various grit sizes, and the stones may be rounded, or angular and sharp. Large, sharp-edged grains are not suitable for species that sift the substrate when feeding or that dig habitually; rough stones may also cut or scratch bottom-dwelling fish. With coarse-grade gravel, uneaten food can become trapped in the gaps between stones, where it may rot, polluting the tank. Softwater aquariums require lime-free gravel; your dealer can advise you. To test gravel for lime content, add some

STANDARD AQUARIUM GRAVEL

vinegar to a small sample. If the gravel fizzes (as the acid reacts with calcium), it contains lime. Gravel is available in a number of colors. Black can make a very attractive aquarium, but other shades often look unnatural. Dark colors are ideal for species from shady habitats, while light colors can make fish appear washed out and may cause them to behave timidly.

FINE GRAVEL

RED GRAVEL

FILTRATION SAND

Sand is a good alternative substrate for freshwater tanks. Types that compact, such as builder's sand, are unsuitable; use filtration sand, which is inert (having no effect on the water) and non-compacting, with rounded grains that allow the free passage of water and plant roots. Its one drawback is that it is difficult to use to create terraces for fish that like gentle slopes and banked areas. Fine sand can clog easily, and is not ideal when using an undergravel filter.

CORAL SAND

Marine aquariums usually contain coral sand either as the sole substrate or as a top layer over dolomite gravel or crushed cockle shells. Be certain not to let the sand clog the filter or mix with the gravel if used as a top layer. Alternatively, calcareous (chalky or limey) gravels can serve as marine substrates, with or without coral sand, and also in small amounts as pH buffers in hard freshwater tanks, for which coral sand is particularly not recommended.

WATER

WATER MAY SEEM TO BE a very simple component of a tank setup. Yet, for aquatic organisms, the correct water quality is critical to life. Every species of fish has an optimum range of conditions for survival, and its metabolism depends on a variety of factors, including the water's degree of hardness, acidity/alkalinity, temperature, and level of oxygenation.

Water management is therefore just as vital as understanding the operation of any item of aquarium equipment in providing and maintaining a healthy environment for your fish. The chemistry of water can be altered readily, and it is easily contaminated by airborne and waterborne agents; unfortunately, this pollution may not be evident until it is life-threatening.

FRESHWATER AQUARIUMS

Except for the initial fill, never add water to an aquarium direct from the tap. Tapwater can contain a number of toxins, including chlorine and fluoride.

Before transferring water to your tank, let it stand for about 12 hours to allow the chemicals to dissipate. To accelerate the process, place a finger over the tap outlet, forcing the water to jet into a bucket. The bubbles in the jetstream help to release the gases in the water; expelled chlorine has a particularly pungent smell. After the bucket is full, an air stone may be applied to agitate the water further. With this method, the water should be usable within an hour or two. There are also convenient commercially prepared solutions that can be added to water to make it usable more quickly.

For all aquariums, water added during a partial water change should be similar in chemical content (pH and hardness) and temperature (within 3.5°F/2°C) to the remainder of the tank water. Soluble additives can help you to adjust the water quality to match tank conditions.

MARINE & BRACKISH-WATER AQUARIUMS

Marine and brackish-water aquarists must modify tapwater to render it saline. Use only proprietary marine salt, never table or cooking salts. For marine fish, mix the required amount of salt, following the manufacturer's instructions, with water in a plastic bucket to achieve a specific gravity (SG) of between 1.023 and 1.027 (fresh water has a SG of 1.000). This range, if maintained, will suffice for most species and some of the hardier invertebrates (others require somewhat different conditions). For brackish-water fish, mix salt to no more than half the strength suggested for marine aquariums, to reach a specific gravity of 1.002–1.007. This level need not be kept constant, since these species in nature often inhabit areas subject to tidal flow, with accompanying variations in salinity throughout the day.

For initial filling of the tank, the salt must be at least partially dissolved; during partial water changes, first check the aquarium salinity using a hydrometer, and make sure the salt is completely dissolved so that the correct tank SG is achieved almost immediately. When evaporation occurs, only pure water is lost; all salts remain in the aquarium. Therefore, check the salinity before topping up the tank with more salt water. If evaporation has been excessive, as in midsummer, refilling the aquarium with fresh water will safeguard against increasing the SG.

Decor and Accessories

ALL ITEMS SELECTED to furnish a tank should be non-toxic, have no adverse effect on water chemistry, and suit the fish's natural requirements. Retiring species must be given seclusion in the form of rocky caves or woodwork, while constant swimmers need plenty of open space. Beyond such essential considerations, decor choice is a matter of personal taste. Although many hobbyists prefer a natural look, others opt for a variety of novelty ornaments, including models of deep-sea divers and sunken galleons!

Rocks

Rocks are readily available at aquarium shops. Do not collect your own unless you have a firm knowledge of geology; some rocks can leach toxins or adversely affect water chemistry. Marble, for instance, contains arsenic, while limestone will make water hard and alkaline. Rocks supplied by your dealer will be inert for aquarium use, but should always be scrubbed clean first under running tapwater.

Select rocks of similar color and texture, and for a natural look align any stratification lines when placing them. Do not pile successive layers of rock too high without cementing them together with silicone sealant. A fish can easily undermine a low-level rock,

collapsing the entire structure.

Lightweight, highly porous tufa rock is widely used in marine aquariums, but is equally suitable for hard freshwater tanks. Ocean rock, which also hardens water, is much heavier and displaces more water. In freshwater or brackish-water aquariums, a small area of rounded pebbles laid on the substrate makes an attractive feature.

TUFA ROCK

PEBBLES

Wood

Wood is suitable only for freshwater and brackish-water tanks, and is sold in three main forms: bogwood, vine root, and curio wood. Bogwood is largely the remnants of dead tree roots that have remained either submerged or covered in moist earth for a number of years. It leaches tannins into the water, which will acquire a brownish tinge, but this usually does not affect fish (especially species that prefer soft, acidic water). Nevertheless, soak bogwood or curio wood, a similar trade item, in regularly replaced water for two weeks to release excess tannin; agitation with an airstone will quicken this process. Scrub wood before use. Vine root is a dried material often sold by florists. It does not leach tannins to the same degree, but should also be soaked and scrubbed; once waterlogged, woods sink more readily to the tank bottom.

BOGWOOD

CURIO WOOD

CORALS AND SHELLS

Many attractive dead corals are available, but these are suitable only for marine aquariums, since they will harden fresh water and increase pH. Some also have sharp edges and can lacerate the skin of delicate fish. Since dead corals are the skeletal remains of once-living creatures, they should be boiled for an hour or two before being added to the tank to avoid polluting the water. Alternatively, choose artificial corals, which help conserve the environment and look remarkably lifelike once they have acquired a cover of algae.

Shells may be provided for fish that in nature use these items for shelter. Make sure the fish cannot be trapped inside the shells, which should be boiled clean first.

ARTIFICIAL ALTERNATIVES

At one time, plastic plants were quite unappealing, but today they are often indistinguishable from the real thing. They are particularly useful when keeping fish that dig up or eat vegetation. Replicas of marine algae such as *Caulerpa* spp. are a good alternative to the real plants, which can be difficult to cultivate in an aquarium.

Artificial wood, rock, and coral are also available, made of plastic or denser materials. Although the range of shapes and colors is limited, these products are totally inert, and need not be extensively scrubbed, soaked, or boiled. Unlike items such as "living rock," encrusted with minute mollusks or crustaceans, there is also no risk of introducing unwanted organisms.

TANK BACKGROUNDS

Aquarium fish behave most confidently and naturally if given the secure shelter of a tank background. The simplest way to provide this is to paint the outer face of the rear glass black; this gives an impression of depth to the finished tank, and hides any wall covering behind. Plastic sheet backgrounds bearing a variety of images, such as a coral reef, are also available; lightly glued at the edges to the outside of the tank, these can be changed with ease.

Internal backgrounds such as plastic panels, often representing terraced rocks, can be fitted to the inside rear tank face. Fix the panel to the glass before filling the tank, to avoid trapping any fish behind it.

ADDITIONAL MAINTENANCE EQUIPMENT

ESSENTIAL

- Bucket
- Siphon tube: ideally about ½ in (10-15 mm) bore and approximately 7 ft (2 m) long
- Nets: sized to suit your fish; a minimum of two is recommended to help catch elusive fish
- Thermometer: simple stick-on varieties that change color with temperature are a good indicator, but nothing can beat an accurate alcohol or electronic thermometer; keep a spare alcohol type in case of breakage
- Hydrometer: for marine and brackish-water installations only, to measure salinity
- Replacement filter medium (if using filtration that requires it)
- Test kits: to measure a wide variety of water chemistry conditions; use these to analyze the water if problems are suspected

ADVISABLE

- Reference books on fish: for information on identification, keeping, and breeding
- Spare parts: seals for filters, bearings for water pumps, and diaphragms for air pumps are inexpensive and useful to have on hand; stock up on replacement parts periodically
- Spare heater/thermostat: can be invaluable if a unit fails at an inconvenient moment
- Spare fuses for plug tops: these too can fail
- Fish medications: stock only a couple of the most commonly required remedies; medications have a limited shelf life, and are best bought when needed
- Algae scraper
- Tolerant partner/family members: you will inevitably spill a little water on the carpet, and the smell when servicing a filter can be pungent!

SETTING UP YOUR AQUARIUM

Installing an aquarium is not a simple, quick job, but you can make the task much easier with good planning and preparation. Although there is a general sequence to follow, it is useful to compile your own personalized checklist; you can then consult this while you work. Allow plenty of time – a tank that has been set up incorrectly will not operate effectively, if at all. As you add each component, follow the manufacturers' instructions to the letter. For safety, have a qualified professional connect any electrical items. To help guide you, this section includes basic installation procedures along with some recommended freshwater, brackish-water, and marine setups.

◁ REEF FISH SUCH AS THESE FIREFISH (*NEMATELEOTRIS MAGNIFICA*) ADAPT WELL TO AQUARIUM CONDITIONS

PREPARING FOR INSTALLATION

IT PAYS TO PLAN carefully at every stage of setting up an aquarium. The first step, before buying any equipment, is to decide on the size of the tank and where it is to be sited, ensuring that the floor will support the weight of the final product. Finish any home decorating beforehand, since even a small installed aquarium is extremely heavy and cannot be moved without being completely dismantled. Locate the tank in a place that is quiet and unobtrusive, yet easily accessible for maintenance and water supply. Avoid a position in direct sunlight, since this can increase algal growth and hamper temperature control.

Once you have determined the basic tank layout and collected all necessary items, complete any preliminary jobs that must be done in advance or which will save time during installation.

TOOLS AND EQUIPMENT CHECKLIST

- Tank ✓
- Tank stand ✓
- Hood (if not integrated)
- Baseboard (if used) ✓
- Polystyrene tiles
- Background
- Substrate (sand or gravel)
- Undergravel filter plate (if used)
- Rocks and/or wood
- Corals and/or shells (if used, corals for marine tanks only; shells for marine or hardwater freshwater tanks only)
- Filtration system ✓
- Heater/thermostat(s) (if used) ✓
- Lighting system
- Air pump, air line, air stone(s), and non-return valve (all if used)
- Thermometer ✓
- Glass cover or condensation tray
- Multi-plug adaptor (if used)
- Spirit level (or water-filled air line)

- Wire cutters/strippers
- Pliers ✓
- Screwdriver(s) ✓
- Scissors ✓
- Sharp knife ✓
- Adhesive tape ✓
- Insulation tape ✓
- Electrical plugs ✓
- Cable ties/clips
- Bucket ✓
- Colander
- Silicone sealant
- Scrub brush or nail brush ✓
- Plastic sheets
- Towel ✓
- Siphon tube
- Rubber bands, fishing line, and drill for constructing decorations (if used) ✓
- Marine salt (for brackish-water or marine tanks)
- Hydrometer (for brackish-water or marine tanks)

Planning Your Tank Design

Plan the layout of your aquarium on paper first, deciding where the tank equipment, plants, and decor (including rocks, wood, corals, or shells) will be placed. Prior to any purchase, it is worth asking your dealer if you can arrange items in a similarly sized empty tank to gauge the overall effect and fit. Site the heater/thermostat(s) so it is accessible for maintenance, yet hidden from view. It should also be located where the water is not still, to prevent temperature gradients. If necessary, place an air stone near the heater for improved circulation throughout the tank. Position filter pipes and spray bars where they will cause minimal damage to delicate plants while still allowing free passage of water to the intake pipe and from the outflow (if using a spray bar). If the filter features an intake tube (as do most external units), when setting up your tank ensure that the open tube end lies just above the substrate and that the strainer basket provided is fitted, so that fish are not sucked into the filter.

Pre-installation Tasks

If you are using an adhesive plastic tank background, attach it to the external rear face of the aquarium. Paper backgrounds should not be fixed until the tank has been positioned; otherwise, they may be torn. Alternatively, paint the rear tank face black (or other color as desired) and allow it to dry thoroughly. Cork tiles can also be used as a background; attach these with silicone, allowing 24 hours for the adhesive to dry.

If you have somewhere to store your gravel or sand, wash this beforehand. New substrate is often very dirty, and should be cleaned under running water until it drains clear; take care not to block sinks and drains with spills. Rinse the substrate in a kitchen colander, or stir small amounts in a bucket to remove dirt and debris. Use your hands or a wooden spoon; like all other aquarium equipment, this should be reserved exclusively for fishkeeping. If you have no storage space, you will need to clean the substrate little by little on the day of installation, tipping each washed portion directly into the aquarium. Bear in mind that this is a time-consuming job.

Scrub the rocks and/or wood with a brush, using hot, but not soapy, water. If this is done in advance, then a quick rinse will suffice on the day of installation. To prevent wood from floating, it should be soaked for about two weeks in regularly replaced water. This also helps to remove tannins from the wood, which would otherwise give the tank water a harmless but unattractive brown tinge, like weak tea.

You may wish to glue rocks or pieces of dead or imitation coral together to make a terrace, cave, or stacked pile, or to anchor wood or cork bark to a slate base. For stable construction, choose pieces with flat undersides as foundations. Use a silicone sealant, and secure items with tape or rubber bands while drying. Let each join dry before adding further sections, and when finished allow at least 24 hours for the silicone to cure. If you are planning to attach plants such as Java Fern to pieces of wood, drill small holes in the wood so that fishing line can be passed through these later when securing the plants. Assemble your internal box or external power filter, and fill it with media. As with all aquarium equipment, read the manufacturer's instructions carefully; familiarity with a unit's features and construction makes subsequent maintenance tasks much easier.

Although it is possible to install an aquarium singlehandedly, enlist someone to help you lift and position the tank. It is particularly reassuring to have an experienced assistant; your dealer may be able to put you in contact with your local aquatic society, whose members are usually willing to share their knowledge and expertise. On the day of installation, clear the area in which you will be working, and cover carpets and nearby furniture with plastic sheets to protect them from water or gravel spills. Keep young children and pets well out of the way. Above all, allow yourself plenty of time.

FRESHWATER TANK SETUP

BEFORE BEGINNING to install your aquarium, give yourself enough space to work comfortably and make sure that you have all the items you will need. Review the basic sequence of events with your assistant, and proceed slowly and carefully; it is much better to get things right the first time than to have to go back and fix an incorrect setup.

INSTALLING EQUIPMENT AND DECOR

1 ▷ Position the tank stand and ensure that it is level and stable. Place the base board and polystyrene tiles on the stand, then put the tank on top; if your tank is large, you may need help to lift it. Check that the tank is level and the stand does not wobble. Wash out the tank using clean, warm water; do not use detergent of any kind. Allow it to dry thoroughly. If using an undergravel filter plate, fit this with an uplift tube and place it in the base of the tank.

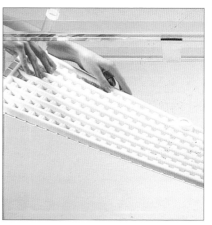

2 ▽ Connect the air line to the uplift tube. For a more efficient airlift (but one requiring more air pressure from the pump), attach an air stone to the air line and position it near the base of the uplift tube. Or, in place of the air line, fit a power head to the end of the tube; trim the tube with a sharp knife if it will not fit under the tank hood.

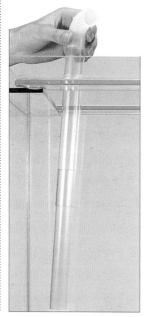

3 Add a small amount of washed substrate in which to bed the hard decor; a 1 in (2.5 cm) layer is sufficient. Smooth the gravel evenly across the base of the tank. If keeping bottom-dwelling fish or other species that dig in the substrate, it is often safer to add the gravel after positioning hard decor items. Large rocks are less likely to be undermined if placed directly on the undergravel filter plate or tank bottom. Lighter rocks, flowerpots, or wood need not be bedded on the tank bottom, and can simply be placed on the surface after the rest of the substrate has been added, with additional gravel filled in around them if needed.

4 ▷ Position the rockwork, bedding all items firmly. If not using pre-constructed arrangements that have been glued together with silicone sealant, choose flat-bottomed rocks as foundations for stacked structures, and ensure that added pieces rest securely. Never lean rocks against the glass, and make sure piles cannot be knocked over. Remember to leave space for tank equipment. Taking care not to dislodge the pile, fill in around it with additional substrate, to a total depth of about 1½ in (4 cm). Then smooth the surface, sloping it gently upwards from front to back.

5 ◁ Add wood if desired. Large pieces can be strategically placed to conceal equipment such as heater cables. Flowerpots, whole or broken, can also be employed as decor (though not in softwater tanks). They are not strong enough to support rocks, but can be used to elevate pieces of wood or in the center of, but not supporting, rocky caves. Make sure that any cave entrances are clear. Unless waterlogged by pre-soaking, wood may float and should be wedged down temporarily with rocks, tied to heavy items with fishing line, or weighted with a piece of slate pre-glued to the underside (using silicone sealant) and then buried in the substrate.

6 Attach the heater/thermostat(s) to the rear or side tank glass, using the suction devices provided. Position these at an angle, rather than vertically, for best heat distribution. Your unit(s) may be fully submersible or its top may need to be above the water level. If you are using plastic plants, these may be added now.

7 ▷ Fill the tank with water; this may come direct from the tap, since it will mature in the tank before fish are added. To avoid disturbing the gravel, carefully pour the water onto a rock or a saucer placed on the substrate. Or, for less disruption, siphon the water into the tank from a bucket.

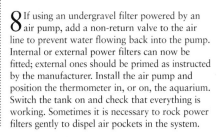

8 If using an undergravel filter powered by an air pump, add a non-return valve to the air line to prevent water flowing back into the pump. Internal or external power filters can now be fitted; external ones should be primed as instructed by the manufacturer. Install the air pump and position the thermometer in, or on, the aquarium. Switch the tank on and check that everything is working. Sometimes it is necessary to rock power filters gently to dispel air pockets in the system.

9 Wait 2–3 days before purchasing and adding your plants, to allow the water temperature to stabilize; sudden immersion in cold water can traumatize tropical vegetation. Use this period to ensure that all your equipment is operating correctly and that the heater/thermostat(s) is heating the water to the desired temperature. It is much easier to change faulty items now rather than later, when plants may be disrupted or damaged.

ADDING PLANTS

1 After a few days have elapsed, you will be ready to add plants. Siphon out some water into a bucket (and retain it) so that you can work in the aquarium without spilling water over the sides (or getting your sleeves wet!). If purchased in bunches, separate cuttings and plant these individually to avoid damaging the delicate stems. Consulting your original tank design plan, add one group of plants at a time, and keep those you are not working with warm and damp. For a natural look, and to create adequate refuges for your fish, plant each species together in small clusters or thickets. Contrast colors, textures, and leaf shapes throughout the tank to lend added appeal.

2 Plant the rear and sides first, building a background of relatively tall vegetation. Place smaller plants towards the front and position one or two main feature specimens as focal points in the tank. Bury only the roots of the plants, leaving the crowns just above the surface. To add height, carefully attach suitable plants to decor items using fishing line, ensuring that the line does not cut into the plant's rhizome. As you work, take care not to dislodge any rocks, wood, or equipment.

3 When you have finished and are satisfied with the result, put the reserved water back in the tank. Make sure that the water is being heated to the right temperature and turn on the lighting. Initially, the completed arrangement may seem cluttered, but over the next day the plants will straighten, and within a few more days their roots should start to take hold in the substrate. Although the water is likely to look rather murky directly after planting, the filter will soon clear it.

COMPLETING THE INSTALLATION

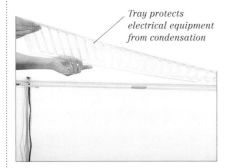

Tray protects electrical equipment from condensation

1 Place a condensation tray (or cover glass) over the top of the tank. Fit the hood with clips to hold the fluorescent light tube. Screw the lighting control unit to the outside of the hood, or fit it in the compartment provided (if any). Thread the two tube leads through the ready-made (or purpose-cut) holes in the hood, and fit the damp-proof caps to the ends of the tube. Gently press the tube in place. Spotlights, if used, must be wall- or ceiling-mounted, a task for an electrician. If you are uncertain about wiring any of your equipment, seek professional advice; an error could kill you!

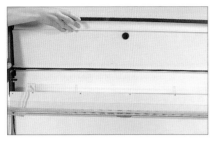

2 Place the hood on the tank. If using a multi-plug adapter, connect the heater/thermostat(s), lighting unit, air pump, and filtration system. It is wiser, however, to have three separate power sources: one for the heating system, one for the filtration and air pump, and one for the lighting. Then, if one fuse blows, only one system will fail, whereas with a single adapter, both heating and filtration will be lost. Neatly secure all excess lengths of cable with cable ties or tape; if left trailing loosely, they are likely to cause accidents.

INTRODUCING FISH

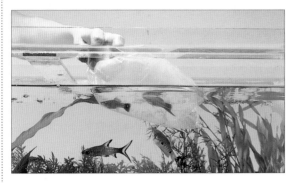

1 Initially, do not remove your new fish from the plastic bag used to transport them. Float this in the aquarium for about an hour, to allow the water temperature inside the bag to equalize with that in the tank. During this period the fish will come to no harm if the bag is left closed. However, if you prefer to open the bag, roll the top back and anchor it to the side of the tank with a clothes peg.

2 After an hour, release the fish. It is best not to introduce any water from the plastic bag to the aquarium, to prevent potential contamination. Many fishkeepers release new specimens in a bucket first, then net them and place them in the tank. Others use a small net in the bag, but this can be awkward and must be done carefully to avoid damaging the fish. Although some aquarists advocate mixing a small amount of tank water with that in the bag to help acclimate the fish, this is pointless, since it takes several hours for a fish to adjust to any drastic change in water chemistry.

TROPICAL FRESHWATER TANK

The aquarium below is a recommended setup for a general, planted, tropical freshwater community tank suitable for a novice. It comprises relatively small fish, some of which will breed readily. An alternative selection is also suggested, with fewer, medium-sized, species accommodated in the tank. Tank conditions for both choices are: temperature 72–75°F (22–24°C); pH 7.0–7.5; dH 10–12°.

If, like many beginning aquarists, you hanker after a particular fish, a third option gives you the opportunity to try your hand with either Oscars or piranhas. However, before buying several attractive young specimens, remember that these will quickly outgrow your tank and require rehousing.

Bear in mind that you will also need a far more efficient filtration system than that installed for general setups, to cope with the vast amount of waste these fish produce. Piranhas can be kept with large plants such as Amazon Swords (*Echinodorus* spp.), *Sagittaria platyphylla*, or Java Fern attached to rocks. Artificial plants, or none at all, are best in tanks with Oscars, which love digging and uprooting things. Java Fern tied to rocks may resist their attentions.

If you opt to make your own selection of fish for a freshwater community tank, check their compatibility and dietary and water requirements before you buy, and remember that schooling species must be kept in groups.

EQUIPMENT, DECOR, AND STOCK

- Equipment: 36 x 12 x 12 in (100 x 30 x 30 cm) tank, glass cover or condensation tray (if not integrated), heater/thermostat(s), undergravel filter, air pump, air line, fluorescent light(s)
- Substrate: standard aquarium gravel
- Rocks: granite or similar rock
- Plants: choose from *Bacopa caroliniana*, *Cabomba caroliniana*, *Cryptocoryne affinis*, *Echinodorus* spp., *Hygrophilia polysperma*, *Ludwigia repens*, and *Vallisneria spiralis*
- Pair x *Ancistrus* spp. *(page 40)*
- 6 x *Barbus titteya (page 64)*
- 6 x *Brachydanio rerio (page 66)*
- 2 x *Corydoras paleatus (page 39)*
- 2 x *Crossocheilus siamensis (page 70)*
- 2 pairs x *Poecilia reticulata (page 80)*
- Pair x *Trichogaster leeri (page 37)*
- Pair x *Xiphophorus helleri (page 82)*
- 4 x *Xiphophorus maculatus (page 83)*

ALTERNATIVE FISH SELECTIONS

Pair x *Ancistrus* spp. *(page 40)*

Pair x *Aplocheilus lineatus (page 77)*

4 x *Corydoras barbatus (page 39)*

Pair x *Melanotaenia boesemani (page 85)*

6 x *Phenacogrammus interruptus (page 45)*

Pair x *Trichogaster trichopterus (page 36)*

Or, for a 48 x 15 x 15 in (120 x 40 x 40 cm) species tank (juvenile specimens only):

2 x *Astronotus ocellatus (page 56)* or

3–4 x *Serrasalmus nattereri (page 50)*

SOFTWATER TANK

When setting up a softwater aquarium, it is essential to use lime-free sand, gravel, or pebbles – make sure that you can obtain these. Although water softeners are available to achieve the correct water chemistry, this will be in vain if the substrate or pebbles then revert the water to its previous, or a higher, hardness. Remember, if you need to make drastic alterations to the parameters of your water supply, you will have to repeat this every time you carry out a water change.

The tank below features a variety of fish, but you can create an equally impressive display using just three species, as in the suggested alternative selection. If you intend to keep deep-bodied Discus and/or Angels,

then a minimum tank depth of 18 in (50 cm) is preferable, with the aquarium sited in a particularly quiet spot. For these species, you need not plant the tank fully but have just a few large specimen plants, such as Amazon Sword, with perhaps some Java Fern attached to wood. For a general community aquarium, provide some areas of open substrate, plenty of plant cover, and a few caves fashioned from wood or half coconut shells; earthenware flowerpots are not suitable for softwater tanks. You may add one or two flat stones to serve as potential spawning sites.

Maintain the following tank conditions for both community selections: temperature 72–75°F (22–24°C); pH 6.0–6.4; dH 5–6°.

Equipment, Decor, and Stock

• Equipment: 36 x 12 x 12 in (100 x 30 x 30 cm) tank, glass cover or condensation tray (if not integrated), heater/thermostat(s), external power filter with spray bar return, fluorescent light(s)
• Substrate: filtration sand
• Wood: bogwood and/or vine root
• Plants: choose from *Barclaya longifolia*, *Cryptocoryne balansae*, *Echinodorus paniculatus*, *Echinodorus tenellus*, *Limnophilia aquatica*, *Ludwigia repens*, *Nymphaea stellata*, *Synnema triflorum*, and *Vesicularia dubyana*
• 4 x *Botia sidthimunki (page 74)*
• 6 x *Moenkhausia pittieri (page 47)*
• 6 x *Nannostomus beckfordi (page 49)*
• 4 x *Otocinclus affinis (page 41)*
• Pair x *Papiliochromis ramirezi (page 55)*
• 10 x *Paracheirodon axelrodi (page 47)*

ALTERNATIVE FISH SELECTIONS

10 x *Carnegiella strigata (page 48)*

Pair x *Crenicara filamentosa (page 54)*

25 x *Paracheirodon axelrodi (page 47)*

Or, for a 36 x 18 x 18 in (100 x 50 x 50 cm) species tank:

4 x *Pterophyllum scalare (page 57)* or

4 x *Symphysodon* spp. *(page 57)*

(or keep a pair of each species; if either pair breeds, it may become necessary to remove the other)

RIFT LAKE TANK

With African Rift Lake cichlids, it is important to avoid mixing species that originate from different lakes. Not only do Lake Malawi and Lake Tanganyikan fish have incompatible behavior patterns, they also require different water conditions, stocking levels, and tank layouts.

If your choice is Lake Malawi cichlids, establish rockwork that reaches nearly to the water surface, providing numerous crevices and caves as hiding places and areas to defend. Seat the rocks securely to prevent the fish from undermining them by digging, and position equipment so that access for maintenance can be gained by removing only one or two rocks. Plants are not essential.

Lake Tanganyikan cichlids require more swimming space, and will benefit from an area of open substrate in the center of the aquarium with rock piles at either end, plus a few thickets of plants such as *Vallisneria* spp. or *Cryptocoryne* spp. Scatter a few small shells on the substrate for the shell-dwelling *Neolamprologus brevis* to use as homes and spawning sites.

Both types of cichlid require very clear, well-filtered, highly oxygenated water at a temperature of 74–79°F (24–26°C). For Lake Malawi fish, maintain pH at 7.5–8.0 and dH at 8–10°. Species from Lake Tanganyika require conditions that are slightly more hard and alkaline (pH 8.0–8.5; dH 15–20°).

EQUIPMENT, DECOR, AND STOCK

• Equipment: 36 x 15 x 15 in (100 x 40 x 40 cm) tank, glass cover or condensation tray (if not integrated), heater/thermostat(s), undergravel filter with uplift tube(s) and power head(s), fluorescent light(s)
• Substrate: standard aquarium gravel
• Rocks: granite or similar rock as recommended, piled at back of tank nearly to top (a small amount of tufa rock may be added as a pH buffer)
• Plants: none
• 3 x *Labeotropheus trewavasae (page 60)*
• 3 x *Labidochromis caeruleus (page 60)*
• 3 x *Melanochromis johanni (page 61)*
• 3 x *Pseudotropheus estherae (page 61)*
• 3 x *Pseudotropheus livingstonii (page 61)*
• 3 x *Pseudotropheus zebra (page 61)*
(Ideally, each trio should comprise two females and one male, to reduce aggressive behavior by the male during spawning)

ALTERNATIVE FISH SELECTION
(LAKE TANGANYIKAN CICHLIDS)

4 x *Julidochromis dickfeldi (page 58)*

2 pairs x *Neolamprologus brevis (page 59)*

4 x *Neolamprologus leleupi (page 59)*

Include at least one small snail shell as a dwelling/spawning site for each pair of *Neolamprologus brevis* (use shells of the Lake Tanganyikan *Neothauma* snail, or of edible snails obtained from a restaurant), and provide plant cover (*Vallisneria* spp. or *Cryptocoryne* spp.).

COLDWATER TANK

The most popular coldwater fish, the Goldfish, can be kept in a planted aquarium, but it is often practical to opt for artificial plants, which will not be dug up or eaten. Goldfish are notoriously mucky fish, and require good filtration to deal with the copious waste they produce and the debris they stir up from digging in the substrate. For the other coldwater species recommended here, it is advisable to provide plants for cover and, in some cases, to serve as spawning sites.

Many aquarists keep either single-tailed or twin-tailed goldfish, since single-tailed types can become too large and boisterous to mix with the "fancy" varieties. While the fish shown below and those in alternative selection 3 will be quite happy in a totally unheated tank, with a temperature range of 50–68°F (10–20°C), the fish in selections 1 and 2 do not prefer it below 59°F (15°C) and 64°F (18°C) respectively, and the aquarium may need to be heated during chilly winter months. Conversely, in hot weather the tank water will warm, reducing its oxygen content. To prevent distressing your fish, carry out a partial water change, cut back on feeding, and check that the filtration system is working efficiently. The species in selection 3 prefer a current of well-oxygenated water, which can be provided by a spray bar return from a power filter. For all four selections, maintain pH at 6.8–7.4 and dH at 8–10°.

EQUIPMENT, DECOR, AND STOCK

• Equipment: 36 x 12 x 12 in (100 x 30 x 30 cm) tank, glass cover or condensation tray (if not integrated), heater/thermostat (if required), undergravel filter, air pump, air line, fluorescent light(s)
• Substrate: standard aquarium gravel
• Rocks: granite or similar rock as recommended within your area (wood may be added if desired)
• Plants: Choose from *Ceratophyllum demersum* (floating or planted), *Egeria densa*, *Ludwigia repens*, *Vallisneria spiralis*, and *Vallisneria tortifolia*; artificial specimens may be used as an alternative
• 10 x 2 in (5 cm) common *Carassius auratus* or total of 10 x 2 in (5 cm) mixed Goldfish varieties (selected from Comet, Fantail, Moor, Oranda, Pearlscale, and Shubunkin *(pages 90–91)*

ALTERNATIVE FISH SELECTIONS

Selection 1:
4 x *Enneacanthus chaetodon (page 88)*

6 x *Notropis lutrensis (page 92)*

4 x *Rhodeus* spp. *(page 92)*

Selection 2:
10 x *Gambusia affinis (page 78)*

10 x *Tanichthys albonubes (page 67)*

Selection 3:
4 x *Cottus gobio (page 89)*

2 x *Gasterosteus aculeatus (page 93)*

4 x *Gymnocephalus cernuus (page 93)*

BRACKISH WATER TANK SETUP

SETTING UP A brackish water tank is an enjoyable challenge for the experienced aquarist. Since evaporation can be a problem in a partially filled aquarium such as the one below, designed to simulate a shoreline mangrove swamp, be sure to place the heater/thermostat well below the water level. Complete the installation with a cover glass or condensation tray, hood, and lighting.

INSTALLING EQUIPMENT AND DECOR

1 Cover the base of the tank with a 1½–2 in (4–5 cm) layer of washed filtration sand. Pot the plants to restrict their growth (half-pots are least conspicuous) and position them at the rear, where they can be concealed. Use palm shoots in place of mangroves if unavailable.

2 Add rocks and wood strategically to hide the plant pots. Fill in any gaps with pebbles or sand, to ensure stability and to eliminate crannies where debris can decay unnoticed. Include one or two large, flat-topped rocks as resting platforms for fish such as Mudskippers or *Anableps* spp.

3 ◁ To create the sandbank, pile the sand at one end, bolstering it with rocks and wood. Fill the tank with water of the correct salinity to just above the sandbank height. Add some twigs to protrude above the water, like roots in a swamp.

4 ▽ Fit the heater/thermostat and thermometer, ensuring that they are submerged, and install the external power filter. Switch the tank on and position the spray bar just above the water surface so it directs a gentle current along the length of the tank; a strong flow will disrupt the sandbank.

MARINE TANK SETUP

THIS BASIC MARINE design features tufa or ocean rock stacked to provide plenty of nooks, crannies, and terraces; place the rocks gently to avoid damaging the tank. As with a brackish water installation, ensure that you include no metallic items; these will corrode in saltwater, polluting the tank. Add a condensation tray or cover glass, hood, and lights to finish the set-up.

INSTALLING EQUIPMENT AND DECOR

1 Fit the aquarium with an undergravel filter plate, uplift tube, and power head (air line is not required). Cover the filter plate with 1 in (2.5 cm) of well-washed dolomite gravel. Spread the substrate evenly across the base of the tank before adding a gravel layer on top.

2 Cover the gravel with a 2 in (5 cm) layer of coral sand; make sure the sand has been pre-cleaned thoroughly, since any remaining dust will cloud the water. Distribute the sand in an even layer over the base gravel so that it will act efficiently as a filter bed.

3 ▷ When placing rocks in the tank, add the largest first and seat them securely in the substrate. Then carefully build up the rockwork, checking that all structures are stable. As you position the rocks, create a few caves as hiding places. These can be constructed in advance, gluing the pieces together with silicone sealant (leave for 24 hours to set).

4 ▽ The finished layout should allow swimming space for the fish, a free flow of water through the tank, and access to all equipment for maintenance. Fit the heater/thermostat(s), thermometer, air pump, and (if desired) a protein skimmer. Fill the tank with prepared saline water and switch the system on.

BRACKISH-WATER TANK

Brackish-water aquariums are perhaps the most trouble to manage, being neither completely marine nor freshwater, and with the specific gravity of the water often fluctuating. In a natural brackish-water environment, salt levels vary with the ebb and flow of the tides, so do not worry too much about keeping the salinity completely stable. Rather, ensure that any changes are gradual and that water quality is maintained. Aim at these optimum tank parameters: temperature 77–82°F (25–28°C); pH 7.6; dH 12–15°; SG 1.002–1.007. When preparing water, mix marine salt at half the recommended strength.

The fish featured in the tank below grow into large, active creatures and will eventually require rehousing in a larger tank. Those in the alternative selection, which includes sedentary bottom-dwellers and open-water species, will stay a manageable size and be content to remain in their original tank. Do not try mixing fish from the two selections; this is likely to produce a war zone, with the smaller fish coming off worst. Plants are beneficial, but choose them with care, ensuring that they can survive in brackish conditions. The species suggested are those most likely to withstand any nibbling. As with marine tanks, check that there are no metal objects in contact with or near the water, since these will corrode, releasing toxins. Monitor conditions regularly with a hydrometer.

EQUIPMENT, DECOR, AND STOCK

• Equipment: 36 x 12 x 12 in (100 x 30 x 30 cm) tank, glass cover or condensation tray (if not integrated), heater/thermostat, external power filter with spray bar return, fluorescent light(s)
• Substrate: standard aquarium gravel
• Wood: bogwood and/or vine root (rocks may be added if desired)
• Plants: Choose from *Ceratopteris thalictroides*, *Cryptocoryne ciliata*, *Microsorium pteropus* (attached to wood, this lends height to a plant arrangement; clumps may be purchased already established on wood), *Sagittaria platyphylla*, and *Sagittaria subulata*
• 2 or 3 x *Arius seemani* (page 95)
• 2 or 3 x *Monodactylus argenteus* (page 98)
• 2 or 3 x *Scatophagus argus* (page 99)
• 2 or 3 x *Toxotes jaculatrix* (page 101)

ALTERNATIVE FISH SELECTION

6 x *Brachygobius xanthozona* (page 96)
4 x *Chanda ranga* (page 96)
Pair x *Poecilia latipinna* (page 99)
2 x *Stigmatogobius sadanundio* (page 97)
6 x *Telmatherina ladigesi* (page 95)

TROPICAL MARINE TANK

With marine aquariums, it is especially important to observe the correct maturation period before introducing livestock. Time, patience, and plenty of research to ensure the compatibility of your fish are the keys to success with marines. All equipment must be suitable for use in salt water; items made of metal, such as hoods or heater clips, will contaminate the tank. Rockwork should be securely seated on the base glass and filled in with coral sand.

The novice marine aquarist should begin with a fish-only tank rather than mixing fish with invertebrates, since lighting is less critical, stocking levels are easier to establish, and diseases can be more easily treated. Close monitoring of conditions remains essential, however; marine species are sensitive to any build-up of toxins, such as nitrites or ammonia. Take particular care not to overfeed, so that uneaten food will not decompose and pollute the water. Regular tank maintenance, including partial water changes, will reduce the risk of this. Keep conditions at: temperature 75–79°F (24–26°C); pH 8.3–8.4; SG 1.023–1.027.

Do not attempt to stock your tank at levels higher than those recommended here; marine fish require far more space than freshwater species. The alternative selection listed includes larger, and therefore fewer, fish than are accommodated in the tank below.

Equipment, Decor, and Stock

- Equipment: 36 x 12 x 12 in (100 x 30 x 30 cm) tank, glass cover or condensation tray (if not integral), heater/thermostat(s), external power filter with spray bar return, fluorescent light(s)
- Substrate: coral sand
- Rocks: ocean rock or tufa rock (artificial corals may be added if desired)
- Plants: none (some algae may grow spontaneously in the tank)
- 2 x *Amphiprion clarkii (page 114)*
- 6 x *Chromis cyanea (page 117)*
- 1 x *Coris gaimard (page 134)*
- 2 x *Dascyllus aruanus (page 118)*
- 1 x *Labroides dimidiatus (page 135)*
- 2 x *Paracanthurus hepatus (page 131)*

ALTERNATIVE FISH SELECTION

4 x *Anthias squamipinnis (page 137)*
1 x *Calloplesiops altivelis (page 136)*
1 x *Chaetodon chrysurus (page 125)*
1 x *Gomphosus varius (page 135)*
1 x *Zebrasoma flavescens (page 131)*

REEF TANK

The keeping of marine invertebrates in a reef-type setup requires some degree of experience in caring for fish and managing water. It can often take several months to get everything running smoothly, so be prepared to wait; rushing the process frequently ends in disaster. Choose invertebrates with care; many have very specific needs regarding lighting levels, temperature, pH, and other factors, and are highly sensitive to any changes in their environment. Some also require quite specialized feeding.

Mixing fish and invertebrates can be fraught with compatibility problems, since some fish thrive on a diet of invertebrates. Fish diseases may be harder to cure, since invertebrates often react badly to treatments, and can even die. Do not be discouraged, though; if you have experience with freshwater fish or a fish-only marine tank, try cutting your teeth on anemones and clownfishes. With a bit of luck, you may actually manage to breed the fish, and be well on your way.

Monitor the aquarium carefully and carry out regular water changes and maintenance. Keep conditions at: temperature 75–79°F (24–26°C); pH 8.3–8.4; SG 1.023–1.024. After a few months, once the tank has settled and you are confident in maintaining your livestock, consider adding a further feature specimen, such as a dwarf angelfish or a Mandarinfish, to complete your reef display.

EQUIPMENT, DECOR, AND STOCK

• Equipment: 36 x 12 x 12 in (100 x 30 x 30 cm) tank, glass cover or condensation tray (if not integrated), heater/thermostat(s), undergravel filter with power head(s) and protein skimmer, fluorescent lights (2–3, to cover spectrum)
• Substrate: coral sand
• Rocks: ocean rock or tufa rock (artificial corals may be added if desired)
• Plants: algae *(Caulerpa sertularioides)*
• 6 x *Amphiprion ocellaris (page 115)*
• 1 x *Centropyge bispinosus (page 123)*
• 1 x *Fromia monilis (page 152)*
• 3 x *Heteractis malu (page 151)*
• 4–6 x *Lysmata amboinensis (page 152)*
• 1 x *Pseudocolochirus axiologus (page 153)*
• 1 x *Synchiropus splendidus (page 139)*

ALTERNATIVE FISH AND INVERTEBRATE SELECTION

2 x *Heteractis malu (page 151)*

4 x *Lysmata amboinensis (page 152)*

2 x *Opistognathus aurifrons (page 141)*

Pair x *Premnas biaculeatus (page 115)*

4 x *Sabellastarte* spp. *(page 150)*

4 x *Sphaeramia nematoptera (page 138)*

CARING
FOR
YOUR FISH

STOCKING AND RUNNING YOUR AQUARIUM

A healthy, well-balanced tank is easily recognizable. The water is clear and odorless, any plants have good color, and the fish are neither listless nor congregate at the surface, gasping for oxygen. This is your goal as an aquarist, but remember that it cannot be achieved overnight. Patience is essential, especially in the early stages: adding stock before a tank has stabilized may result in disaster. Once you have invested the time and effort to establish the right conditions, and taken care to introduce fish appropriately, maintenance is its own reward. A little regular attention will keep your fish contented and well, and the aquarium looking its best.

◁ TROPICAL FRESHWATER COMMUNITY TANK

PREPARING TO ADD LIVESTOCK

NOVICE AQUARISTS ARE often impatient to acquire their first fish. Introducing stock in haste, however, can cause a great deal of trouble, since a tank that has not stabilized may not support life. Wait until your aquarium is ready and you are certain that everything is functioning properly before adding your fish.

Livestock should be introduced slowly, to avoid straining the newly setup filtration system, which will still be establishing its colony of beneficial bacteria. Ensure that you stay within reasonable limits by calculating the correct stocking level for the size of your tank and the type of fish being kept.

TANK MATURATION

A newly installed aquarium cannot sustain livestock until it has an established nitrogen cycle. During the first nine to 10 days, the concentration of ammonia in the water may be lethal to any introduced fish. Thereafter, as ammonia levels diminish (virtually disappearing after 15 days), the development of toxic nitrites increases, peaking 29 days after the original tank installation. Over the next seven days, these nitrites are rapidly converted into harmless nitrates. Only now, 36 days from setting up the tank, do you have a well-balanced aquarium. There is no shortcut to this process, other than using water from another mature tank, and "seeding" the new filter with media from an established one. Even then, time must be allowed for the water chemistry to settle before adding fish. In freshwater aquariums, plants assist tank maturation by absorbing damaging

chemicals, salts, and gases (particularly carbon dioxide) during daylight hours. In marine tanks, proteins can reach critical levels; until the concentration stabilizes, maintain your protein skimmer by clearing foam from the collection trap twice a day.

It is possible to introduce hardy, nitrite-tolerant freshwater fish earlier in the maturation period, after 14–20 days, once the ammonia stage of the cycle is complete. Nitrite-tolerant species include some of the livebearers, particularly platies and mollies, as well as the Three-spot Gourami. Watch for signs of distress and imperfections to the body and fins; if fish withstand these early conditions, their waste products help to feed beneficial bacteria in the filter bed. For marine aquariums, the full 36-day cycle must be completed before adding fish or invertebrates; observe a further settlement period of at least a week before introducing particularly delicate species.

Put the maturation period to good use by checking the reliability of your equipment. Regulate the thermostat if required to achieve the desired water temperature. Inspect the sealing of external filters; filters should be operational from the outset so that they reach stability at the same time as the tank water. Monitor water chemistry to ensure that appropriate levels of acidity/alkalinity (pH) and hardness (dH) are established before adding stock. For marine and brackish-water aquariums, correct salinity must also be maintained.

Introduce livestock gradually to any newly established tank, beginning with relatively hardy species such as this Three-spot Gourami.

STOCKING LEVELS

In an aquarium, living space is extremely confined; even with just one fish in a tank, the population density is greater than in a natural aquatic habitat. The aquarist must strike a balance to ensure that a tank is vibrant with life, yet not overcrowded. In an overstocked aquarium, correct filtration and oxygen levels are harder to maintain, disease can spread more quickly and uncontrollably, and water chemistry is less stable. The fish may become more intolerant of each other, with weaker individuals suffering the most.

When stocking a tank, the most critical factor is surface area, rather than the total volume of water. The aquarium depth is irrelevant; it is the water/air interface at the surface that determines the amount of dissolved oxygen needed to support life. A 35 gallon (160 liter) tank, if 39 in long x 16 in deep x 16 in wide (100 x 40 x 40 cm), will have a surface area of 625 sq in (4000 sq cm); alternatively, it may be 30 in long x 20 in deep x 16 in wide (75 x 52 x 40 cm), with a surface area of 480 sq in (3000 sq cm). Although both tanks hold the same amount of water, the one with the larger surface area will support more fish. To find the correct stocking level, first calculate the surface area by multiplying the tank length by its width. Then establish the adult body length (excluding the caudal fin) of the fish you plan to keep in the tank; for each 1 in (2.5 cm), you will require 12 sq in (75 sq cm) of tank space for tropical freshwater species, 28 sq in (180 sq cm) for coldwater freshwater fish, and 47 sq in (300 sq cm) for tropical marine species.

In certain cases, fish may require more or less space than average. For example, the Discus, which grows to 6 in (15 cm), is best kept in pairs with little else in the tank. Only in this way are you likely to grow these fish to maturity and have them breed. With good water turnover and efficient filtration, stocking levels may be slightly increased. However, do not rely on equipment to support a heavily stocked aquarium; mechanical failure could prove disastrous. Remember also that fewer fish often look far more impressive than a tank crammed with bodies.

TROPICAL FRESHWATER TANK

A tropical freshwater tank that is 36 in (90 cm) long and 12 in (30 cm) wide has a surface area of 430 sq in (2700 sq cm). It will support 18 fish sized 2 in (5 cm) each, or an assortment of fish with a combined body length of 36 in (90 cm). The area needed per fish, shown far right, is much smaller than for coldwater or marine species.

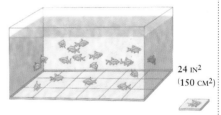

24 IN² (150 CM²)

COLDWATER FRESHWATER TANK

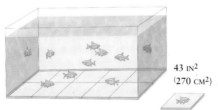

43 IN² (270 CM²)

A coldwater freshwater aquarium 36 in (90 cm) long and 12 in (30 cm) wide can comfortably house 10 fish measuring 1½ in (3.75 cm), or a varied group of fish totalling 15 in (37.5 cm) in body length. Do not be tempted to overstock with young specimens that will outgrow your tank.

TROPICAL MARINE TANK

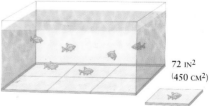

72 IN² (450 CM²)

In a 36 x 12 in (90 x 30 cm) marine tank, the population should not exceed a total body length of 9 in (22.5 cm). This equates to six fish, with each 1½ in (3.75 cm) long. Stocking levels are particularly critical for all marine species, and this is the recommended minimum aquarium size.

BUYING FISH

FOR THE BEST RESULTS with your new aquarium, it is essential that you know which fish to buy, how to identify healthy specimens, and where to obtain reliable stock. It is most important to choose species that will be compatible tankmates, and whose needs you will be able to meet. The key is research – before making any purchases, find out all you can about the fish you would like to keep. Be prepared and well informed; this will help you to choose with confidence and avoid making costly mistakes.

SOURCES OF STOCK AND INFORMATION

Well-run shops are clean and tidy, with staff to guide you in your selections. Visit dealers with some species in mind, plus a few alternatives.

There are numerous sources of fish: general pet shops with an aquatic section; specialist aquatic outlets; fish auctions; bring-and-buys organized by fishkeeping societies; and friends who breed fish and have excess stock. Beware, however, of accepting fish from friends – they may wish to be rid of certain specimens because they are troublesome or unsuitably large. Aquatic societies can be an invaluable source of information; do not let inexperience deter you from contacting a fishkeeping club – all hobbyists have to begin somewhere! At shows and auctions it is possible to purchase healthy, homebred fish, and to get advice from the breeder on how to rear them.

It is important to find a reputable retailer; compare as many establishments as possible before buying, and get recommendations from any friends who already keep fish. A good dealer will have time for you, will ask questions to see if you understand why you should choose a particular combination of fish/invertebrates/plants, and may even refuse to sell you incompatible items. If you request a pair of fish, and the species is sexable, that is what you will receive. It is quite normal for a respectable dealer to hold a caught fish in the net against the front glass, not only so that he can inspect it but also for you to check – you can learn a lot about sexing fish this way! A good dealer will not try to sell you unnecessary equipment, but will prefer to ensure that, as a satisfied customer, you will return to buy your dry goods, such as food and filter media. Bad dealers are easily identified – they have no time for customers and care little about what they sell. Avoid them like the plague!

Do not immediately acquire all the fish that you want. Stock must be introduced gradually to avoid overloading the filter, which may not contain enough bacteria to cope with the sudden volume of waste.

DO'S AND DON'TS FOR NOVICE FISHKEEPERS

DO

• Go into shops and look around. You need not buy, but you can see whether the place is clean, the tanks are well stocked with lively fish or invertebrates, and the plants look healthy.

• Ask questions, even if you know the answers! Good outlets will spend time giving advice, from setting up your equipment to choosing compatible stock. Try to choose a quiet time to do this – a busy Sunday afternoon is not ideal!

• Check livestock for signs of disease; a good dealer will have any sick fish in quarantine.

• Join your local club; fishkeeping societies are found in most large towns and cities, and the advantages of membership are well worth the initial effort of making contact. You can receive help and advice with all sorts of situations, from moving large fish, to checking your tank while you are on holiday, to borrowing a piece of equipment when yours has failed and the shops are closed.

• When buying, ask what the fish are being fed, and ensure you have the same foods for them.

DON'T

• Be impatient. A fully stocked aquarium takes weeks to achieve; shortcuts can lead to disaster.

• Buy on impulse. A rash decision can be costly, financially and in terms of your fish's health.

• Purchase fish from a dealer who has no time, or is unwilling, to answer your questions or to catch a particular fish for you.

• Buy any fish that appears diseased, is hanging at the surface, swims irregularly or listlessly around the tank, or is emaciated.

• Allow the livestock to become chilled or overheated on the way home. A coolbox is ideal for transporting bagged fish.

• Buy fish from a tank containing a dead specimen. Fish do die of old age, but you can never be sure, and you risk inadvertently introducing disease to your own aquarium.

• Purchase fish when you are a great distance from home, since the water conditions may vary from those in your own tank. As a novice, you will have neither the expertise nor the facilities to cope with this.

SELECTING HEALTHY FISH

A healthy fish will behave naturally; for each species, research can guide you on exactly what that means! Most fish should be swimming around with their fins extended; others that live on the bottom will be grubbing in the substrate or resting on, or under, rocks and wood, while surface-dwellers can be found flitting around just beneath the water surface. Whatever their habits, they should not appear stressed or have signs of disease (such as spots, inflammation, or fungus) or any physical damage. Healthy fish have good color, clear eyes, and complete fins, and interact normally. Specimens that hide away in corners, hang near the surface, have split fins, or scratch and flick against rocks and plants could be suffering from a number of problems ranging from mishandling or bullying to poor water conditions. If you have any doubts about a fish's health, don't buy it.

Do not worry about buying from a dealer who has a tank with a quarantine sign on it. This is a responsible precaution, indicating that the fish in that tank are not completely well and are being nursed back to full health before being sold. It is to the dealer's credit that he acknowledges a problem and is acting to rectify it. Some retailers maintain such good stock that it is not unheard of for people to purchase fish and have them spawning within days, or to acquire show-standard specimens.

Healthy fish, such as this pair of pencilfishes, show strong color and finnage, and may even display to each other in the dealer's tank.

CHOOSING SUITABLE FISH

When selecting stock for your aquarium, the fish's water requirements and behavior are far more important considerations than their looks. Although colorful softwater tetras would contrast well with the cichlids seen here, it would be wholly inappropriate to add them to this hardwater setup.

When stocking a tank, select species that will be compatible. Some fish are more belligerent than others, some seek a quiet environment with little activity, while others thrive in a busy tank, swimming interminably either in schools or alone. The mixing of active predators with smaller, placid fish is a route to disaster.

In accordance with their natural habitats, different species may live in disparate parts of the aquarium. Some require the seclusion of rocks or wood, while others are patterned for concealment among plants. Some fish (such as freshwater butterflyfish) spend much of their time sedentary at the surface; others (including many tetras) move constantly as a school in mid-water; yet others (such as *Corydoras* catfish) tend to cluster in small groups at lower levels of the water column. Aquarists must consider the behavior patterns of each species when planning both fish selection and tank decor.

The vast majority of fish likely to be kept in an aquarium are fairly placid. Fish of a nervous disposition, particularly some of the dwarf South American cichlids, feel most secure in the presence of smaller "dither" fish, which act as patrolling guards, their reactions signaling nearby danger.

Many large fish start life as attractively colored beasts, with attention-grabbing personalities – but take heed before you buy. For example, a charming 2 in (5 cm) Snakehead will quickly grow into a formidable predator, grateful for having been provided with so many smaller

companions to dine on! Cichlids can be territorially aggressive, and may harm weaker fish while setting up their domain. They can be kept with fish of a similar size, if numbers are kept to a minimum.

Often, fish that are initially unfriendly tankmates manage to settle peaceably once a "pecking order" has been established. Carefully research any fish that you are planning to buy, investigating its habits, feeding requirements, and likely adult size; some small, innocuous fish are more predatory than other, more intimidating-looking species. Any good retailer will help you to make an appropriate choice.

CHECKING COMPATIBILITY

• Choose fish that require the same water conditions; variables such as pH, hardness, and temperature should always be kept well within a species' natural range.

• Know each fish's territorial requirements and ensure that they can be met without compromising the needs of others.

• Avoid mixing relatively large, boisterous fish with smaller, more quiet species. The larger fish may bully the smaller ones, and will often capture most of the food.

• Be aware of potential dietary problems, either difficulties in providing the right foods, or the presence of a lone predator that is slowly consuming all its tankmates.

• Do not overcrowd one level of the tank; select a mix of fish that inhabit the top, middle, and bottom regions.

CARE REQUIREMENTS

Your fish's quality of life depends on you; the responsibility is equal to that involved in keeping a dog, cat, or any other pet. Whatever a fish's size or temperament, you must be prepared to provide it with a satisfactory lifestyle. Although big fish make an impressive display, they require an aquarium that will not just accommodate them but also allow adequate swimming space. Similarly, smaller, peaceful species should not be forced to endure the stress of sharing living quarters with larger, more aggressive fish.

When stocking an aquarium, the fishes' well-being must be your primary consideration. The first step in buying a fish is to acquire a sound understanding of its requirements. Key questions to be answered include: Do the fish's required water conditions match those in the tank in which is to be housed? Can its dietary needs be met? Can it peacefully interact with other species in the aquarium?

Usually, provided that extremes of pH and hardness are avoided, most fish introduced into a freshwater tank will be fairly tolerant of the water chemistry. With marine fish and invertebrates, it is best to obtain your dealer's advice on the required salinity level and any special water parameters or feeding requirements. With all aquariums, conditions must be monitored at regular intervals and the water changed periodically, maintaining the same chemistry and temperature. Regardless of the species being kept, tanks should always be situated in a quiet area, away from passing distractions; any undue stress can lead to disease.

ADULT OR JUVENILE?

Novice aquarists are often uncertain whether to purchase adult or juvenile specimens. Buying adults generally assures that the stock are physically robust. Any irregularities, such as malformed or damaged fins, can be more readily seen, and the fish's deportment will lend testament to their good health. On the other hand, buying juveniles allows you to enjoy your fish longer; a mature adult may be well into its full lifespan. Young specimens are also less expensive, and you will have the added pleasure of watching their development. Provided the fish are healthy, it is not essential to buy fully grown specimens, unless you are seeking exhibition-sized examples from the start. The choice is yours; for instance, in the past I have bought Congo Tetras and various rainbowfishes as juveniles and enjoyed raising them to adulthood, breeding them along the way. I have also on occasion purchased adult fish purely for their aesthetic value, to enhance the overall appearance of the aquarium or for use as breeding stock.

A beautiful, mature specimen will create an instant impression in a home aquarium. However, it is more affordable, and often far more satisfying, to purchase young fish, such as this juvenile Blue-faced Angelfish, which you will then be able to nurture, observe, and enjoy as they grow into adults in your own tank.

INTRODUCING NEW FISH

HAVING CHOSEN YOUR fish with care, ensuring that they are compatible and healthy, remember that it is equally vital to transfer them safely to your tank. Keep the journey as short as possible, and make sure that everything is ready to receive the fish at home. Plan ahead so that you have adequate time to care for them during this initial period; a gentle introduction will minimize stress on your new livestock. If you are adding fish to an established aquarium, observe them closely to check that they are settling in peacefully. Careful monitoring should quickly alert you to any problems, which are most easily cured with prompt attention.

HANDLE WITH CARE

Every new fish deserves gentle handling and careful attention. The process by which wild-caught or farmed fish are delivered to your local aquarium shop can be very arduous – it may take between four and eight weeks for livestock to pass from exporter to wholesaler to the retail outlet. This imposes huge stress on the fish, as they are repeatedly caught, transported, and placed in waters of varying quality. Food may also have been withheld for short periods to reduce the production of waste.

Despite the efforts of all parties en route to ensure that they arrive in the best of health, some fish succumb to stress-related diseases, most commonly *Ichthyophthirius*, or White Spot. You may see such fish in quarantine at retail premises.

Even if your new purchases appear to be the picture of health, remember that the journey from the shop to your home tank is the final leg of a long ordeal, and take special care to make the transition as untraumatic as possible.

GETTING YOUR FISH HOME

Fish are usually transported in clear plastic bags, secured at the top with a rubber band or other tie. Do not be alarmed at the small amount of water the retailer will put in the bag. The ratio of water to air should be one-third water to two-thirds air. If bagged correctly, the air will have been trapped so that it balloons the bag. As the dissolved oxygen in the water quickly depletes, it is replenished by the air above the water, particularly if the fish disturbs the water surface while swimming. To maximize oxygen supply, some dealers inject pure oxygen into their bags.

The plastic bag should be placed inside an opaque, preferably brown, paper bag. This will minimize stress on the fish as it is taken out into the daylight and exposed to hectic activity. If the shop does not offer a paper bag, demand it. Some dealers provide plastic bags with a rounded shape, to prevent the fish from darting into a corner, rupturing the bag. Alternatively, fold the corners in and tape them, or seal them off using a rubber band tied tightly above them. Spiny-finned fish can easily puncture the plastic bag, and should be double- or triple-bagged to reduce the chances of leakage. With many spiny marine invertebrates, such as certain urchins, a plastic bag is inadequate. Place the bag in a sealed, hard plastic container, transporting one specimen at a time to prevent them damaging each other in transit. A coolbox is a good investment for carrying bagged specimens of all kinds.

Do not leave your fish in the car for long periods; exposure to sunlight can cause them to overheat. If there is no alternative, place them in the trunk, covered with insulating material to avoid temperature extremes. This is particularly important for coldwater species being transported in the heat of summer.

ACCLIMATING NEW FISH

The short trip home should not cause a dramatic reduction in temperature. Once home, float the bag containing the fish in the tank for about an hour so that the temperature of the bagged water regulates with the tank. It is often advised to mix some of the tank water with that in the bag, so the fish will gradually become accustomed to the change in chemistry. This is a myth, since it takes several days for a fish to adjust fully to such differences.

Check that the newcomers are not being harassed by the other fish, and allow them to establish themselves before offering food. The length of time needed for new fish to settle varies, but in most cases they can be fed after a couple of hours. Watch to see whether they are feeding, but do not panic if they fail to eat immediately; it can take 24–48 hours for a fish to accept food. Make sure, however, that no fish is being prevented from eating by a dominant tankmate.

CONTROLLING TERRITORIAL AGGRESSION

Aggressive behavior by established fish towards new livestock must be accepted to some extent, but a subtle rearrangement of the rocks, wood, and plants just prior to the newcomers' introduction can help to control antagonism. The revised decor will keep all the tank inhabitants busy re-establishing territories and pecking orders, detracting attention from the new arrivals. If this tactic does not curb bullying, you may have no option but to transfer the culprit to another tank or, alternatively, to remove the victim. In extreme circumstances, there is no other solution.

Sparring is not always an act of aggression. If neither fish is injured or thereafter permanently hides away, this may be a pair preparing to spawn.

QUARANTINING

New fish are sometimes quarantined to contain and cure any latent disease. The procedure requires a small, bare tank, reserved exclusively for this purpose. Fish should be contained within this holding station for about four to six weeks to allow any disease to become evident and subsequently be treated. All equipment used, including nets, should not be employed elsewhere without sterilization.

The effectiveness of the quarantining procedure is open to some question. In my own experience, the best preventative for stress-related diseases is to introduce a fish at the earliest opportunity to the main tank, where it is usually calmed by the surroundings and by the peaceful activity of other fish. The stress imposed by delaying this transfer until completion of quarantining may in itself be sufficient

to trigger disease. Only if the fish is in obvious ill health should quarantining be necessary. However, when in doubt, this measure is a wise precaution.

Place the quarantine tank in a quiet place, where the fish will not be disturbed by passing activity, and keep lighting levels subdued. Feeding should be minimal. If the suspected disease is due to free-swimming pathogens, such as that which causes White Spot, then an ultra-violet sterilizer is a useful addition to the tank.

Quarantining is not just for new fish, but also for those that have become diseased and require individual treatment. Under these circumstances, I would exercise quarantining without hesitation. For such eventualities, always keep a spare small tank to hand, complete with heater/thermostat and a small filter.

OBSERVING YOUR FISH

ONCE YOUR TANK IS filled with livestock, you can at last begin to enjoy the experience of watching a living underwater picture in your home. However, this is still a time of learning. Observe how your fish interact, and note which species are active during the day, and which appear only in the early morning or late evening. Be aware of your fish's customary behavior, and do not ignore any sudden changes. As you gain experience as an aquarist, you will discover that familiarity with your fish is the best way of ensuring that they remain healthy and content.

MONITORING BEHAVIOR

Once your fish are installed in the tank, take time to observe their lifestyle and habits. Most fish are diurnal – active mainly during daylight hours. Some, however, are nocturnal (active at night-time) or crespucular (active at dawn and dusk), and their feeding times should be scheduled accordingly. A low-wattage red tungsten bulb placed over the tank will give enough illumination to observe nocturnal activity without disturbance.

One of the most pleasurable aspects of keeping fish is observing their behavior and the interaction between different individuals and species. Most fish lead a fairly structured existence. Observant aquarists will quickly note that many fish have a fixed pattern of movement, following set routes with cycle times as long as 3–4 minutes. Skilled aquatic photographers study a fish's swimming routine to obtain the best picture.

Knowing your fish's normal behavior patterns is of great help in the early diagnosis of problems. If activity seems accelerated, or if your fish are sluggish and hugging the substrate when they would normally be schooling serenely in mid-water, then the cause is probably incorrect temperature. Hyperactivity can also indicate the onset of spawning. If fish hang at the surface, this could be the result of poor filtration and/or excessively warm water. The sooner that you spot unusual behavior of any kind, the more promptly you can take appropriate action.

Remember that when you add livestock to a tank, some of the standard behavioral patterns of established fish may change as they adapt to the newcomers, which are, effectively, invading their territory. Ensure that no harm comes to either party.

Most aquarists find that the daily feeding of their fish is the ideal opportunity to check that all tank inhabitants are fit and well. Observe them as they eat, to make sure that each fish is taking food. If some are not eating, vary the mealtimes or the size or type of foods being offered, and curb any bullying by dominant fish.

HANDLING FISH

INEVITABLY, IT WILL BE necessary to catch your fish, either to move them to a different tank or to treat them for ailments. This must be done carefully; swinging a net around the tank, hoping to snare the fish, will result in uprooted plants, floating debris, and frightened or even injured livestock. Catching fish requires some skill to master, but is not difficult.

USING A NET

Fish nets should be made of a fairly fine mesh, particularly if used to catch fish with hard fin spines, such as cichlids, gouramis, and catfishes; otherwise, the spines may become entangled, potentially damaging both fish and net. Should this occur, there are two courses of action. The first is to allow the fish to disentangle itself. This is often the best approach with fish that extend special spines for defence, such as *Ancistrus* catfish and certain loaches. The other option is to carefully cut the net away.

White-colored nets can be less effective than green ones, which a fish may more readily swim into, believing it is seeking sanctuary among plants. It is advisable to use two nets, one to guide the fish into the other. Alternatively, one of the nets can be substituted by a clear plastic bag, which the fish will enter without realizing its presence. After use, all nets should be sterilized to

Wield the net gently in the tank when catching or returning fish. Do not thrash about wildly in pursuit of an elusive specimen.

prevent transmission of disease. Do not use bleach or similar household products in place of purpose-made solutions. These are inexpensive and easy to use; simply dilute in a bucket of water and dip in the net.

GLASS DIP TUBES

A few years ago, one could buy glass dip tubes for catching fish, but unfortunately these are rarely seen nowadays. They resemble a smoker's pipe with a large bowl at one end leading to a tapering, narrow tube. In use, the aquarist approaches the fish with the bowl end, holding the neck vertically with the thumb placed over the tube end, causing air to be trapped inside. Once within reach of the fish, the thumb is removed, releasing the air and allowing water to be sucked in, along with the fish. The clear glass helps to conceal the device from the fish. This apparatus is in more common use on mainland Europe, and is most effective in the catching of fry.

CATCHING BY HAND

With practice, fish can be caught by hand, at your own risk. If adequate care is taken, this is the best means of catching spiny fish such as catfish, and other large, sedentary specimens. Make sure that your hands are not spiked by the fin spines, and hold your fingers so that they will not be trapped between the powerful pectoral fin spine and the fish's body. A catfish should be grasped near the tail with one hand while supporting the underside with the other, flattened, hand. Catching large specimens can be made easier by lowering the water level. Needless to say, never handle venomous species directly, or those that discharge high-voltage electricity.

WATER MANAGEMENT

EACH AQUATIC SPECIES requires specific water conditions in order to survive and flourish. Factors such as hardness, acidity/alkalinity, and salinity must be maintained at appropriate levels, and for this, aquarists need a basic understanding of water chemistry. Once you have established a mature tank, check the chemistry regularly, using commercially produced test kits to monitor any fluctuations, and restabilize conditions as necessary. A wise fishkeeper will always have an accurate thermometer on hand and, if keeping marine or brackish-water fish, also a hydrometer to measure the specific gravity of the water.

ACIDITY/ALKALINITY

The chemical content of natural bodies of water is usually affected by the substrates through and over which they flow. For instance, water from a limestone cave or spring will be alkaline, whereas springs or waters lying in peat ground become acidic. The degree of acidity or alkalinity is measured on the pH scale, which ranges from 1 to 14 (pH, *pondus hydrogenii*, represents the weight of the hydrogen ions in the water). Water with a pH of 7.0 is neither acidic nor alkaline and is referred to as being neutral. Above 7.0 pH, water is considered alkaline, and below that, acidic. Few organisms, especially fish, can tolerate conditions at either extreme of the scale. In fresh water, the pH is usually between 6.5 and 7.0, with a few species requiring levels just outside these limits; levels below 5 or above 8 are generally lethal. For marines, the range is far more restricted; the pH level must be highly alkaline (8.3 being the norm), with variations limited to within 0.2.

There are various pH test kits available. Some use a reactive liquid that, when added to a water sample, changes color to indicate the pH level. Others have dip sticks coated with reactive dyes that work in the same way. All items employing a chemical reactive substance have a limited shelf life and should be renewed annually. Electronic meters, introduced fairly recently, are expensive compared with other devices but much more accurate and quick to use.

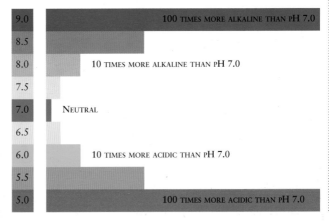

The pH scale is logarithmic, with each increment of 1.0 representing a tenfold increase in acidity or alkalinity. Once this is understood, it is easy to see that differences that, numerically, seem quite small can have dramatic consequences for fish. Regular monitoring of pH values, particularly in marine aquariums, is therefore a vital task in water management.

9.0	100 TIMES MORE ALKALINE THAN pH 7.0
8.5	
8.0	10 TIMES MORE ALKALINE THAN pH 7.0
7.5	
7.0	NEUTRAL
6.5	
6.0	10 TIMES MORE ACIDIC THAN pH 7.0
5.5	
5.0	100 TIMES MORE ACIDIC THAN pH 7.0

HARDNESS

Water hardness is affected in nature by the substrate over which the water flows, but is always high in the case of marine water. Hardness is a measure of certain metallic ions (particularly calcium and, to a lesser extent, magnesium) in the water. More often it is the general hardness (GH) value that is relevant to fishkeepers, though this includes a significant amount of calcium hardness (KH). There are several ways of designating the general hardness, the most common unit being °dH. The chart below shows the relation of calcium concentration to levels of hardness as represented in the dH scale. There are dH test kits similar to those available for the measurement of pH, using reactive substances that change color. A more accurate and quick, though relatively costly, method is to measure the conductivity of the water.

WATER HARDNESS

PPM CaCo₃ (parts per million calcium carbonate)	DH	WATER TYPE
0–50	3°	Soft
50–100	3–6°	Moderately soft
100–200	6–12°	Slightly hard
200–300	12–18°	Moderately hard
300–450	18–25°	Hard
over 450	+25°	Very hard

SALINITY

Saline water is used only in marine and brackish-water aquariums. The amount of salinity is measured by a hydrometer, which displays the specific gravity (SG) of the water. Specific gravity is the ratio of water compared to that in an equal volume of distilled water at 39°F (4°C), which is given a specific gravity of 1.000. Marine water has a higher specific gravity than fresh water, owing to the presence of salts and some trace elements, and this is why it is easier to float in the sea than in fresh water. While pure fresh water has an SG of 1.000, tropical marine water is in the range 1.020–1.027. The specific gravity of brackish water (found in nature where marine and fresh water mix, such as in mangrove swamps, estuaries, and the lower reaches of some rivers) lies between the two.

To regulate the specific gravity of a marine aquarium, add marine salt to increase the SG, or fresh water to lower it. Ensure that the water is at the required tank temperature before measuring the specific gravity, since salinity varies with heat, decreasing as the temperature rises. When making artificial marine water, use only commercially available marine salt mixes; under no circumstances should ordinary domestic cooking salt be used.

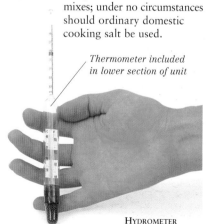

Thermometer included in lower section of unit

HYDROMETER

CONTROL OF WATER CHEMISTRY

Salinity, hardness, and pH can all be adjusted, but this must always be done gradually. Any large changes in water chemistry will be detrimental to livestock. In freshwater tanks, the decor can be exploited to help regulate water chemistry. Abundant vegetation will generally soften the water slightly, as the plants extract dissolved salts. The use of wood, particularly bogwood, will make the tank slightly acidic through the leaching of tannins. This provides an ideal environment for many South American tetras and angelfishes. Conversely, when keeping hardwater fish such as many African Rift Lake cichlids, crushed corals, shells, or limestone may be used as a substrate or in the filter, where the calcium concentration will harden the water. Marine water tends to stabilize at a pH value of 8.3–8.4 and remain fairly hard, but it can be modified by acidic excretions from fish and invertebrates. The most common causes of poor water quality and chemical fluctuations are inefficient filtration, overstocking, and overfeeding. Monitor conditions regularly using appropriate test kits. Buffer solutions are available to adjust water chemistry as required.

If you need to alter your tapwater to maintain your fish, remember that these adjustments must be made for every water change. The replacement water may have to be prepared a day before it is required.

NITRITES

Toxic ammonia from fish excretion and uneaten food is converted, via the nitrogen cycle and filtration systems, first to less harmful nitrites, and then to nitrates, which are returned to the tank via the water return line from the filter. Any accumulation of nitrites can cause great distress to livestock in aquariums, particularly marine tanks. The most common causes of nitrite build-up are overstocking, inadequate filtration, overfeeding, and infrequent water changes. Also, some domestic water supplies can be high in nitrites due to contamination. Test kits are available for measuring levels of both nitrites and ammonia.

Although a water change should immediately reduce nitrite and ammonia levels, you must investigate why the action has become necessary. If the cause is not identified and conditions corrected, the problem will soon recur. Fish are often lost because the aquarist has failed to notice and prevent dangerous rises in toxins. Regular observation of your fish's behavior, coupled with the judicious use of test kits, is the best defense against this.

WATER CHANGES

To help control nitrate and ammonia build-up, partial water changes should be performed once every 10–14 days. To avoid interfering with the nitrogen cycle, replace no more than 10–15 percent of the total volume of tank water at any one time. The replacement water should be similar in pH, chemical make-up, and temperature (within 3.5°F, or 2°C) to that remaining in the tank. If you need to modify your regular water supply to add to your tank, allow yourself adequate time to make these adjustments. With brackish-water or marine aquariums, the salinity should be tested using a hydrometer and adjusted if necessary with proprietary marine salt mixes. Ensure that the replacement water is at the correct temperature before measuring the specific gravity, which changes with temperature.

Introduce the replacement water slowly. During water changes it is also advisable to renew some of the filter media with fresh material. Do not replace all of the existing media; the helpful bacteria it contains will colonize the new filter wool and assist in breaking down waste. While siphoning water out of the tank, remove any debris that has collected on the substrate or among plants or rocks.

TANK MAINTENANCE

WHATEVER TYPE OF aquarium you have, it is essential to establish a routine for caring for your fish. This program should cover all aspects of maintaining their life-support system. Keep a log as a planning aid and begin with the guidelines given below. Factors such as stocking levels, the particular species being kept, and the amount and types of food given will have a bearing on your individual regime. As you learn to live with your tank, you will develop your own schedule for maintenance, including the regular replacement of equipment and the addition of new stock or plants.

ESSENTIAL MAINTENANCE TASKS

DAILY	• Check livestock • Check temperature • Check that equipment is working efficiently • Feed fish and remove any uneaten food • Empty protein skimmer (marine tanks)
WEEKLY	• Clean glass cover or condensation tray • Top up water lost through evaporation • Remove any algae from aquarium glass, using algae scraper
EVERY 2 WEEKS	• Carry out water change – amount will depend on stocking level • Remove dead leaves from plants and trim any growing too long • Check pH and dH • Check ammonia, nitrate, and nitrite levels • Check specific gravity (marine and brackish-water tanks) • Check filter flow and clean as necessary • Stir top of substrate and siphon off debris
EVERY 2–3 MONTHS	• Replace carbon in filter • Clean protein skimmer (marine tanks) • Service power filter(s) and air pump, replacing worn parts; purchase replacements for any spares used during servicing • Clean all filter pipework – check spray bars and clear any blocked holes with a pin • Clean quartz sleeve of UV sterilizer
EVERY 6 MONTHS	• Check lighting (make sure end caps still fit correctly and ends of fluorescent tubes do not appear darkened) and replace tubes if needed • Replace UV sterilizer tubes

FOODS AND FEEDING

Feeding fish is one of the most pleasurable aspects of the hobby. Many aquarists insist that their fish come to see them when they want food. Remember, though, that some species are naturally inquisitive, while others are defensive; an eager approach has nothing to do with hunger. Be very careful not to overfeed – a hungry fish is a healthy fish. Feeding foods of the wrong type or size, or too much of one kind, can also be harmful. Provide a balanced, varied, and suitable diet, and you will have achieved one of the keys to successful fishkeeping.

◁ GOLDFISH ANTICIPATING FEEDING TIME

FISH AND FOOD

AQUARISTS CAN GAIN a reasonable understanding of the correct diet for a particular fish by considering its natural habitat and the food sources found there. Fortunately, aquatic retailers usually do this research for us, by ensuring that stock offered for sale are fully acclimated to a tank environment and are feeding well on appropriate, readily available products. Before purchasing a fish, especially a species with which you are unfamiliar, ask your supplier what it is feeding on and how often it is being fed. Reputable dealers will be more than happy to advise you, and can help you to avoid any subsequent feeding problems.

NATURAL FOOD SOURCES AND DIETS

In an aquatic habitat, each level of the water column provides food. Tiny creatures live both on and in the substrate, plants grow at various depths, and algae flourish on any surface that receives sufficient light. Small invertebrates swim freely, while animals and insects fall onto the water's surface – some floating, some sinking. Terrestrial plants overhang and/or grow into the water. All are sources of food for something, and fish have evolved to occupy particular feeding niches.

Broadly, fish are carnivores (which eat other animals), herbivores (which eat plants), or omnivores (which eat both animals and plants). However, these groups can overlap, and within each there are specialized categories. Among carnivores, the degree and type of flesh-eating can vary enormously. For example, piscivores feed on other fish; some take only live fish, but many others can be weaned onto dead, meaty foods. Molluscivores eat mollusks, such as snails, while insectivores feed on small aquatic invertebrates, including *Daphnia* and mosquito larvae. Limnivores sift through mud to extract edible morsels.

Plant-eating herbivores exist solely on vegetation, but range in habit from species that eat relatively large aquatic plants to those that graze predominantly on algae.

Omnivores are opportunist feeders, scavengers that will accept just about anything – from nibbling at a carcass drifting in the river, to sampling waste thrown from boats or barges, or grubbing along the bottom in search of titbits.

Bottom-dwelling species such as this *Corydoras* catfish spend much of their time sifting through the substrate for food, which is easily picked up with their downturned mouths. Many catfish are omnivorous, eating most foods; others primarily eat insects in the wild. Some species, however, are strict herbivores.

FEEDING HABITS

When pursuing food, each species of fish follows instinctive behavior patterns. The size, shape, and position of the mouth largely determines where and how a fish will feed. Surface feeders will ignore food that falls to the bottom, while bottom-dwellers bypass floating material. Even predatory fish with capacious mouths are selective, and do not waste time chasing small fry. Both feeding strategy and posture are pre-determined by nature, and can be modified only partially in an aquarium environment. Species also feed at different times of day. Although most eat during daylight hours, some are crepuscular and eat at twilight; yet others feed by night. In captivity, fish often adapt their habits, but some will eat only at their preferred times.

The freshwater Creek Chub (*Semotilis atromaculatus*) schools in shallow waters and feeds by capturing prey as it descends through the water and scavenging along the bottom. This fish has snared a worm that will just about fit its mouth.

AQUARIUM NUTRITION

Fish kept in aquariums, although removed from their natural environment, must still be given the specific foods for which their digestive systems are designed. If a fish is fed the wrong diet, its body will be unable to cope. It may suffer both short-term and chronic health problems. Carnivores have short digestive tracts because high-protein foods are quickly digested, while herbivores' digestive tracts are long, since vegetable matter requires more extensive processing by the body. Piscivorous (fish-eating) species will refrain from consuming plants, while plant eaters will not always ignore meaty foods. It is the responsibility of each aquarist to know the needs of the fish that they plan to keep before stocking the tank, and to ensure that an appropriate diet can be provided. Do not be tempted to buy an attractive fish with "difficult" requirements unless you are prepared for the inconvenience and expense of keeping regular supplies of the correct foods.

Most barbs, including this large Lemon-fin, normally feed by grubbing in the substrate. However, being opportunists, in captivity they quickly adapt to take food from the surface.

Aquarium Foods

THERE IS A WIDE range of prepared products available both off the shelf and in frozen form, which makes feeding fish a relatively simple task, whether keeping freshwater or marine, tropical or coldwater species. Aquarists can also draw upon other sources, including the garden, kitchen, and local bodies of water. At times, it is still beneficial to culture your own foods – normally when running a breeding program. A supply of live items such as brine shrimp is essential for conditioning stock and rearing fry.

COMMERCIAL DRY FOODS

The development and production of fish foods is a thriving industry, offering a wide selection of items for the modern aquarist. From the early days of fishkeeping, when a basic flake food and items such as ants' eggs were the only products available, the choice has grown to include very specialized foods such as spirulina (algae) flakes, sponge-based foods, and protein-rich carnivore diets. Your local aquarium shop will stock a range of dry foods in flake, pellet, stick, tablet, and wafer form; these should form the basis of your feeding regime.

FLAKES

Yet, as with humans, your fish will relish, and benefit from, a more varied diet. Dry foods contain no coarse roughage, needed for a healthy digestive system. Since they swell when moistened, they can also bloat a fish's stomach, with fatal results, if given too freely.

TABLETS

PELLETS

HOMEMADE FORMULA

Experienced aquarists often find a particular food or combination of foods that works well for them. For example, dried nettles (available from health food stores) can be made into a paste to feed young loricariids. Coat pebbles with the paste and allow it to dry before placing the stones in the rearing tank. Combinations of fish and meaty foods can also be liquidized to form a base, adding vitamins, vegetable matter, and cereals. Foods can be deep-frozen in ice-cube trays for ready-meals. Take great care, however, if you are intending to create your own high-protein diet. Force-feeding fish will produce overweight, unhealthy stock.

FROZEN FOODS

Frozen foods are a very convenient option. Some types come in cube-shaped portions that are easily thawed and dispensed into the tank. There is a large variety available, including bloodworm, *Daphnia*, mosquito larvae (for small fish such as tetras and barbs), *Mysis* shrimp, cockles, chopped mussel, sand eels, and plankton (for marine fish and invertebrates), as well as specialist items such as spinach (for herbivores) and a menu for Discus. Such packaged products are excellent for growing fry and for conditioning fish prior to spawning. Used in conjunction with dry foods, they add valuable roughage to the diet.

FRESH HOUSEHOLD FOODS

A number of fresh household foods can be used in your aquarium. Peas, lettuce, cucumber, zucchini, and potatoes are all good for feeding herbivores. Lettuce may be "planted" in the substrate, while defrosted frozen peas should be squashed between finger and thumb to remove the seed coat. Cucumbers, zucchini, and potatoes can all be sliced and dropped into the aquarium. Zucchini and potatoes are best part-cooked (but not made soft) and cooled before adding to the tank. Fresh fish and shellfish can also be given in small amounts, but be sure to remove any uneaten material so that it does not pollute the tank. Although some aquarists like to feed liver and ox heart, these should be offered sparingly, since fish can quickly become overweight on such a rich diet. With all fresh foods, remember to chop items to a suitable size before feeding.

LIVE FOODS

If you look in small streams, ponds, and puddles, you will discover a host of small aquatic invertebrates that make excellent food for your fish. They provide useful fiber and are rich in nutrients for conditioning breeding stock. The most notable found live foods are *Daphnia*, *Cyclops*, mosquito larvae, bloodworm, glassworm, and *Tubifex*. Of these, *Daphnia*, bloodworm, and *Tubifex* are frequently available from retailers; buy *Tubifex* frozen or freeze-dried, since live ones can carry disease. Alternatively, many live foods can be collected using a fine mesh net, but take care not to introduce predators such as dragonfly larvae into your tank, where they can eat or harm fish. Another common live food, brine shrimp, can be purchased in aquarium shops or cultured.

From your garden it is possible to harvest earthworms and aphids, provided you do not use insecticides. Earthworms, relished by large fish, may be chopped for feeding to smaller species. Woodlice can also be collected to feed fish whose mouths are sufficiently large. Buckets of old tank water left to stand will yield a good crop of mosquito larvae, and, if you have a water barrel, you can seed this with *Daphnia* to ensure a regular supply year round.

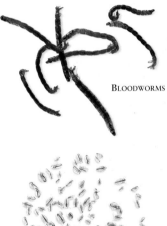

BLOODWORMS

DAPHNIA (WATER FLEAS)

ARTEMIA (BRINE SHRIMP)

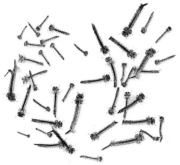

MOSQUITO LARVAE

CULTURED FOODS

There are numerous organisms that you can culture to feed to your fish. The most well known of these are brine shrimp and whiteworm, but others include grindal worms, microworms, rotifers, and infusoria. Algae can also be cultivated for herbivorous (and omnivorous) fish, and may be necessary if algal growth in the tank is minimal. Leave flat stones or pebbles outside in shallow trays of water. When they have developed a good coating of algae, place the stones in the tank for the fish to feed on. Later return the stones to the outdoor trays to regrow the algae.

HATCHING BRINE SHRIMP (*ARTEMIA*)

This is the staple food when rearing fish. Nauplii (newly hatched shrimp) are ideal first foods for fry. To hatch brine shrimp eggs, you will need clear glass or plastic bottles with screw-top lids made of plastic, not metal. Fill the bottles three-quarters full of salt solution, made using just under 1 oz (25 g) of marine salt per 1¾ pt (liter) of water, or as instructed on the egg packaging. Add a pinch of brine shrimp eggs to the salt water. Keep the containers in a warm place, such as on top of an aquarium or in a fish house. The eggs must remain in suspension, and should be aerated vigorously using an air stone, connected to an air pump with air line. Thread the air line into the bottle by punching a hole in the lid, and place the air stone so that it rests near, but not on, the bottom of the bottle.

Hatching will take between 12 hours and three days, depending on the type of eggs you are using. To harvest the nauplii, discontinue aeration and allow the empty eggshells to settle. The water should appear slightly pink with shrimp. Siphon off the shrimp using a piece of air line and strain them through a very fine sieve, to avoid introducing salt water into your rearing tank. Rinse the shrimp in fresh water and feed to your fry. Finally, replace the air stone in the hatching bottle and resume aeration. Cultures are viable for about two to three days. One or two days after starting your first culture, set up a second bottle, followed by a third and fourth at 2-day intervals. Use these in rotation to maintain a continuous supply of shrimp, starting each culture for as long as required.

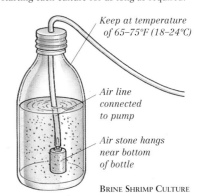

Keep at temperature of 65–75°F (18–24°C)

Air line connected to pump

Air stone hangs near bottom of bottle

BRINE SHRIMP CULTURE

CULTURING WHITEWORM

Whiteworms are bought as starter cultures either at fish shows or, more usually, by mail order. They can be cultured in a large, shallow plastic container with a lid. Fill the container half- to three-quarters full of compost in a level layer, then add the starter culture. Place a piece of damp bread on top, and cover most of the compost's surface with a sheet of glass. To keep the culture dark, add the lid, perforated with holes to maintain good ventilation.

After a few days, small worms should appear on the glass. Add more bread as required and remove any pieces that have become moldy. If the pieces are too large, they may become foul before the worms have time to eat them; to prevent this, use relatively small portions of bread. Once the culture is well established, harvest the clean worms from the glass.

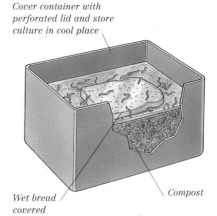

Cover container with perforated lid and store culture in cool place

Wet bread covered with glass

Compost

WHITEWORM CULTURE

FEEDING YOUR FISH

FEEDING TIMES ARE a very enjoyable part of fishkeeping, and perhaps the best opportunity for you to observe your fish and monitor their well-being. How often and how much to feed will depend on the number of fish kept in the tank, and their size and dietary habits. Take care to establish the optimum routine for your fish. Be sure to provide enough of the right foods for each species, and for growing fry, but always offer modest amounts. Decayed leftovers or excessive fish waste can soon overload your filtration system, with potentially disastrous consequences.

HOW TO FEED

For general community aquariums, feeding once or twice a day is usually fine, but you must check that all your fish are receiving food. Flake foods that float on the surface will be taken by surface-dwellers and mid-water swimmers. The latter will continue to feed as the food softens and descends through the water column, so there may be nothing left for bottom-feeders, which could starve. Therefore, ensure that you add sinking foods (one or two tablets) for bottom-dwelling fish.

Peas are also a good dietary supplement for fish that feed from the bottom.

Herbivorous fish feed almost continually, grazing on leaves and algae. While this habit usefully controls algal growth, it can devastate the plants in an aquarium. The solution is to "plant" a lettuce leaf in the substrate, or anchor it down with a stone. This caters both for mid-water herbivores, which will feed downwards only to a certain level, and for bottom-dwelling catfish, which will graze their way along the leaf.

OVER- AND UNDERFEEDING

It is easy to overfeed a fish that eagerly pushes forward to receive food. Resist the temptation, for this contributes to obesity, which can shorten the fish's lifespan and may also cause sterility. Remember that aquarium life offers limited exercise. In the wild, fish must work to find food and may eat only once every two days. Fry need to be fed steadily, but not to excess, if they are to grow well.

Underfeeding can also create problems, especially with young fish. Incorrect feeding regimes are the most common cause of death among fry. To raise a healthy brood, have adequate stocks of correctly-sized food, and maintain a steady supply throughout the growth period. Underfed fry will become stunted and may suffer deformities. Without a balanced diet to complete their growth, they will never develop into good-quality adults.

PROBLEM EATERS

Fish may fail to eat if they are given foods of the wrong type or size. No matter how much you feed, if the items are too large, your fish will starve in the land of plenty. Mouth size can be a deceptive guide: a plankton feeder has a capacious mouth, but requires large quantities of very fine foods that it can filter from the water. Conversely, lurking predators that are designed to hunt large prey to fill their mouths will not bother chasing smaller fish. Carefully research the needs of the species you intend to keep, and resist buying any fish for which you may be unable to provide an appropriate diet. A piscivore, for example, must be fed live fish. Do not assume that you can persuade it to accept dead foods; the fish may well refuse them. Some herbivores can also be finicky; offer home-grown algae as an appealing, natural food.

KEEPING YOUR FISH HEALTHY

Just like humans, fish will become
unwell if given the wrong diet or
living conditions. In an overstocked
tank, they will be starved of oxygen.
If overfed or not given enough space
to swim, they can become obese, and
may die prematurely. Ill health is often
caused by poor tank maintenance,
or by setting the aquarium in an
inappropriate spot, such as a smoky
kitchen, where pollutants in the
atmosphere are introduced into the
water, or in a busy, cramped hallway,
where fish may feel threatened.
For fish to thrive, they need an
environment that will allow them,
as far as possible, to pursue their
natural lifestyle. Provide this, and
you will have the reward of seeing
your fish in prime condition.

◁ HEALTHY SWORDTAILS DISPLAY LUSTROUS
COLOR AND STRONG FINS

BASIC HEALTH CARE

THE BEST MEANS of keeping your fish healthy are routine observation and diligent tank maintenance. The signs of disease are not always obvious. By regularly monitoring your fish's activities, you will find it much easier to spot subtle changes that could signal the onset of an ailment. Never ignore anything that appears unusual; abnormal behavior, such as loss of appetite, clamped fins, or rubbing to alleviate itching, is often the first symptom of an environmental problem or an outbreak of disease. Be prepared to isolate and treat any diseased fish if necessary; prompt action may help avert a full-scale crisis.

Watching your fish is not enough; it is equally vital to keep a close eye on tank conditions; the small, enclosed ecosystem of an aquarium is highly vulnerable to chemical imbalance and bacterial overload. Make sure that your tank is set up correctly at the outset, then maintain it with care. Prevention is always better than cure.

GUARDING AGAINST DISEASE

Careful observation is an invaluable aid in maintaining a healthy aquarium. As a novice, you will initially rely on reference material and advice from more experienced hobbyists to guide you, but you will soon begin to develop your own instincts. It is very useful to keep a logbook, noting water conditions and the fish's behavior; this will help to identify tank fluctuations that have an adverse effect. Follow a regular maintenance schedule; this will alleviate many common problems, and make it easier to recognize when your fish are behaving abnormally or the plants are unhealthy. If water changes become required more frequently than usual, a piece of tank

Poor water quality and boisterous companions will adversely affect these Harlequin Rasboras.

equipment may be due for replacement.

Most fishkeeping problems are caused by the aquarist – a forgotten water change, the introduction of an incompatible fish, or overfeeding. Such mistakes impose stress on fish, leaving them more susceptible to disease. Pathogens may lie dormant in an apparently healthy aquarium, only to attack when the fish are weakened, usually by environmental conditions or trauma. For example, White Spot may be introduced to a tank by a new fish, but is also commonly induced and exacerbated by stress.

TREATING AILMENTS

In aquariums that are generally healthy, most diseases are relatively easy to cure. Do not panic and grab the nearest remedy; carefully identify the problem before applying the correct treatment.

When dosing the aquarium, follow the manufacturer's instructions precisely. A cure will not be instant; it will take days, or, occasionally, weeks. If after 24 hours the treatment does not appear to have worked, resist the temptation to try another remedy – mixed medications can be a lethal cocktail for fish. Remember also that many pathogens can be eradicated only during the free-swimming stage of their life cycle, and therefore the complete cycle must be allowed to take place for treatment to be effective.

Some fish are very sensitive to certain substances. For example, treatments that contain copper can be toxic to some species. Check the instructions before use to see if any of your fish may be affected. Treatments can also harm plants and bacterial beds in filters. In this case, it may be wise to transfer any ailing fish to a hospital tank for treatment. A hospital tank is also a sensible option if the treatment requires that you catch the affected fish at regular intervals – for example, to apply medication directly to an open wound. With pathogens that have a free-swimming stage, fish should be treated in situ; unless the organism's life cycle is broken, it will remain in the tank to infect new hosts. If you are using carbon in your filter, remove it, since this will flush the treatment from the water.

Fish will occasionally die even in a healthy aquarium. This is not a cause for concern if you suspect that death is due simply to old age.

Sadly, at some time you may have to destroy a sick or injured fish. The most humane method is to sever the spinal cord just behind the head, using a sharp knife. If you are unable to do this cleanly, ask your vet or another person to do it for you.

SETTING UP A HOSPITAL TANK

Have a spare aquarium available at all times to use as a hospital tank. You may wish to convert a tank usually set up for quarantining or breeding. That is fine, as long as you always have an empty tank available for emergencies. If using an air-operated sponge filter in one of your main aquariums, you will quickly be able to set up a hospital tank, using the polyfilter and the main tank water, which will be well matured and harboring plenty of beneficial bacteria.

The base of the tank can be left bare or have a fine covering of gravel or sand. Add a plant, a piece of wood, or a plant pot to provide the sick fish with some security, and transfer it gently from the main aquarium. Set the hospital tank in a quiet place to prevent frightening the fish; if necessary, keep the tank darkened.

Keep hospital tank decor fairly sparse, for cleanliness, but provide some areas of shelter.

FIRST-AID KIT

Have a fish first-aid kit on hand, but keep it basic. A White Spot cure, a bactericide, and a fungicide will solve most problems. Although medications have a shelf life, this is not always listed on the packaging. Write the date of purchase on each bottle or packet you buy, and replace it after a year, whether you've used it or not. Also remember to keep spares for equipment such as filters and air pumps, which are your fish's life-support systems.

MAJOR FISH AILMENTS

THE VAST MAJORITY of diseases have environmental causes, and pathogens often remain dormant until a fish is weakened by stress or poor water quality. Correct identification of health problems is the first step in finding a cure. Most diseases can be treated successfully, but administering a panicked succession of remedies can be lethal. If unsure, seek advice from an experienced aquarist. Remember also that ailments are likely to recur if unsuitable tank conditions are left uncorrected.

ANCHOR WORM (*LERNAEA*)

Symptoms: Fish swims erratically, scratching itself against rocks, wood, or the substrate; small, worm-like organisms are seen on the body, and whitish-green threads may hang from inflamed skin.
Cause: The adult parasite *Lernaea*, which buries its anchor-shaped head into the host fish; pond fish are most frequently affected.
Treatment: Remove the fish from the tank and carefully pull out the worm using tweezers; do not break off the head. Treat the wound with antiseptic. For serious infestations, administer Metriponate (1.125–1.8 mg per gallon/4.5 liters).

CONSTIPATION

Symptoms: Irregular and insufficient action of the bowels; if untreated, an affected fish will become severely weakened. Constipated fish do not feed, produce few (if any) feces, rest on the substrate, and may develop a distended belly. Severe cases, where the abdomen is swollen, can be mistaken for dropsy.
Cause: Poor or incorrect diet and, in some cases, overfeeding.
Treatment: Dose the tank with half a level teaspoon of magnesium sulphate (Epsom salts) per gallon (4.5 liters) of water. If the fish recovers, improve or correct its diet.

DROPSY/MALAWI BLOAT

Symptoms: Swollen abdomen; scales may protrude from the body. The term "dropsy" refers to all diseases that make the belly swell abnormally; these ailments often cannot be distinguished from each other without an autopsy. Chronic dropsy develops slowly; in acute cases, swelling is sudden. Malawi Bloat is a type of dropsy that affects cichlids.
Cause: Either organ failure or environmental factors: excessive sodium chloride levels, high nitrate levels, bacteria, or poor/unsuitable diet.
Treatment: None. Improving or correcting tank conditions and diet may help.

FIN ROT

Symptoms: Inflammation (reddening) of the fin rays or degeneration of the fin membranes (or barbels, in catfishes). Fish with long, trailing fins are most susceptible.
Cause: Bacterial infection triggered by poor water quality. Other contributing factors include damage caused by fin-nipping or net-catching, and a poor, vitamin-deficient diet.
Treatment: Improve water quality and correct any environmental causes. Remove the fish and treat the affected area with a proprietary bactericide (Myxazin) or gentian violet. Seek specialist advice in severe cases.

FISH LICE (*ARGULUS*)

Symptoms: Fish scratches against rocks, wood, or the substrate. Small, disk-like, transparent parasites are clearly visible, lying flat against the skin.
Cause: Fish lice attach themselves to the host with suckers, then penetrate the skin to feed on its blood. Females leave the host to lay eggs; the hatched young then seek out new hosts.
Treatment: Remove fish and pull out the parasite with tweezers; treat the wound with antiseptic. Dose the tank with a proprietary remedy to kill larvae. For serious cases (usually in ponds), add Metriponate (1.125–1.8 mg per gallon/4.5 litres).

FUNGUS

Symptoms: Fluffy, cotton-like, fungal growths that occur in patches, or an overall dirty appearance to the skin. Fungus affects areas of the body and/or fins where the protective mucus coating has been damaged.
Cause: Secondary fungal infection to an existing wound or site of parasitic infestation, or poor water quality; often originates from White Spot.
Treatment: Treat the entire tank with fungicide to cure an outbreak. Determine the initial cause of the fungal attack, such as poor conditions or injuries from fighting, and rectify it.

GILL FLUKES (*DACTYLOGYRUS*)

Symptoms: Labored or fast breathing (but this can also indicate other conditions); in severe infestations, may have glazed eyes, heightened color, inflamed gills, and disorientation, as oxygen supply to the brain is reduced. The fish may rub its gill covers on rocks or other objects in the tank to relieve itching.
Cause: Infestation of the gill membranes by tiny, worm-like parasites just visible to the naked eye.
Treatment: Administer a proprietary treatment, such as Sterazin, available from aquatic dealers. However, *Dactylogyrus* eggs are very resilient and the treatment may not be effective until they hatch.

HOLE-IN-THE-HEAD (*HEXAMITIASIS*)

Symptoms: Sensory pores on the head and along the lateral line become enlarged and pus-filled; feces are light and stringy. Discus are susceptible. Similar disease HLLE (head and lateral line erosion) in marine species.
Cause: *Hexamita*, a parasite often found in intestines of young cichlids and gouramis; usually harmless until fish weakened by stress, old age, or poor environment.
Treatment: Dose the tank with prescription drugs Metronidazole or Di-metronidazole (50 mg per gallon/4.5 liters), mixed with water before use; repeat after 3 days. Or, mix the drugs with food. Vitamin A, C, and E supplements may aid healing.

INTESTINAL PARASITES

Symptoms: A well-fed fish gradually becomes emaciated; in severe cases, parasites may be seen protruding from the vent. Most often occurs in newly imported wild-caught fish, but in some instances may not become apparent for several months after import, depending on the specific internal parasite.
Cause: Various species of intestinal worms that penetrate the tissues and feed on blood and other body fluids.
Treatment: Consult your vet. Obtain a suitable anthelmintic to be administered with food. Dose the tank with a proprietary remedy to kill the parasite.

LEECHES

Symptoms: Fish scratches against rocks, wood, or the substrate; worm-like parasites are seen on the skin; these contract when touched.
Cause: Leeches, attached to the fish by suckers on both ends. The adult parasite detaches itself to lay eggs on rocks and/or plants; when hatched, the young seek new hosts.
Treatment: For minor infestations, remove leeches carefully with tweezers; treat the sites of attachment with antiseptic. For major infestations, treat the tank or pond with Metriponate (1.125–1.8 mg per gallon/4.5 liters) and replace the substrate.

POP-EYE (*EXOPHTHALMIA*)

Symptoms: Eye protrudes from the socket and may look inflamed; weight loss often accompanies.
Cause: Usually poor water quality or minor damage due to careless handling or fighting, resulting in increased vulnerability to infection. Pop-eye, characterized by the development of inflamed nodules behind the eye, is usually caused by bacterial septicemia, tuberculosis, or (occasionally) parasites.
Treatment: Rectify tank conditions; recovery is slow. Treat septicemia with prescribed antibiotics. The condition is incurable if caused by tuberculosis or parasites. Remove and euthanize affected fish.

SKIN SLIME

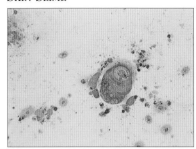

Symptoms: Dulled coloration with a very fine, gray-white covering of mucus on the body; gill damage or general weakness may be evident. Fish often shimmy or scratch against objects to relieve itching.
Cause: Poor water conditions that break down the body mucus, allowing attack by parasites such as *Chilodonella*, *Ichthyobodo*, and *Cyclochaeta*.
Treatment: These parasites are very resilient, making treatment problematic. If the disease is noted before it reaches the gills, treat the tank with a proprietary remedy. At later stages, treat the fish to a short-term formalin bath, but only under expert guidance.

SWIM BLADDER DISEASE

Symptoms: An affected fish will have difficulty maintaining its equilibrium, often losing its balance, swimming upside down, or on its side.
Cause: Damage or bruising to the swim bladder by careless handling or fighting; secondary bacterial infection; poor water conditions; congenital disorder.
Treatment: Identifying the source of the problem can be difficult. With bacterial infections, improve water quality and administer prescribed antibiotics. If an external cause is suspected, isolate the fish in a hospital tank with shallow water; if there is no improvement after 7 days, consider euthanasia.

VELVET

Symptoms: A yellow-gold, velvety covering on the body and fins (or gills, in marines), resembling gold-dust; increased breathing with rapid gill movements. The fish may rub against objects to relieve itching.
Cause: The parasites *Piscinoodinium* (in freshwater fish) or *Amyloodinium* (in marines), which penetrate skin cells with "roots" through which they feed.
Treatment: Administer a proprietary treatment; this is toxic to invertebrates, which should be removed. Also remove any activated filter carbon, which can eradicate the medication from the water. Shade the tank to rob the parasite of light energy, which it uses.

WHITE SPOT (*ICHTHYOPHTHIRIUS*)

Symptoms: Small white spots appear on the body and fins, increasing in number rapidly over 3–4 days; rapid gill movements are seen in a badly affected fish.
Cause: *Ichthyopthirius* (or *Cryptocaryon* in marine fish), a common parasite that lives under the skin. To reproduce, it burrows out of the fish's body, leaving a hole open to secondary infections, and forms a cyst. This eventually bursts, releasing many young.
Treatment: Administer a proprietary treatment either before the cyst forms or after it has burst; at other stages treatment is ineffective. Remove invertebrates and activated carbon from filters first.

BREEDING AQUARIUM FISH

Although aquarium fish can be readily purchased, it is fun to breed your own stock. You can encourage your fish to spawn by providing the right conditions and foods. Of course, you must ensure that you have at least one pair in the first place! If everything is to the fish's liking, they will breed. However, fish that appear fit and healthy may fail to spawn because one or more critical factors have been overlooked, such as the species' particular breeding habits, preferred water parameters, nutritional needs, courtship and territorial requirements, or the number of fish involved in the spawning procedure. Many freshwater species can be aquarium-bred using the basic setups described in this section. Marine fish must be left to their own devices!

◁ FEMALE RAM TENDING TWO-DAY-OLD FRY

BREEDING YOUR FISH

NOVICE AQUARISTS' first experience of fish breeding is often when a female livebearer unexpectedly produces a brood in the community tank. Many of the aquarium inhabitants will regard this as an opportunity for a good meal, and most of the fry are likely to be lost. Although a spare tank can be brought into service to raise the fry, this may already be in use for quarantining new or sick fish, or you may be forced to commandeer equipment that should be reserved for emergencies. With species that provide parental care, a fair number of young may survive; however, this can in turn result in overcrowding.

Avoid such problems by planning breeding programs in advance. Carefully consider which fish you should breed, where you will house spawning pairs and fry, and whether you can provide them with adequate supplies of the right foods. Breeding fish is a hugely enjoyable challenge, but requires time and dedication.

CHOOSING BREEDING STOCK

If you are uncertain whether a species spawns as pairs (as shown here) or as a group, purchase five or six specimens to cover both possibilities.

Before deciding to breed a particular species, consider how many fry you can cope with – some fish produce hundreds of eggs. It is far better to raise 30 healthy fry than to rear 100 poor-quality specimens.

For breeding, select healthy young adults with good coloring and no body or fin deformities. Alternatively, some aquarists prefer to buy very young stock that they can raise to maturity, controlling food intake and living conditions.

If fish have already pair-bonded in the dealer's tank, it is sensible to purchase in pairs; however, the option of buying juveniles and allowing them to establish their own partners is equally valid.

CONDITIONING YOUR FISH

Having selected a pair, trio, or group of fish as your breeding stock, your next task is to condition them for spawning; it is often best to separate the males and females at this time. Feed each specimen well to ensure that it will produce plenty of viable eggs or sperm. Some species require very specific foods such as mosquito larvae, which are rich in the amino acids that females need for egg production.

Water quality is also important; poor conditions can deter fish from spawning.

Prepare a special spawning tank, where the eggs can be left to develop and hatch. Conditioning may also take place in this aquarium, provided that it is immaculately maintained to protect the eggs from bacterial or fungal infection. Reduce the risk of contamination by conditioning your breeding stock elsewhere.

RITUALS AND RIVALRY

In species where there are courtship rituals and male rivalry, the males are usually more boldly colored than the females. When they are about to breed, this coloration intensifies as the males jostle over territories and attempt to attract a female to their chosen site. Males of some species display their enlarged fins to desired mates. For other fish, courtship may entail vague posturing near the female, or the male nudging the female close to her vent. Some male catfish use the bristles on their cheeks to stimulate the female.

The cleaning of the spawning site, which may be anything from a plant leaf, the aquarium glass, a filter pipe, or a piece of slate or rock, is an established behavior among many fish, including cichlids, which will then defend this area to protect their eggs and, later, brood.

Courtship rivalry is often mistaken for simple aggression; the weaker fish is usually unharmed, but should be removed if seriously attacked.

SPAWNING CARE

With pairs and trios of territorial species, females must first be allowed to establish themselves in the spawning tank, before introducing the males. The reverse procedure – adding the female to the male's territory – is a recipe for disaster.

Observe your fish during spawning; ardent males may mercilessly pursue, and even kill, a spent female. Remove over-aggressive males and continue conditioning for a few days before trying again, or provide clumps of Java Moss or synthetic spawning media to give the female shelter.

School spawners can be introduced to a breeding tank as a group; they should spawn within 24–48 hours. If they do not, try a water or temperature change (check the requirements for your fish). If this has no result, remove the fish for reconditioning and attempt spawning later. *Apistogramma* cichlids are unwilling to spawn unless there are smaller "dither" fish present, whose constant activity offers reassurance that the area is free from predators.

These Rams have just finished spawning; as part of their breeding ritual, they will later move their fry from place to place around the aquarium.

SPAWNING TRIGGERS

• Raising or lowering the water temperature by a few degrees (depending on the species) can activate the spawning urge. If reducing the temperature, make a substantial water change with cool water, to simulate natural rainfall.
• Locate the spawning tank in an area that is exposed to morning sunlight; this will stimulate many fish to spawn.
• To encourage difficult fish, or ones whose breeding habits are unknown, try spawning an easily-bred species of egg-scatterer (such as tetras or danios) in the same aquarium; the release of their hormones into the water may act as a trigger for the other fish to breed.

AFTER SPAWNING

All fish are weakened after breeding, and require peaceful surroundings and a steady supply of nutritious food. If you simply wish to have the pleasure of observing your fish's natural behavior, leave the parents to raise their brood. It is not uncommon, however, for young pairs to eat their offspring; if this continues after repeated spawnings, hatch and rear the fry separately.

Fish that give no parental care may eat their eggs and/or fry, and should be separated from the eggs after spawning. Some species will care for their eggs, but leave the fry to fend for themselves; in these cases, move the parents to another tank when the eggs hatch. For other fish, such as bubble-nest builders, it is essential to leave the male to defend and repair the nest until the fry become free-swimming, while the female(s) should be removed after spawning to avoid harassment from the overprotective male. With some species, such as the Bristlenose Catfish,

the pair may be left in the main aquarium, provided there is enough cover for the female to retire to, leaving the male to guard the eggs and fry. In certain cases, parents and offspring cannot be separated – for example, Discus and their fry, which feed on the adults' body mucus.

Mouthbrooders can be left to their own devices, although many aquarists and commercial breeders move the brooding parent to another tank when it is about to release the fry. If left in the original tank, the young may fall prey to other fish.

Female livebearers may be moved to a breeding tank just before giving birth. Be gentle during the transfer and do not stress the female by placing her in too confined a space. After the birth, she may be returned to her original tank.

With substrate-spawning killifishes, the parents should be removed after breeding and separated, since the females take much longer to recover than the males.

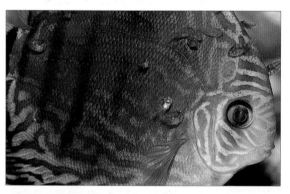

To raise high-quality Discus, it is essential to keep the young with their parents, since the fry feed on the adults' skin secretions prior to taking newly hatched brine shrimp.

Like most cichlids, Rams guard their eggs and tend the fry until they can fend for themselves. Just four days after hatching, this young brood clusters around the protective parents.

REMOTE HATCHING

To maximize the number of surviving fry, it is generally best to remove the eggs at regular intervals for hatching in a separate tank. If deposited on plants or artificial spawning mops, transfer the eggs still attached. If your fish have spawned on the aquarium glass, remove the eggs using a razor blade. Hold a fine mesh sieve (such as those sold for grading live foods) against the glass just beneath the eggs, and slide the razor blade gently between the eggs and glass, so that the eggs fall off

Some fish, such as this freshwater angelfish, can be left to care for their own young, but when hatching eggs away from the parents, promptly remove any fungused or infertile (white) eggs.

into the sieve. Suspend the sieve in the hatching tank near the flow from an air-operated sponge filter. If the eggs have been deposited on a rock or leaf, they will also require a gentle, well-oxygenated flow of water over them, such as their parents would have provided by fanning the eggs with their pectoral fins.

Keep the tank scrupulously clean, and check the eggs regularly. Remove any that are infertile (these usually turn white) or grow fungus (a hairy appearance) so they do not affect the rest. Some aquarists add a small amount of fungicide or bactericide to the tank to help prevent infections; alternatively, the introduction of a Water Louse or Sow Bug (*Asellus* spp.) will act as a biological control. This small creature lives naturally in streams and ponds, feeding on micro-organisms and decaying vegetable matter. One or two specimens added to a clutch of eggs will roam over the eggs, eating any that are infected while leaving the healthy ones undisturbed. When eggs begin to hatch, the Water Louse can be moved to another batch of eggs or returned to its pond or stream.

HAND-REARING FRY

One of the keys to rearing fry successfully is having sufficient stocks of the correct foods. Tiny fry must be fed with cultures of infusoria, followed by newly hatched brine shrimp. Larger young may be able to eat small *Daphnia* and flake foods. Herbivores require a steady supply of algae; if this is not available, peas, lettuce, or spinach can be used.

Young fish require regular meals two, three, or even four times a day. To prevent bacterial infections, siphon out uneaten food before offering the next meal.

In the excitement of having a large batch of fry, it is easy to overlook the amount of growning space that will be required. As fry mature, they must be transferred to a larger aquarium, or divided between several different tanks; otherwise, they will become stunted. For some carnivorous species, the fry may be cannibalistic; separate them into

individual tanks or divide your aquarium into compartments to prevent losses.

At this stage, the importance of cleanliness cannot be over-emphasized. A little extra care can make the difference between raising healthy stock or ending up with a few weak specimens.

For proper growth, fry must be fed diligently. Before deciding to raise a brood, ensure that you will be able to provide a steady supply of foods of the correct type and size.

Breeding Tank for Egg-scatterers

Egg-scattering fish produce either adhesive or non-adhesive eggs. Those with adhesive eggs, such as tetras, require a clump of Java Moss or other fine-leaved plant (or a similar synthetic material) to act as a site of attachment. For all egg-scatterers, plants are useful to provide cover for spent females. In breeding setups for fish with non-adhesive eggs, such as danios, cover the bottom of the tank with a layer of marbles; the eggs will fall between these and escape being eaten by the parents. Alternatively, a mesh net can be used to let the eggs fall safely free. Requirements regarding tank size and water conditions (including temperature) depend on the particular species being bred. The number of individuals needed for spawning also varies: for some species, a pair will suffice; for others, you will require a mixed-sex school of four or more fish. After spawning, the parents should be removed to prevent egg predation.

Tank Setup with Marble Substrate

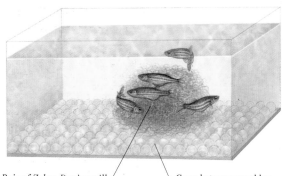

Pair of Zebra Danios will break from school to spawn over plants or marbles

Gaps between marbles provide ideal safety zone for eggs

After cleaning all materials, cover the base of the tank with a single layer of marbles. Do this gently to avoid breaking the glass. Fill the tank with water, fit a heater/thermostat (if used), and install an air-operated sponge filter. You may wish to include a clump of Java Moss. Check that the temperature is correct before adding the conditioned parents, and place a cover glass on top. Once spawning is complete, remove the parents. Then remove the marbles; this will make it easier to keep the tank clean during hatching and raising of the fry.

Tank Setup with Mesh Netting

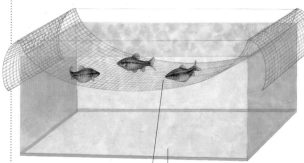

Keep two female Cherry Barbs to one male, so no individual female is excessively harassed

Base of tank must be kept clean to prevent bacterial or fungal infection of eggs

Clean the tank well and fill it, then add a heater/thermostat (if required). Rinse the mesh to remove any dust and debris and drape it carefully across the tank, leaving no way for the adult fish to escape. Anchor it in place using clothes pegs or adhesive tape on the outside of the tank. Check the temperature, then place the parent fish in the aquarium and add a cover glass. After spawning, remove the parents and the mesh. Fit a small air-operated sponge filter and maintain conditions while the eggs hatch and the young grow.

BREEDING TANK FOR EGG-DEPOSITORS

Depending on the species, egg-depositors may place their eggs on plants, on the substrate, or on surfaces that are ritually cleaned prior to spawning. Java Moss is usually used in breeding setups, but for fish that spawn over a number of days (such as rainbowfishes and some killifishes) artificial spawning mops are preferable, since these can be removed and replaced at regular intervals for remote hatching of the eggs. Construct several mops in advance; if dealing with a species you have not bred before, make some mops with long strands and some with short, to cater both for fish that prefer to spawn near the surface and those that prefer the bottom. Cichlids deposit their eggs on flat surfaces, such as rocks, cave roofs, or leaves. If not provided with a suitable site, they may spawn on the tank glass or other equipment. With all egg-depositors, research the species to determine if it is appropriate to remove one, both, or neither of the parents after spawning.

TANK SETUP WITH SPAWNING MOP

Clean the breeding tank and fill it with water. Fit a heater/thermostat (if used) and an air-operated sponge filter. Include two spawning mops or two clumps of Java Moss, or one of each. Once the temperature is correct, add the fish – either a pair or a trio, depending on their breeding habits. After spawning, remove the parents and care for the eggs and fry as appropriate for the species.

MAKING A SPAWNING MOP

Spawning mops can be used in place of fine-leaved vegetation as a site for fish to attach their adhesive eggs. They may be made either to float or to be placed on the tank bottom; eggs will be found scattered throughout the mop. To construct a mop, you will need synthetic knitting yarn (in a light color that will not bleed dye), a sturdy piece of card, a cork or piece of polystyrene (or a large marble if you want the mop to sink), and a pair of scissors. Wind the yarn around the card, tie it at the top, then slip the hank of yarn off the card. Cut the loop of yarn opposite the tie and attach the knotted end to the cork, polystyrene, or marble.

TANK SETUP WITH ROCKS AND CAVE

Thicket at side of tank provides refuge for female to rest during spawning

Clump of Java Moss gives added shelter at cave entrance

Start with a clean tank and add a fine gravel substrate. Fill the tank and fit a heater/thermostat (if needed) and an air-operated sponge filter. Add a thicket of broad-leafed plants to serve both as a spawning site and a retreat for the female. Provide flat rocks and a plant pot "cave" as further surfaces for egg deposits. Before adding the fish, check the temperature and the breeding details (with some species, the female should be introduced a day or two before the male). Fit a cover glass. After spawning, remove one, both, or neither parent, as appropriate.

BREEDING TANK FOR EGG-BURIERS

The most notable egg-burying fish, also referred to as peat-divers, are annual killifishes. These small, highly colorful fish are demanding, both to keep and to breed. Careful preparation is vital for successful spawning; the breeding pair must be conditioned with plenty of live foods. With some species, the male pushes the female into the substrate as she lays her eggs; for these, a 1 in (2.5 cm) layer of peat at the bottom of the tank is sufficient. Other species dive into the substrate to release the eggs; this requires 2–4 in (5–20 cm) of peat, depending on the size of the fish. Provide a clump of plants or a spawning mop as cover for the females, who may be harassed and even killed by ardent males. Tank cleanliness is vital, since the peat containing the eggs is stored in warm conditions for as long as several months (depending on the species), during which time any contaminants, such as uneaten food, will become foul.

TANK SETUP FOR EGG-BURIERS

Clean the tank and cover the base with a layer of peat (see details below). Fill with water and install a heater/thermostat; a filter is unnecessary. Add a spawning mop and/or a clump of Java Moss as a refuge for the female(s), then place the fish (either a pair or a trio) in the aquarium. If conditioned properly, they should spawn within hours. Observe them closely to ward off any attacks on the spent female(s) by the overattentive male. After spawning, remove the fish and follow the procedure below for handling and hatching the eggs.

Small 10 x 8 x 8 in (25 x 20 x 20 cm) breeding tank is ideal for killifishes

To induce spawning, raise water temperature slightly above original level

HANDLING PEAT AND HATCHING THE EGGS

Use either aquarium peat or sphagnum moss peat containing no additives. Most aquarists boil the peat to ensure that it sinks; this is a smelly process best performed in a well-ventilated room, using a saucepan reserved specifically for this purpose. Allow the peat to cool, then cover the base of the tank to a depth appropriate for the species being bred.

Once spawning is complete, remove the fish and drain off the tank water. Strain the remaining water and peat using a large, fine-meshed net, then gently squeeze the peat to remove excess moisture. The peat should be crumbly, with small eggs visible. Place the damp peat and eggs in polythene bags, then seal the bags and label them with the species name and spawning date; you may also wish to note the earliest hatching date (this must be researched specifically for your fish). Record the same details in your aquarium log; if you do not keep a log, now is the time to start! Finally, store the bags in a warm, dark place.

When the eggs are ready to be hatched, fill a small, clean tank with about 4 in (10 cm) of water at 72–75°F (22–24°C) and add the peat/egg mix. Within an hour, you should see some tiny fry; transfer these very carefully to a separate rearing tank. Repeat the process of straining, labeling, storing, and rehydrating to yield a second and third hatching. Killifish eggs are designed to survive drying out, and a single spawning will result in several broods.

Breeding Tank for Mouthbrooders

While cichlids are the best known of the mouthbrooders, this breeding strategy is also practised by some anabantids and catfish. Mouthbrooders, which produce small numbers of fry and provide good parental care, do not require a special breeding tank. They need only a small area of substrate on which to spawn, after which the eggs are taken into the mouth of one parent and brooded. Although the brooding parent may remain in its usual aquarium, it can be transferred to a separate rearing tank to maximize the number of surviving fry. Choose a tank that is suitable for the size of the adult and the expected brood. The aquarium need not contain substrate, but should be furnished with some potted plants or a few rocks as shelter; otherwise, the parent will become stressed. When the fry are released, the adult can then be returned to the main aquarium, leaving the fry to be grown on in protective isolation.

Parent Brooding Eggs

Since mouthbrooders spawn in their original aquarium, it is important to know how to spot when a male or female (the gender of the brooder varies with species) is carrying eggs. Usually, the fish has a distended mouth and throat; novices often ascribe this to illness or injury from fighting. Once brooding, the fish will not eat and may seek refuge in a quiet area of the tank. Do not be alarmed if the fish appears to be chewing the eggs; it is merely moving them to ensure a steady flow of water around them as water is taken in and then expelled.

Release of Fry

The eggs hatch in the parent's mouth and the fry continue to be brooded there, feeding on their yolk sacs, until they are large enough to fend for themselves. The parent then releases the young, which will swim nearby, swiftly returning to the safety of the parental mouth should danger threaten (whether in the form of a tankmate looking for a quick snack, or the aquarist doing routine tank maintenance). The duration of the brooding period varies according to species, and can range from a few days to a week or more.

Breeding Tank for Nest-builders

Breeding setups for nest-builders must contain the materials that the fish need to construct their nest. A nest can consist of an elaborate structure made with plant matter (as with the Stickleback); a foamy structure (or bubble-nest) at the water surface, requiring a floating anchorage point such as a large leaf or a piece of polystyrene (typical of some gouramis); or a depression dug in certain types of substrate (as with various cichlids). The tank shown below is a typical setup for

fish that build bubble-nests. The dimensions of the breeding aquarium must be chosen to suit the size of the adults; a 18 x 10 x 10 in (50 x 25 x 25 cm) tank is adequate for small species. Remember also to check the correct water temperature range for the fish being bred. With most bubble-nest builders, the male guards the nest and fry. Females should be removed to allow them to recover from the rigors of spawning before they are attacked by the overprotective males.

Bubble-nest Tank Setup

In spawning embrace, pair position themselves below the bubble-nest

Thicket of plants will supply immediate cover for the spent female

Clean the tank well, then add substrate and two thickets of fine-leaved plants; these must be tall enough to reach the water surface, to serve as an anchor for the floating bubble-nest. Fill the tank, using some water from the parents' original aquarium, and position the heater/thermostat. A filter is not required; excess disturbance of the water surface will destroy the nest. When putting the fish in the tank, add the female first and allow her 6–12 hours to establish herself before introducing the male. Finally, install a tight-fitting cover glass.

Guarding the Floating Nest

Fish that construct bubble-nests need a little more help from the aquarist than those that build nests on the substrate, since their eggs are near an alien environment (the air). The floating nest is guarded by the male, which continually blows bubbles to replace those that have burst. A secure cover glass is essential to prevent any cold drafts on the nest. When the fry hatch, the male guards them until they are free-swimming. Keep the cover glass in place to maintain high humidity just above the water, or the young will become chilled and die.

BREEDING TANK FOR LIVEBEARERS

Unlike most fish, livebearers do not lay eggs, but give birth to fully formed young. To help prevent the adult female from eating its offspring, set up a breeding tank with a layer of fine-leaved floating plants and clumps of Java Moss for the fry to hide among. Commercial breeding traps offer more effective protection, but are too confining for all but the smallest adults. Alternatively, suitably-sized mesh may be used to allow the fry to swim free from the parent, as in the set-up for egg-scatterers (*see page 240*). For best results, specially-built breeding tanks with V-shaped inserts are ideal; they allow plenty of swimming space for both parent and fry, and, after birth, the insert can be removed and the fry grown on. Choose a tank large enough to accommodate the expected brood; a 18 x 10 x 10 in (50 x 25 x 25 cm) aquarium will suffice for most species. Water temperature should be as in the adults' original tank.

TANK WITH "V" INSERT

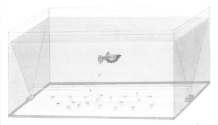

For serious breeding, it is worth making a special aquarium. In the design shown above, two panes of glass are fitted in the tank to form a "V". The glass is held in place by a slotted block, leaving a gap at the bottom of the "V" to allow the fry to drop through while retaining the female in the insert section. Fit a heater/thermostat, air-operated sponge filter, and cover glass to finish the setup.

TANK WITH BREEDING TRAP

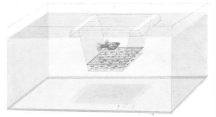

Breeding traps are convenient for small species. With the floating type seen here, the fry fall through a slatted partition safely into the base. Fill the tank using some water from the parents' original aquarium, then add a heater/thermostat, an air-operated sponge filter, and a cover glass. After the birth, remove the female and release the fry into the breeding tank for growing on.

GIVING BIRTH

If left in its main aquarium, a female livebearer that is ready to give birth will often retire to a quiet part of the tank where it can rest among plants. Although fine-leaved vegetation or floating plants such as Riccia offer some shelter to the free-swimming newborn fry, many will inevitably fall prey to larger tankmates. Brood size varies considerably between species; some livebearing fish produce only a few young, while others have a prodigious number of very tiny fry. The larger the offspring, the better are their chances of survival.

COMMERCIAL BREEDING

THE ENDURING popularity of fishkeeping has made the modern aquarium trade a thriving industry. In many developing nations, the commercial breeding of freshwater and marine fish for the hobby plays an important role both economically and in the conservation of the local environment. Some species, especially those that are notoriously difficult, if not impossible, to breed in captivity, must still be collected from the wild; a notable example is the Cardinal Tetra. Today, such fishing is carefully restricted to sustain wild populations, and certain vulnerable marine species in particular are actively protected through captive breeding programs. Ongoing improvements in methods of collecting, acclimating, and farming fish have made available an ever-increasing variety of high-quality, well-acclimated, tank-bred specimens for the aquarium trade.

FARMED FISH

Many tropical and coldwater freshwater fish are bred commercially, and the number of farmed marine species is steadily rising. Both aquarium and pond fish are farmed around the world, with well-established trades in Singapore, Hong Kong, Malaysia, South Africa, Sri Lanka, Israel, and the US (Florida). In many Third World countries, the exportation of tropical species is an important source of income and, to conserve this lucrative resource, numerous traders have set up their own breeding and collecting stations to supply the industry. In warm climates, fish can be reared in outdoor ponds or in built-to-order fish houses. Such is the market for high-quality tropical fish that specimens are now being bred in relatively cool regions, notably Poland and Czechoslovakia where, even with the added heating costs, suppliers are still able to compete in the international market. Coldwater species, notably the Goldfish and the much larger Koi (usually kept as a pond rather than tank fish), are also produced in large numbers worldwide.

Fish farms generally specialize in certain groups of fish, for example anabantids or livebearers. Some work with just a single species, such as the Guppy, creating new varieties with different coloration, body shapes, or fin forms to introduce to the trade. Other producers may concentrate on breeding fish that are seasonal in the wild, so that they can be supplied year-round.

Commercial fish farms range from large, self-contained units to relatively modest collecting stations where out-breeders with much smaller facilities produce fish. The livestock is then transported to central export points for packing and shipment abroad.

TRADE-DEVELOPED VARIETIES

The aquarium trade continually develops new strains of fish to meet customer demand. Goldfish have been line-bred over generations to produce the wide variety seen today. With tropical species, many color forms have been produced, with further selective breeding to enhance finnage, creating new types such as long-finned danios and Oscars. It has been debated whether these developments, while commercially profitable, are in fact beneficial for the fish. Some consider it cruel to produce a fish that struggles to swim because it is weighed down by excessive finnage, while others find such exotic strains beautiful. Inbred fish are also generally less hardy than the original species and can easily fall victim to disease.

Other controversial trade developments include the introduction of a number of color-injected species. The best known of these is the Glassfish (*Chanda* spp.), where fluorescent dye may be injected to add a brilliant arc of color to the fish's normally transparent body. Although the result is attractive to some, its effects on the fish's health are unknown. Reputable dealers no longer stock such specimens.

Beauty is in the eye of the beholder. People usually either love or loathe fancy manmade varieties such as the Bubble-eye Goldfish. This fish requires special care to protect its extremely delicate enlarged eye sacs.

CONSERVATION OF SPECIES

There are many fish noted by the Convention on the International Trade in Endangered Species (CITES) that are officially banned from trade, although a few have become reestablished. The Dragonfish (*Scleropages formosus*), for example, is now bred commercially in the Far East, with second-generation specimens allowed for export, electronically tagged and certified as farmed.

In the conservation of aquatic life, much has been achieved with the captive breeding of marine species, especially seahorses, to ensure their survival. Many zoos and public aquariums have breeding programs, occasionally assisted by established hobbyists, which help to maintain stocks of endangered fish. These can then be bred (if only in small numbers), either for reintroduction into the wild or simply to preserve species whose habitats have been destroyed by man or natural disaster. Initiatives to reform indiscriminate fishing techniques, including practices such as the release of cyanide on marine reefs, have also contributed to conservation goals. The aquarium trade is playing a part too, by backing projects that promote and teach captive breeding techniques (dealing not just with fish but also with aquatic plants), and by supporting research to maintain the status of wild species.

Public aquaria, such as this one in Monterey, California, USA, aid conservation both with breeding programmes and by providing huge display tanks so that we can better observe and understand the interactions between species.

FISH INDEX

GENERAL INDEX

ACKNOWLEDGMENTS

The author would like to thank: Keith Banister
and Brian Walsh for allowing me to pick their
brains and discuss various pertinent points,
sometimes at great length; and to my family –
Mike, Jenny, Elaine, and Rowan – for managing
to survive while I have been otherwise
occupied. Finally, there are Tigger, Wiffle, and
countless others (some sadly now departed),
who have maintained my interest in fish for
many years, not to mention Vlad, for keeping
me company in the wee small hours.

Dorling Kindersley would like to thank:
Frank Greenaway, of the Natural History
Museum photography department, for his
boundless creativity and patience in setting up,
maintaining, and photographing our feature
tanks, pictured on pages 151t, 156r, 184–185,
186–187, 188–189, 190–191, 194–195,
196–197, 198–199. We are also grateful to
Jason Rainbow and James McKeown at Syon
Park Aquatic Centre for supplying fish and
equipment, Robin James at Weymouth Sealife
Centre for advice and assistance, and Margaret
McCormack for compiling the index.

The publisher would also like to thank the
following for permission to reproduce the
photographs indicated below.
Key: l=left; c=center; t=top; r=right; b=bottom.

Ardea London Ltd: 11t, P. Morris 93b, 148b;
Biofotos: 231cb; Biophoto Associates: 105r,
157bl, 157tl; Bruce Coleman Ltd: Franco Banfi
115b, 127b, Jane Burton 221b, Kevin
Cullimore 12–13, Andrew J. Purcell 16br, 146,
147b, 148t, 149, Hans Reinhard 89t, Kim
Taylor 101b; Nick Dakin: 163; R. K. Doyle:
60r, 61tr; Fisheries Western Australia: 231b,
233t; JPH Foto: Michael Jensen 208, 220,
232cb; Frank Lane Picture Agency: Gerard
Lacz 50b, F. W. Lane 18cr, 42b, Linda Lewis
118t, 218–219, 237t, 238t; B. James 104l;
Natural Science Photos: Hal Beral 134, David

B. Fleetham 139b; N.H.P.A.: A.N.T. 84, 85t, G.
J. Cambridge 154, Nigel J. Dennis 246, Gerard
Lacz 108tl, 228, Trevor McDonald 204, B.
Jones & M. Shimlock 153t, Norbert Wu 211;
Oxford Scientific Films: Kathie Atkinson 151b,
George I. Bernard 232ct, Max Gibbs 1, 4, 9,
11b, 13t, 17br, 21cr, 39t, 40b, 41t, 49l, 52–53,
54, 55b, 57t, 61tl, 70b, 72–73, 75b, 77b, 79b,
80b, 81b, 82t, 86–87, 91cr, 94, 96t, 97, 100t,
101t, 114, 125t, 128–129, 130, 131t, 135t,
137b, 138, 140b, 141b, 142t, 143b, 144–145,
158–159, 176–177, 202–203, 207, 209, 212,
226–227, 230, 231t, 231ct, 232t, 233ct, 233b,
234–235, 237b, 238b, 239t, 243b, 244b, 245b,
247t, Howard Hall 153b, Richard Herrman
247b, Paul Kay 150, 155, Breck P. Kent 221t,
Rudie H. Kuiter 152t, Zig Leszcynski 123b,
156l, Hans Reinhard 89b, K. G. Vock 58b;
Photomax: 2, 6–7, 8, 14, 30–31, 32–33, 91tl,
91br, 110–111, 112–113, 157br, 157tr,
160–161, 170–171, 200–201, 206; Photos
Horticultural: Michael and Lois Warren 105l;
Planet Earth Pictures: Vaughan Bean 125b,
Gary Bell 126t, 141t, Georgette Dounma 135b,
Chris Huxley 243t, Ken Lucas 61bl, Paulo
Oliveira 232b, 236, 239b, Linda Pitkin 152b,
Carl Roessler 127t; Mike Sandford: 10, 16tl,
16cl, 16tr, 16cr, 17cr, 18tl, 18bl, 20cl, 20cr,
21tl, 21cl, 21tr, 25, 35b, 36t, 36br, 37br, 37t,
39b, 40t, 42t, 43bl, 43t, 44–45, 46l, 47tl, 47bl,
47cr, 47br, 48, 51t, 56t, 57b, 59, 60l, 61br, 62,
64, 66b, 67t, 68b, 69t, 71b, 74, 77t, 79t, 81t,
83b, 83tr, 85b, 88, 91cl, 92t, 93t, 95, 96b, 99,
100b, 102–103, 104r, 121, 122b, 132–133,
136, 137t, 139t, 140t; Tetra: Dr Pool 233cb;
Jerry Young: 3, 16bl, 17tr, 19b, 20bl, 21bl, 22,
28bl, 28br, 29, 34, 37bl, 41b, 43br, 50t, 51b,
55t, 58t, 65t, 76, 80t, 81tl, 91bl, 91tr, 92b,
115t, 116, 117t, 118b, 119, 120, 122t, 123t,
124, 126b, 131b, 142t, 147t, 168c, 169.

Illustrations by: Kuo Kang Chen 15, 23, 24, 27,
164–165, 166–167, 168b, 224; Carl Ellis 205,
240–241, 242, 244t 245t.